CRIMINAL JUSTICE RESEARCH IN LIBRARIES AND ON THE INTERNET

This book is a revision of
Criminal Justice Research in Libraries: Strategies and Resources
by Marilyn Lutzker and Eleanor Ferrall.

CRIMINAL JUSTICE RESEARCH IN LIBRARIES AND ON THE INTERNET

Bonnie R. Nelson
Marilyn Lutzker, Advisory Editor
Foreword by Edward Sagarin

GREENWOOD PRESS

Westport, Connecticut • London

Library of Congress Cataloging-in-Publication Data

Nelson, Bonnie R.
    Criminal justice research in libraries and on the internet / Bonnie
R. Nelson ; foreword by Edward Sagarin. — Rev. ed.
        p.   cm.
    Rev. ed. of: Criminal justice research in libraries / Marilyn
Lutzker and Eleanor Ferrall. 1986.
    Includes bibliographical references and index.
    ISBN 0–313–30048–8 (alk. paper)
    1. Reference books—Criminal justice, Administration of.
2. Criminal justice, Administration of—Bibliography.   3. Criminal
justice, Administration of—Computer network resources.
I. Lutzker, Marilyn. Criminal justice research in libraries.
II. Title.
Z5703.4.C73N45   1997
[HV7419]
364'.07'22—DC21   97–16124

British Library Cataloguing in Publication Data is available.

Library of Congress Catalog Card Number: 97–16124

ISBN: 0–313–30048–8

First published in 1997

Greenwood Press, 88 Post Road West, Westport, CT 06881
An imprint of Greenwood Publishing Group, Inc.

Printed in the United States of America

The paper used in this book complies with the
Permanent Paper Standard issued by the National
Information Standards Organization (Z39.48–1984).

10   9   8   7   6   5   4   3   2   1

Contents

Foreword to the Revised Edition

I liked this book when Eleanor Ferrall and I first wrote it in 1986. I like it even better now!

The nature of information has not changed since the first edition; but the speed with which information in computerized formats has joined that in traditional formats has enlarged the parameters of criminal justice research. Thus, it is fitting that the author of this second edition should be a specialist in computer information systems as well as in criminal justice.

The addition of a chapter on Forensic Science, ably authored by Professor Katherine Killoran, fills a gap that was evident in the first edition.

Both beginning and accomplished researchers will continue to find in *Criminal Justice Research in Libraries and on the Internet* the tools for efficient and successful research.

Marilyn Lutzker

Foreword to the First Edition

Crime is often said to be as old as time, or at least as old as life. These are metaphorical statements, for what is meant is that crime is as old as *Homo sapiens*. No other species, form, or variety of living organism has the wisdom to make laws nor the urge, motivation, and ability to violate them.

To paraphrase a famous sentence in sociology, written not about crime but about social inequality, crime is traced back to antiquity and extends to ubiquity. Although criminal behavior had been noted for centuries in the first criminal codes and by literary artists and philosophers such as Sophocles and Aristotle, the first serious inquiry into the nature of lawbreaking and what ought to be done with those responsible for harm to others did not occur until the eighteenth century.

The great literary event that marks the birth of the literature on crime came in 1764, when Cesare Beccaria, a young Italian nobleman with no experience or previous knowledge in the field, wrote his treatise on crimes and punishments. His theories were based on the premises that governmental policy should seek the greatest good for the greatest number of people, that surety of punishment, not severity, effected security and order, and that the severity of punishment should be scaled to the severity of the crime. He taught that anything in excess of these principles led to tyranny. Beccaria's small book attracted attention and had an influence throughout Europe that must have taken its author by surprise. It was almost immediately translated into English, French, and numerous other languages. It seriously influenced the thought of such diverse and important thinkers as Voltaire in France and John Stuart Mill in England, and it led to legislative reform of criminal justice practices in western Europe, England, Russia, Sweden, and eventually America. The followers of Beccaria's theories became known as the *classical school* of criminology, its first and founding school.

In revised form, Beccaria's influence was most undeniably felt in the early years of the nineteenth century when the Napoleonic Code was promulgated. That Code, reflecting the influence of Beccaria but with modifications which allowed for some mitigation and flexibility, became the basis for the criminal code in most continental European and Latin American countries. The revisions in Beccaria's theories, however, were sufficient to give this development a slightly different name; it was to be called the *neoclassical school*. In some instances it showed a remarkable similarity to what was to appear a century and a half later under the concepts of just deserts and retribution.

To trace what has happened in the literature of crime, and eventually what came to be known as criminal justice, in the almost two centuries since the Napoleonic Code, would be a formidable task requiring several volumes. Here only a few highlights will be mentioned and a few landmarks cited; many will be omitted, deliberately or inadvertently.

The early and middle years of the nineteenth century brought two developments of great importance to the social sciences and to criminology. The first was the study of social events in a systematic, scientific manner, following the rigorous methodology of the physical sciences. The most important single name associated with this work was probably Auguste Comte, who coined the term "sociology" and conceived of the study of social phenomena as something that would be in the nature of what was called "social physics." His influence was wide; the setting was established for the birth of what is today termed the social sciences.

The second event of equal or perhaps greater importance in the eyes of many was the publication in 1859 of *The Origin of Species* by Charles Darwin, initiating what some have called "the century of Darwin." For Darwinians, biology was paramount, and all aspects of the world could be thought of in terms of evolution and survival of the fittest.

Directly related to these two events was the emergence of what has been called the social survey or social reform movement. Born in response to the extreme social problems of the nineteenth century, this was a movement not of scholars but of philanthropists, journalists, and other individuals who united for social action. They felt that amassing all the facts about the human social condition would lead to solutions for such problems as poverty, health, education, housing, crime, and prison discipline. The writings of these people were not intended as scholarly and scientific works, but were social statements aimed at informing and molding public opinion and influencing social policy.

The synthesis of the two great philosophical forces represented by Comte and Darwin was manifested by the emergence, in the latter quarter of the nineteenth century, of Cesare Lombroso. An Italian physician who worked with criminals, particularly in the Army, he founded with many of his contemporaries what came to be known as the *positivist school* of criminology. Its controversial nature notwithstanding, it soon gained prominence and, temporarily at least, left the classical and neoclassical schools as nothing more than moments in history. Lombroso's name is often associated, particularly by people who have only the most superficial knowledge of his work, with born criminals, atavistic evolutionary throwbacks, and physiological signs (or stigmata) by which such persons could be recognized as criminals. In the totality of his work, however, and particularly in its later stages, he thought of many of these criminals as having developed because of social conditions and others as having inborn criminal tendencies or predilections that made them vulnerable to crime under certain conditions. This position was remarkably similar to that taken in the latter part of the twentieth century by researchers promulgating what is now called the biosocial basis of violent behavior.

Thus, with Beccaria's social philosophy and Lombroso's statistical studies and systematic investigations, there came into existence criminology, and later, in a distinction that is still not entirely clear, criminal justice.

On the European continent, criminology and criminal justice developed as subdivisions of criminal law and were dominated by people learned in the law and occasionally in psychology. In England and the United States, a separate course of development took place. Criminology came to be taught almost entirely within sociology departments, but it was taught as a concentration on crime, delinquency, and, a little later, deviant behavior, within the larger field of sociology.

Neither of the two approaches proved adequate for two reasons. The first is that crime, with its form and shape, its frequency, its perpetrators, and the nature of the reaction against it, has to be studied in an interdisciplinary fashion. This means that theories and writings from the disciplines of political science, economics, psychology, anthropology, philosophy, and criminal law, to name a few among many, must be integrated with one another.

A second reason that criminology or criminal justice could not be adequately served as a subdiscipline of either sociology or criminal law was the growth of a separate, independent literature seldom studied by those trained either in criminal law or in sociology, although it was not entirely ignored by either. That literature specialized in police science and administration on the one hand, and punishment, imprisonment, rehabilitation, and what came to be called so optimistically and euphemistically "corrections," on the other.

This brings us to a few more highlights which are necessary to describe how we got to where we are. Throughout the nineteenth century, theories of imprisonment and punishment attracted great attention in the United States. What came to be known as corrections had its associations, conferences, and position papers in America considerably before sociology, criminal justice or criminology had gained any academic or scholarly recognition.

Not until the later years of the nineteenth century, with the dominating figure of William Graham Sumner at Yale University did American universities first grant recognition to sociology. In 1893, the University of Chicago offered what is believed to be the first doctorate in sociology, and two years later it initiated publication of the *American Journal of Sociology*, which continues to be published. In 1905 a group of sociologists met and formed the American Sociological Society, which several years later initiated publication of its own journal, *American Sociological Review,* which also continues to be published.

The focus of attention and the center of study in sociology during the first quarter of this century was undoubtedly the University of Chicago, where what came to be known as the Chicago school of sociology was taught and practiced. It is difficult to pinpoint exactly what constituted this school, other than its excellence, the large numbers of outstanding people who graduated from it, and the dominant position that it held. The Chicago school urged its students, faculty, and researchers to go out among the people, live with them, and see how they lived in order to study the real world of real men and women. In addition to a focus on crime, deviant people, and lower socioeconomic classes, the Chicago school developed the idea of the "own story" or "life story" of individual criminals, often carefully annotated by a criminologist, a lasting contribution to the burgeoning discipline.

Also in Chicago, but at Northwestern University School of Law, an American Institute of Criminal Law and Criminology was formed, growing out of a national conference. Soon after, the School of Law launched its excellent journal—the only law school journal in which criminal law was not just paramount but exclusive: the *Journal of Criminal Law, Criminology, and Police Science*. It is an interesting title, for it represented a marriage that many did not believe the scholars and the disciplines were ready to put into effect. Police science was later dropped from the title; perhaps it suggested too much the practitioner for a scholarly journal. The journal is today known as the *Journal of Criminal Law and Criminology*.

Many other events of the twentieth century can be quickly recorded. Two organizations in the fields of criminology and criminal justice were formed in addition to the many established in corrections, police, and related areas. Each assumed importance, held national conferences, distributed newsletters, published journals, and established networks of people who came to know each other's work and often to collaborate. The American Society of Criminology started issuing a little journal called *Criminologica*, a title later changed to *Criminology: An Interdisciplinary Journal*. The American Society of Criminology attracted mainly academic people, primarily from sociology but not to the exclusion of professors of criminal law, psychiatry, and other disciplines. Then the Academy of Criminal Justice Sciences (ACJS) was formed, with a greater practitioner emphasis, but nonetheless scholarly, and with some overlap in membership between the two organizations. The ACJS holds an annual conference and publishes *Justice Quarterly*. Yet these are only two of the many journals—regional and specialized, some having ideological views—

that now fill the shelves, or at least the microfilm drawers, of a good library in this area of study.

Academicians, practitioners, and students became increasingly interested in the distinction, if any, between criminal justice and criminology, particularly as the former term began to be used with greater frequency. The development of a field of scholarly studies, based around the practitioner aspects of those involved in the prevention, control, and management of crime and the handling of those found guilty of criminal acts, appeared to many to be both possible and important.

A forerunner in this field in America was August Vollmer. On the West Coast he started a police training program in 1908. Five years later this became the Berkeley Police School. Today, Vollmer's association with the first major effort to bring professionalism to police and scholarship to the study of problems in policing is symbolized by an annual award, named after him, given each year by the American Society of Criminology to an outstanding practitioner. Later, the University of California at Berkeley formed a School of Criminology, as distinct from a school of social sciences or a department of criminology. It taught both the academic and scholarly aspects of criminology, with a sociological emphasis, but it also had a training program in forensic sciences. The political turmoil of the late 1960s led to the disbanding of the school, though not before it had launched some major publications on crime from a radical or Marxist perspective.

To return to the distinction between criminal justice and criminology, some scholars would contend that the names are interchangeable, but others, myself included, disagree. Both have as their focus the understanding of crime, the event, and the perpetrator. Criminology places this in the context of society, power, legislation, and causality and sees crime primarily in terms of the universality of social norms and the causes of and reaction to their abrogation. Criminal justice concerns itself with crime and its societal context but puts equal emphasis on police science and administration, on criminal law and the court system, and on jails, prisons, and alternative forms of punishment.

In 1965 there were 95 academic criminal justice programs in the United States of which only 9 included graduate-level education. Ten years later there were 1,348 such programs, including 185 at the graduate level. The establishment of the Law Enforcement Education Program (LEEP) as part of the Law Enforcement Assistance Administration (LEAA) had had a major effect.

With the increase in criminal justice programs as a result of LEEP and other forces, with the expansion of research as a result of grants from the LEAA and numerous other government and private agencies, and with the tremendous attention given to crime by the public as a result of the great increase in crime and violence from the early 1960s through the 1970s, the amount of information available to the criminal justice researcher started to multiply. As in many other fields, there was an information explosion. At first there were but a few journals printing articles on crime; then came the deluge. There were not only journals specializing in criminal justice but hundreds of others in related fields that included articles on crime. Abstract services were devoted to crime, police, and other fields of study, but articles on crime were also abstracted and indexed in publications devoted to psychology, sociology, and medicine, among others. And then there were the innumerable government documents; the material found as chapters in books (books not edited by the chapter authors and hence not cataloged under their names), in newspapers and in magazines; and countless indexes. There were dictionaries, encyclopedias, histories, biographies, and volume upon volume, row upon row of opinions from numerous courts. All this is in print, in computer files, on microfilm and microfiche.

This veritable deluge of data, statistics, information, ideas, texts, and documents is so overwhelming that one wonders how a young profession could ever have advanced without it. It is also so overwhelming that one is intimidated and does not know where to start or how to get at that small portion of what is there that is essential to one's own needs and interests. The scholar gets lost in a maze because the information is so extensive and so rich. But such information has value only to those who can locate it. That is where the expert, not in criminology but in librarianship, becomes essential. This leads us to this excellent book, so needed that we can only look to the void that it has filled and ask ourselves, in disbelief, how we ever functioned before. The answer is simple: many of us did not know that the gap existed.

Now the drudgery of finding information can be simplified and reduced in time—time better spent on reading, thinking, testing, writing, and going forward from the point where one has stopped learning what others have done. To make this possible, Marilyn Lutzker and Eleanor Ferrall have done a superb job. Our indebtedness to them will be apparent from the first page. I hope for the sake of research and scholarship that our colleagues in other disciplines are as fortunate in finding people equally knowledgeable and devoted to write guides for library research in their fields that deserve to be on the same shelf with this book.

> Edward Sagarin, 1913–1986
> City University of New York

Preface

When Marilyn Lutzker approached me with the idea of revising *Criminal Justice Research in Libraries*, my first thought was "how simple." Marilyn Lutzker and Eleanor Ferrall had produced an excellent guide for criminal justice researchers to the landscape of scholarly sources and library tools; it would be a trifle to go through the book, look for new editions and recently published reference books, and add notes about which ones were now available in computerized form.

My second thought, after rereading the book, was that doing a second edition might prove a bit more challenging. Many of the sources were dated, most of the indexes were now available in computerized form, and library catalogs had changed drastically. Several chapters clearly would have to be rewritten, but the organization was excellent, the narratives were well written, and the task still appeared to be one of simple updating.

It was not until I was well into this project that I really came to understand how completely library research had changed in slightly over ten years. In the Lloyd Sealy Library of the John Jay College of Criminal Justice the card catalog has disappeared, the index and abstract shelves are gathering dust, and students line up for computers that connect to WESTLAW, LEXIS-NEXIS, and the Internet. The new edition reflects all of these changes.

Still, some things have not changed. The basic elements of information flow remain the same, and that initial chapter has been altered little from the first edition, except to add the role that the Internet now plays in scholarly communication. Similarly, the chapter on "Efficiency in Research" remains a model of how to organize a term paper or similar research project; I have added suggestions about dealing with online resources and hypertext links in an organized fashion.

The rest of Part I is new. Bibliographic searching with a computer is now so important that it requires an in-depth explanation of concepts like databases, records, and full text. The Internet, of course, gets a chapter of its own.

Part II is a mixture of old and new. The chapter on the Library Catalog is almost totally new. The chapters on Indexes and Abstracts; Newsletters, Newspapers, and News Broadcasts; Documents, Reports, and Conference Proceedings; and Statistics have been substantially rewritten to reflect the shift to computerized sources, including the Internet, in these areas. The chapters on Encyclopedias, Dictionaries, and Annual Reviews; and Printed Bibliographies have simply been updated with new editions and new titles.

In Part III the chapter on legal resources has been changed to reflect the addition of the myriad legal resources available over the Internet. The chapter on comparative research is almost totally new, while that on historical research is almost unchanged. The chapter contributed by Katherine Killoran on library research in forensic science corrects the most obvious omission in the first edition.

The appendixes have been updated and a glossary of possibly unfamiliar terms has been added.

Marilyn Lutzker and Eleanor Ferrall, in their Preface to the first edition, discussed the challenge of gearing their work to the reader who may be an undergraduate, a full-time practitioner, a professor, or an independent researcher. That challenge remains. Librarians have always tended to complain, somewhat superciliously, that even full professors do not know how to do library research but would never admit it. With the growth of computerized indexes and the Internet, more and more researchers *are* admitting that they feel inadequate to the new tools. And librarians, themselves, are struggling to keep abreast of new technologies that seem to come faster than they can be learned, much less taught. Indeed, I have come increasingly to feel that it was only the process of researching this book that has taught me how to do library research in criminal justice. It is my hope that this book will ease the way for students, practitioners, scholars, and librarians to that same sense of competency.

ACKNOWLEDGMENTS

Authors traditionally thank those who have helped in their research and writing, but how to single out a few from among the many who have aided in so many different ways? I hope that those whom I do not name, whom I may not even know by name, will understand that I appreciate and acknowledge their help.

First, above all, I am grateful to Marilyn Lutzker, who encouraged me to undertake this project, constantly fed me leads on new printed and Internet sources, critiqued the entire book in a near-final form, and was always ready with suggestions for improvement, even when I didn't want to hear them. I thank her also for setting high standards, both in reference and in editorial work, and for never allowing me to shirk from meeting those standards.

Thanks to all my reference colleagues, past and present, at John Jay College, from whom I have learned so much over the years, particularly Kathy Killoran, who read many parts of this work and was always free with advice and time. I am forever indebted to the late Robert Grappone, extraordinary administrator and reference librarian, who wrote many of the John Jay Library research guides that were so helpful in preparing this edition. My colleagues in technical services and collection development, who made the Lloyd Sealy Library such a fruitful place for researching this book, must be noted, particularly Marlene Kandel, who taught me most of what I know about subject indexing.

John Jay College of Criminal Justice, and its Provost, Basil Wilson, were tremendously supportive in providing me with a sabbatical leave, during which some of this work was done, and in truly believing in the importance of libraries and librarians to scholarship and education. The students and faculty of John Jay College are a wonderful community whose questions and comments are a constant reminder of the purpose of libraries.

My colleagues from around the world in the World Criminal Justice Library Network heightened my awareness of the information needs of the criminal justice practitioner, and how improvements in the flow of information in that field can directly benefit the individual.

Last, but not least, of course, I must thank my family for their forbearance, good humor and vital contributions. My husband, Robert, patiently read and edited the entire book, and was always ready to listen and offer advice. My daughter, Miranda, prepared most of the charts and illustrations that are included here. I am intensely grateful to both of them and to the other members of my extended family who tolerated my absences and encouraged my work.

This work, of course, is my own, and I assume all responsibility for any errors.

Introduction

Criminal justice research is usually thought of as the processes of data-gathering, analysis, and theory testing applied to the various components of the criminal justice system. But no research study should take place in a vacuum; the research of today must be informed by the studies of the past. The research through the literature of the field—that essential part of criminal justice research that takes place in libraries and, increasingly, on the Internet before, during, and even after the empirical studies—is the subject of this book.

As Professor Sagarin describes so well in his Foreword, criminal justice has a rich history. Theories have been advanced, ideas have been tested, and procedures have been critiqued in a disciplined way since the middle of the nineteenth century. Because the tradition and history of this social science is a written, not an oral one, the major studies have been written down and published as books, journal articles, and reports. Students and researchers confront an enormous task when reviewing this literature. The chapters that follow should help you find your way through this massive labyrinth of documentary material.

In the nineteenth century the educated public was small, and the circle of scholars interested in the fields of criminology, penology, and criminal justice as a whole was sufficiently limited that most knew each other. They were easily able to stay abreast of the literature of the field. It is probably fair to say that the giant thinkers of the mid- to late-nineteenth century had read almost everything that had been written about criminal justice, plus everything that was possibly related to it in the still-new fields of sociology, psychology, and political science. The information explosion in the twentieth century has made

Chart A
Some Highlights in the Development of Criminal Justice and Some of the
Major Research Tools That Serve It

SOCIAL SCIENCE AND SOCIOLOGY	CRIMINOLOGY	CRIMINAL JUSTICE
1876: First American sociology course at Yale University **1893**: First Ph.D. in Sociology offered at University of Chicago **1895**: *American Journal of Sociology* **1905**: American Sociological Association 　**1907**: *International Index* 　**1928-32**: *Social Science Abstracts* 　**1930**: *Encyclopedia of the Social Sciences* 　**1953**: *Sociological Abstracts* 　**1968**: *International Encyclopedia of the Social Sciences*	**1899**: Lombroso's *The Criminal Man* **1923**: First B.A. with minor in Criminology **1941**: American Society of Criminologists 　**1961**: *Criminology and Penology Abstracts*	**1916**: Vollmer's Police School 　**1929**: Kulman's *Guide to Material on Crime and Criminal Justice* (first comprehensive book-length bibliography) **1963**: Academy of Criminal Justice Sciences 　**1975**: *Criminal Justice Periodical Index* 　**1981**: *Encyclopedia of Crime and Justice* 　**1993**: *NCJRS* Index on CD-ROM 　**1995**: *Criminal Justice Abstracts on CD-ROM*

that impossible now. Today, scholars can read the top journals in their field, and try to keep up with the most important books being published, but they cannot possibly know everything published in related fields, or in less well-known periodicals. For the undergraduate, or even graduate student, this plethora of information may appear overwhelming.

POLICE AND LAW ENFORCEMENT	PENOLOGY and SOCIAL REFORM	ALL DISCIPLINES
	1764: Beccaria's *Essay on Crimes and Punishment* **1790s**: Beginning of experiments in penal reform in New York and Pennsylvania	
1845: New York City establishes first professional police force in America	**1845**: *Journal of Prison Discipline and Philanthropy* **1865**: American Social Science Association **1870**: American Correctional Association	**1848**: William Frederick Poole published what is perhaps the first periodical index **1876**: First edition of Dewey Decimal Classification
1893: International Association of Chiefs of Police **1909**: U.S. Bureau of Investigation (later called FBI) **1931**: *Uniform Crime Reports*	**1897**: *Encyclopedia of Social Reform*	**1902**: Library of Congress begins printing catalog cards
1968: Law Enforcement Assistance Administration **1973**: *Police Science Abstracts*		**1969**: ARPANET, precursor to the Internet, created **1971**: Appearance of MEDLARS database, one of the first online indexes **1980s**: First online library catalogs appear **1991**: Development of the World Wide Web

Fortunately for criminal justice researchers, as for those in other fields, as a discipline matures, its information agents mature as well. Privately published tracts are replaced by scholarly journals. As the books and journals multiply, library catalogs become standardized, and journal indexes develop. Knowledge is summarized and synthesized in textbooks and encyclopedias. The process continues today as the computer transforms card catalogs into online library catalogs and printed indexes into online databases, and begins to blur the boundaries between catalogs, indexes, books, journals, and encyclopedias.

Chart A is a schematic presentation of this process. It shows selected highlights in the historic development of criminal justice studies, as discussed in the Foreword, and some key bibliographic responses to that development.

Unfortunately, to many beginning (and some advanced) researchers, the development of these information tools and their increasing sophistication has come to seem part of the problem, rather than the solution. The modern library with its complex computer networks and, more recently, the new information tool called the Internet, are bewildering to many, and occasionally confusing even to librarians. Nevertheless, in spite of appearances, it really is easier than ever to find the information you need, whether for a term paper or a major grant proposal. The present book is designed to introduce you to the process of bibliographic research, help you decide what kind of information you need, and guide you directly to the most appropriate information resources.

Use this book in the manner in which it was designed. Read Part I, as it says, "Before You Start." Chapter 1, "Communication, Information, and Information Flow," provides a generalized overview of how information is generated and communicated by criminal justice researchers and practitioners. This is the chapter that gives you the theoretical basis for deciding where to start your research.

Chapter 2, "Efficiency in Research," is designed basically for the neophyte researcher, although even the more experienced may find it helpful. It deals with the mechanics of getting started and organized, and contains advice aimed at conserving both time and temper.

Chapter 3, "Bibliographic Searching," focuses on using the computer in doing bibliographic research. Understanding how computers organize information and how that information can then be retrieved makea using computerized bibliographic databases easier, less daunting, and more productive.

Chapter 4 discusses using the Internet. It describes what the Internet is, explains its primary tools, such as the World Wide Web, and explores its role in criminal justice research.

Part II moves beyond theory and methodology. Each chapter discusses a different type of information resource and offers practical details about how and when to use specific items.

Part III expands on four special kinds of research situations: legal research, forensic science research (with a chapter contributed by Katherine B. Killoran), historical research, and comparative research across countries.

The appendixes contain a variety of practical resources: lists of Library of Congress subject headings, directories, and criminal justice commission reports. The glossary helps with some of the less familiar terms.

Part I

BEFORE YOU START

1

Communication, Information, and Information Flow

COMMUNICATION

Criminal justice researchers and practitioners do not work in a vacuum. They need to know what others have done—what theories have been tested, what mistakes have been made—so that they are not starting from scratch whenever confronting a new problem. As Professor Sagarin described so well in detailing the history of criminal justice in the Foreword, the growth of a scholarly discipline depends on the communication of ideas and research results from one scholar to another.

Formal Communication

Publication of research results in reports, journals, and books has traditionally been the formal method of communication. Publication, whether in print or electronic form, usually implies a review of the material either by an editor or by a panel of one's peers in the field. Published sources are in permanent form and are independent of any one individual. This published communication of research results, with subsequent validation, analysis, and synthesis, constitutes the literature of a field.

Formal, published communication is generally publicly available. Research reports may be published in journals, newsletters, on the Internet, or separately by a government agency or research organization. Journals and books are widely sold to libraries and individuals, and increasingly may be available in electronic form through online services. All of these can usually be accessed through bibliographic citations found in library catalogs, printed or computerized indexes and abstracts, published bibliographies and encyclopedias, and as bibliographic notes in other published works.

The formal communication system is structured to allow information to be found, verified, and used to advance knowledge in a field.

Informal Communication

Communication can be informal as well as formal. The informal communication network is basically one person talking or writing to another. Although no attempt may be made to keep the information secret, its existence is not publicly known. Therefore it is unavailable to anyone outside the network of colleagues or friends.

Electronic mail (e-mail) and Internet discussion groups have broadened the reach of informal communication. With electronic mail and electronic exchange of documents, it is possible for researchers to collaborate on projects from a distance, or to solicit and receive comments on research before publication, even in the planning stages. Electronic discussion groups—e-mail distributed simultaneously to hundreds or thousands of subscribers—on the Internet provide researchers with the opportunity to get the kind of comments and feedback on their research that was previously available only after publication. Yet even though this type of communication may involve great numbers of people in a discussion, the text of the discussion is usually not available in permanent form, and the content of the discussion has not been reviewed or monitored by an editor or panel of experts. Although e-mail and discussion lists may have a wider impact than one person talking or writing to another, they are still informal means of communication.

While these loose, unregulated, impermanent methods of communication can often be effective means of exchanging information, misinformation can also be spread, and worthwhile knowledge can easily be lost.

INFORMATION

Communication transmits information in many ways and in many formats. Awareness of the distinctions between primary and secondary information sources, and among scholarly, popular, and professional literature is essential for the researcher.

Information Sources: Primary and Secondary

The distinction between primary and secondary sources can be vital to the scholar and to the student, even though to the world in general it often seems to matter little.

Primary Sources

Primary sources are raw data or information without analysis or interpretation. They are the building blocks from which the analytical literature of the discipline is built.

The form of a primary source may differ from one discipline to another. Failure to understand this is one reason for confusion about the meaning of the term. For the historian, a primary source can be a document written on vellum, an ideograph carved in stone, or a diary. For a political scientist a primary source can be a printout or file of voter records; for a sociologist, a returned survey form or a demographic database. For a scholar in criminal justice it can be any of the above or a report of the results of an experiment in dispute resolution by police officers.

As a source of information upon which to base conclusions, a primary source is always preferable to a secondary one. Nevertheless, primary sources vary in their reliability, or authority. Criteria generally used in evaluating the degree of authority of a primary source are (1) the closer in time and place to the activity documented, the better it is as a record of that activity; the immediate testimony of an eyewitness is probably more reliable than recollections written fifty years later; (2) the less selectivity involved in documenting the event, the more reliable is that documentation; a verbatim transcript of a trial or a press conference is more authoritative than the newspaper story reporting the event. It is not uncommon for the same document to contain primary data of different degrees of authority and also secondary analysis.

Even the most popular communication forms—newspapers and television—can be sources of primary data, but great care must be exercised in evaluating them. Television might have recorded the event, but someone exercised discretion in deciding where to point the camera; the journalist decided which parts of the story to emphasize and whom to interview. These problems are discussed further in Chapter 8.

Secondary Sources

Secondary sources involve the selection, evaluation, analysis, or synthesis of data or information. They may be based on a single primary source or may draw upon multiple sources, both primary and secondary.

Secondary sources most often take the form of articles and books. However, the distinction is in the substance of the material, not in its format. It is possible for a report to be mainly evaluative and analytical, and thus secondary in nature, and for the book format to be used for presentation of primary material.

The same source can be both primary and secondary depending upon how and when it is used. The 1897 *Encyclopedia of Social Reform* is today a primary source for anyone interested in tracing the history of concepts and movements in social reform, although it was a secondary source when published. Today's newspaper editorial describing mismanagement in the prison system is a secondary source for the researcher interested in prison administration but may be a primary source for one interested in attitudes toward prisons and prison administrators. In fifty years it can be a primary source for someone interested in either topic.

The Internet is a fascinating mix of primary and secondary sources. Original research results, survey data, and government statistics can all be found here and are clearly primary sources. Journal articles and books can also be found on the Internet and generally remain secondary source materials. But how should you categorize World Wide Web pages or archives of discussion groups? Again, it depends on how and when they are used.

Information Sources: Popular, Scholarly, and Professional

The distinctions between popular, scholarly, and professional literature are important for the researcher to recognize. However, you must keep in mind that the differences are not necessarily in the substance or quality of the information, but rather in its presentation, which is determined by the intended audience.

Popular Literature

Popular literature is that written for the average adult information-seeker who wants facts or opinions presented clearly and succinctly. Such readers do not intend to replicate the research process, but rely on the author to have used reliable sources and to have covered the topic thoroughly. Detailed descriptions of methodologies employed would be both unnecessary and unwelcome. Rather, illustrations and anecdotes abound. If readers disagree with the conclusions in the article, they either choose not to pursue the topic further or make attempts to find a more congenial author. Popular literature is often well researched, although not always according to strict scientific procedures. There may be a list of suggested readings, and books and articles may be mentioned in the text, but formal footnotes are rare. Examples of popular sources are newspapers and magazines such as *Time* and *Psychology Today*.

Scholarly Literature

Scholarly literature is written by and for a professional audience that needs to know not only the conclusions, but also the manner in which they were drawn. The reader is interested in theory, methodology, and precise identification of sources. Good scholarly articles are written so that the reader learns the derivation of every piece of information and every idea not original to the author; in other words, they are full of footnotes. The text and the notes can be used to retrace the research and check it with the original sources if there is any doubt as to the validity of the conclusions. The style of the article is often dry, highly technical, and full of the jargon of the field. Scholarly journals usually employ a panel of experts to review each article submitted for publication and advise on its merit, a process known as *peer review*. Examples of scholarly journals are *Criminology; An Interdisciplinary Journal*, a commercially produced journal from Sage Publications; and *Justice Quarterly*, an official publication of the Academy of Criminal Justice Sciences.

Professional Literature

Professional literature, a category which sets criminal justice apart from the more traditional academic disciplines, addresses the day-to-day problems of practitioners as distinct from the concerns of academics. As practitioners (although they may be scholars as well), these readers have policy and action as their main considerations. In fact, the position of the person who did the study may be of more interest than its research design and methodology. Practitioners are less likely to seek evaluation of the design of a study than to identify positive results directly applicable to their own problems. Examples of such articles may be found in *Corrections Today*, which is the official publication of the American Correctional Association, and *Police Chief*, published by the International Association of Chiefs of Police.

INFORMATION FLOW

Knowledge starts with an idea, an observation, a concept, or a theory in need of testing or elaboration. An overview of new ideas or theories as they move from inception to acceptance and inclusion in textbooks and encyclopedic tomes shows a generally similar progression through several identifiable stages. This movement is called the *information flow*.

The stages in the flow of information follow a basic pattern, although there are uncounted possibilities for variation due to the complexities of both research studies and researchers. The following hypothetical case is offered as an example of the movement of information within the criminal justice system.

The director of a large halfway house for juveniles believes that a certain type of educational program will reduce recidivism among juvenile offenders. The idea is discussed with staff, friends, and colleagues, both in person and via e-mail and electronic discussion lists, and, after a review of the existing literature, a research study is designed to test the hypothesis. Applications are made for research funding from the institution itself, a government agency, or a private foundation. When the funding is received and work is ready to begin, the project will be announced to criminal justice colleagues in the corrections or juvenile justice newsletters, and to the broader community through local newspapers.

While the project is underway, the director may again bring it to the attention of the criminal justice community by reading a paper at a professional conference. When the study is finally completed, a report of the findings will be written, submitted to the funding agency, and circulated within the criminal justice community. Reports of government and independent research agencies are also increasingly being made available on the Internet. The information in the report is now public.

If the findings appear to be significant, someone within the agency, or perhaps someone from the academic world, may write a journal article discussing them. The article, or the original report, may inspire other researchers to attempt replication of either all or part of the original study, perhaps expanding it to encompass additional related hypotheses. Additional reports and articles will in turn generate further discussion. As the ideas achieve wider circulation, they will be reported and discussed in books. Eventually, if widely accepted, they may appear in summary form in textbooks and encyclopedia articles.

In the above hypothetical example, it is possible to isolate seven distinct points in the flow of information: (1) informal discussion, in person and electronically; (2) announcements in newspapers, newsletters, and on Internet newsgroups; (3) conference papers; (4) formal reports; (5) journal articles; (6) books; and (7) textbooks and encyclopedias. At each of these points the communication occurs in a different format. Since most library research tools are designed to locate information in only one or two formats, access to the information flow varies. The information flow, and its access points, is illustrated schematically in Chart B.

Chart B
Information Flow and Access to Information in Criminal Justice

FORM OF INFORMATION	TO LOCATE THE INFORMATION, USE	FOR DISCUSSION, SEE CHAPTER
WORD OF MOUTH	• Internet • Directories	1, 4 Appendix B
NEWSLETTERS NEWSPAPERS NEWS BROADCASTS	• *Criminal Justice Periodical Index* • Newspaper indexes and databases • Broadcast indexes and Internet	8
CONFERENCE PAPERS	• Indexes to published proceedings • *Sociological Abstracts*	9
REPORTS and DOCUMENTS	• Indexes to reports and documents • Internet	9
JOURNAL ARTICLES	• Journal indexes and abstracts • Full text databases • Bibliographies	7 11
BOOKS and MONOGRAPHS	• Online library catalogs • Bibliographies	5 11
SUMMARIES, OVERVIEWS, HIGHLIGHTS	• Encyclopedias • Annual reviews	6

Although the subject matter at these seven steps may remain the same, at each level of communication there may be a meaningful shift or change in interpretation or conclusion. This can happen as the original idea is expanded or contracted, as unexpected subtleties arise and are dealt with, and as methodologies are refined.

Discussion with Friends and Colleagues

Discussion with friends and colleagues is the informal communication network. Unfortunately, it is available only to those within the "network" of friends and colleagues, although the spreading of these discussions to e-mail and Internet distribution lists has broadened the network considerably. While these discussions provide the most up-to-date information, they are also the most riddled with inaccuracies and unverified gossip. Informal networks exist in both the agency and academic worlds, and in their interstices.

Announcements in Newspapers and Newsletters

When a grant is received and/or a project started, it is announced and hopefully is described in the publications of the granting agency, the newsletters of the criminal justice profession, and possibly in the local newspapers of the community. Although the example with which we have been working involves an agency, research grants for both empirical and theoretical studies are available to academia as well.

Information in newsletters and newspapers is part of the formal information network. It can generally be located through the use of appropriate indexes and abstracts (see Chapters 7 and 8 for further discussion).

Conference Papers

The ideas and possibly some interim reports on the progress of the research, may be presented at a conference of scholars or criminal justice practitioners. Copies of papers presented at such conferences are made available to those who attend the conference. They may also be published in conference proceedings, and occasionally some are summarized in newsletters or newspapers. Some conferences establish World Wide Web pages for a limited time and "publish" abstracts of papers or entire papers presented at the conference. These may remain on the Internet in semi-permanent form, or disappear as soon as the conference is over.

Presentation of papers at a conference is somewhere between the informal and the formal; some information is available in printed or possibly electronic formats, and the careful researcher can locate it, although not always easily. The section of Chapter 9 on conference proceedings has a full description of the available tools (pp. 119–120).

Reports

At the conclusion of the study, a report is written. This report may vary in form from a full-scale book printed in large quantities and widely distributed; to a short, informal document. These reports can be written by an academic, a practitioner, or a person with a foot in each camp.

The formal report of a research project is generally called a research report if it is undertaken by a private agency or individual, and a government document if it emanates from a government agency.

Because of the variety in format, there are many ways to locate reports and documents, ranging from the general library catalog, to highly specialized indexes, to the Internet. It is important for the researcher to know the intricacies of locating these sources, because the information they contain is frequently unavailable in other formats. See Chapter 9 for a full discussion.

Journal Articles

Journal articles are frequently the next stage in the information flow. In the example we have been using, someone responsible for the research may write an article for a professional journal reporting the nature of the study and its conclusions. On the other hand, an academic associated with the project, or one who learns about it and is interested in the subject, may write an article for a scholarly journal discussing the study. In both instances the information conveyed is very likely to have appeared at one of the earlier stages of the information flow.

In the academic world, journal articles often represent the first step, rather than an intermediate one, in the process of information transfer. With the exception of those instances where there have been government grants, the newspaper/newsletter and report stages will not be involved. Scholarly journals are the key devices for transmission of ideas within the scholarly community.

Whether they represent the first stage or an intermediate one, journals are one of the most important sources of information for the criminal justice researcher. Articles may be located by use of the appropriate indexes and abstracts which are discussed in detail in Chapter 7.

Books

With the research reported and communicated to the profession, the ideas can now join the body of analytical literature in book form. Some studies by academics make their first appearance in books. Efficient and effective use of the library catalog to locate books is discussed in Chapter 5.

Summaries and Overviews

As the idea circulates more widely, and becomes accepted and integrated into the literature of the field, it is eventually incorporated into textbooks and encyclopedias (discussed in Chapter 6). The research is now integrated into the knowledge base of the discipline.

INFORMATION FLOW: THE ACADEMIC
AND THE PRACTITIONER

The information flow of criminal justice may be said to move in parallel streams; the academic, the practitioner, and the overlap represented by the person involved in both worlds. It would be nice if we could firmly assert that these streams flow together into a river from the constant interaction between them. In truth, evidence suggests that the ideal is not the actual.

Practitioners and agency personnel, even those with academic connections and backgrounds, are concerned with the vital problems of the here and now. They may not always think in terms of preserving the records of their research, or of ways to make the results available to others. Once a study has been completed and implemented, the written report no longer has any pressing value to the agency. It may be filed and forgotten. Academics and personnel from other agencies may hear about it through the informal information network, but its long-term use to scholars and historians may be largely overlooked in the press of daily agency concerns.

At the same time, practitioners, although they may desire theoretical support for their arguments, frequently have not had access tools readily available to locate the more formal research of their academic colleagues. Even if the tools were available, the time traditionally involved in locating relevant academic research may not have appeared as cost-effective to the busy administrator. There are signs that this is changing, however, due to the accessibility of electronic resources. Tools such as *Criminal Justice Abstracts* and the *NCJRS Document Database* are now available at a reasonable price to anyone with a microcomputer and a CD-ROM drive; many government reports are now available in full-text over the Internet to anyone with access; and news reports and journal articles can now be ordered over the Internet and delivered by fax (see Chapters 3, 7, 8, and 9).

INFORMATION FLOW INTO CRIMINAL JUSTICE

No profession or academic discipline functions in an enclosed bubble uninfluenced by other fields. This is particularly true of criminal justice.

A criminal justice researcher must consider the possibility of obtaining information from the many fields which intersect and feed directly into criminal justice. Although there are variations in the manner of information generation and dissemination in each of these subject areas, the basic movement of information and its relation to access tools are similar. Some interdisciplinary aspects of criminal justice research are quite obvious. It is hard to discuss problems of search and seizure without discussing constitutional law. You cannot consider the problems of literacy in the prison population without considering the education profession's research on adult literacy programs.

Chart C
Information Flow into Criminal Justice

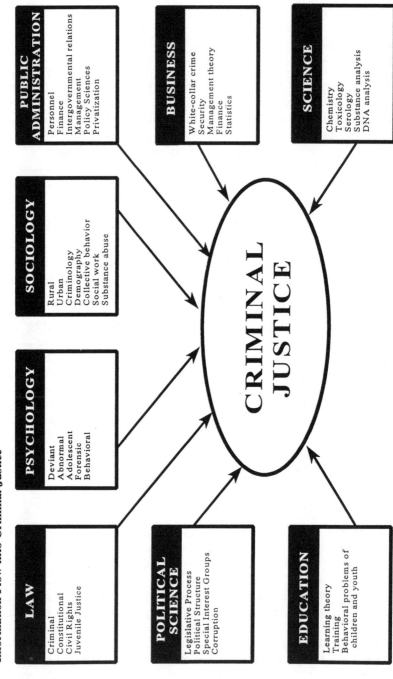

In other cases, more imagination is needed to assess possible information rewards from allied fields. For example, if you are interested in police stress, the literature of psychology will tell you about the psychology of stress; the literature of public administration or business administration may discuss on-the-job stress; and the literature of sociology may discuss the dynamics of constant work in small groups (such as two people in a patrol car). If you are interested in behavior modification as a rehabilitative technique in prisons, you may want to know what psychologists say about behavior modification, but you must also know what the law says about the civil rights of prisoners. To understand violence in American society it would help to read what anthropologists have observed about violence in other societies and at other times. Research studies of any depth into almost any problem in police administration would benefit from information derived from the fields of public administration, business administration, and political science.

See Chart C for a schematic representation of the interdisciplinary nature of criminal justice research.

ENTERING THE INFORMATION FLOW NETWORK

The key point for the researcher is to understand the nature of the information flow, and to decide where to "plug in" to that flow.

If a commanding officer wants to know which departments in the state are currently conducting research on community relations with non-English speaking minorities, and needs the information tomorrow morning, it is best to plug into that informal network in the fastest way possible, possibly with a phone call (perhaps using a directory listed in Appendix B) or a message broadcast on a discussion list. On the other hand, if what is wanted is a thorough review of all such programs currently underway, and you have a few days leeway, it may be best to go beyond the informal, and work down the information flow through newsletters, newspapers, and journal articles.

If, however, you need to get a fast overview of the problems of probation before deciding on a research topic, you may want to start at the other end of the continuum with the synthesizing and summarizing literature of encyclopedias and textbooks.

Breaking into the information flow at an appropriate point is not difficult. Just as there is an overall logic to the manner in which information moves, there is also an overall logic to the tools which enable researchers to access that information.

Reference tools have been developed to serve as connectors between the researcher and both the substantive information and the citations which lead to that information. Knowing the manner in which information flows within the field, and the appropriate reference tools for locating that information, is one key to efficient and effective library research.

2

Efficiency in Research

Only the rare, or lucky, researcher can rush into a library at the last moment, check a few references, digest limited information, and compile an acceptable report. For most persons, library research is a time consuming, sometimes confusing project, followed by the challenge of writing a cohesive report. Although this chapter is directed primarily at the neophyte researcher, even the more experienced may find helpful ideas.

A MASTER PLAN

Every project will benefit from a master plan, the framework of efficient research. Step by step the researcher should

1. Choose a topic
2. Draft an outline
3. Master the arrangements and procedures of the library to be used
4. Consider the information flow
5. Establish parameters
6. Maintain a research record
7. Build a bibliography
8. Locate the needed materials
9. Master a citation format
10. Choose and use a method for taking notes
11. Revise the outline

12. Write the first draft

13. Revise

These steps tend to merge with one another and may not inevitably follow this exact sequence. As you find, read, and analyze material you may be led to additional important citations that induce you to alter your original topic and outline. Following a master plan in general, however, will assure orderly progress toward your goal of efficient research.

1. CHOOSE A TOPIC

Choosing a topic is the first—and often the most difficult—step in writing a paper. Professors may give students the freedom to select a topic, hoping that personal interest will foster finer research. The student, on the other hand, faced with such a broad choice, may be at a loss for ideas. If you are in the latter situation, help is available. You can turn to

- *Encyclopedias.* The overview and organization of material in an encyclopedia may indicate topics worthy of investigation and expansion.
- *Periodical Indexes and Abstracts.* Scanning the subject indexes or tables of contents in recent printed issues may identify topics of current concern.
- *Textbooks.* Chapter headings and sub-headings may suggest areas for research.
- *Discussions.* Talks with professors, professionals, coworkers, librarians, and fellow students can reveal questions in need of answers and comments in need of clarification or rebuttal.
- *Library of Congress Subject Headings.* Your library will have this list of all the subject headings established by the Library of Congress for use in library catalogs. Selected lists of Library of Congress subject headings related to criminal justice are provided in Appendix A of this book. Scan these lists for topic ideas.

Be sure to choose a subject you find interesting. The topic you choose must be sufficiently limited in scope to allow for reasonable coverage, given the length of your project. It also must be sufficiently broad to allow you to locate enough information to write about. If you consider doing a comparison, be wary. Comparisons tend to double the required research and, for most students, time can be in very short supply. You must plan to spend enough time doing the research to capture the essence of your topic.

If actual time in the library, as well as time in general, is your problem, choose your research topic with this in mind. Although every topic requires some work in the library, the relationship between time needed for work in the library and time needed for work at home can vary considerably. Research that centers on recent events and new ideas is likely to require the use of journals and newspapers which, even though they can be photocopied, take considerable library time, especially if they are on microfilm. On the other hand, long-standing controversies and well-established concepts are likely to be well covered by books that can be read at home.

If you are planning to work on a topic that relies heavily on statistical sources, find out if any of the data can be downloaded or copied from a computer network in your library or university, or perhaps downloaded from the Internet, to be analyzed on a microcomputer at home. Realize that, in most libraries, reference books with statistics are noncirculating.

If you are hopeful that most of your information can come from the Internet, and you can bypass the library altogether, think again. While current newspapers, government reports, and authoritative statistics can all easily be found on the Internet, books and journals—the mainstays of the formal communication network—are still largely only available in print and most easily found through libraries. In addition, finding information on the Internet, a medium known for its lack of organization, can be considerably more time-consuming than locating information in libraries, whose *raison d'etre* is the organization of knowledge. See Chapter 4 for more information on using the Internet.

2. DRAFT AN OUTLINE

Your preliminary work does not have to be done in a library. Thinking is a vital part of the research process; it can be done almost anywhere. Thinking carefully about your outline in the beginning can save you time later.

If you did not use an encyclopedia to find a subject, this is a good time to consult entries relevant to your topic for general background information.

Now, write a preliminary outline. It may be very broad. It will probably list questions or concepts rather than specific facts. Keep the outline tentative and flexible, since it will undoubtedly undergo several revisions. This is the time to begin using your computer's word processing program. It will allow you to revise your outline more easily and you can even use your outline as the backbone of your paper.

At this stage if you do not feel comfortable preparing an outline, do more background reading. List questions you need to answer and ask yourself "What do I want to know?" The more you learn about the topic, the easier it will be to prepare your draft outline. If it is not getting easier, you should rethink your choice of topic. You may choose to limit yourself to only one aspect of your original topic, or you may want to select another one.

3. MASTER THE LIBRARY

How many libraries do you have access to? How many libraries will you need to use for your topic? If you need to use more than one library or need to use a library to which you do not normally have access, you may want to reconsider your topic.

To work efficiently in any library you must know how it is arranged. Most libraries in the United States arrange their books according to either the Library of Congress Classification or the Dewey Decimal System; both systems bring together items on the same subject. Even libraries that use the same classification schedules may vary considerably in the arrangement of their resources. Most libraries distribute maps and floor plans to acquaint you with their facilities. Request one. Once you know where things are located you will not aimlessly roam the stacks and waste time.

In becoming acquainted with the library be sure to note where the reference librarians are located. They are the single best source of information in the library. Do not overlook them.

Learn the library's procedures. What materials circulate? What identification do you need to enter the library or to borrow materials? If you find that you need to use other libraries, can arrangements be made to gain access or can you request material through interlibrary loan? How much time must you allow for an interlibrary loan?

4. CONSIDER THE INFORMATION FLOW

If you skipped, skimmed, or did not fully understand Chapter 1, go back and read it now. It is a vital part of organizing your research plan. Note the various forms in which information can be found. Do you really need to use all elements of the flow, or can you intercept the information flow at a specific point? Which type of information source is most likely to yield the material needed for your project? For a short paper a few carefully selected periodical articles may give you all the material you need. For a very long project you may need to do a complete review of the literature, using the entire range of sources. Most research projects fall somewhere in-between.

Always keep in mind the interdisciplinary nature of criminal justice research. For example, in considering prison industries you may have to look at the literature in the fields of business and politics, as well as that in corrections. In researching the use of hypnotism in criminal investigation, you may want to read the opinions of psychologists and people concerned with civil rights law, as well as those of persons concerned with law enforcement. If you are writing on vandalism in state parks you should search public administration resources. In almost every case be prepared to use indexes from related subject areas.

5. ESTABLISH PARAMETERS

Armed with the knowledge of the general pattern of information flow, a subject, and a draft outline, you should decide the parameters of your research before you start. Some parameters are almost mechanical. Either with your professor, or alone, you have determined the length of the work, the currency of the material to use, and the amount of subjectivity which is acceptable. Your outline will help establish parameters on the depth of research required.

6. MAINTAIN A RESEARCH RECORD

Keeping a research record may sound as though it will take extra time. Actually, it is a procedure designed for people who have little time, or who must do their research in small segments of time. Consider the advantages such a record offers:

1. It is a visual record of the sources you will use;
2. It enables you to proceed in an organized fashion;
3. It keeps you from backtracking if you are interrupted;
4. It enables you to use even very short periods of time effectively.

In your record, you should

1. On a separate index card or sheet, list each source to be searched—be it a library catalog, printed index, database available through an online public access catalog (OPAC), CD-ROM database, or Internet resource:
   a. Use this book and consult with your librarian for possible indexes and abstracts to list;
   b. Remember to include indexes to government documents and reports, if appropriate;
   c. Make separate cards or sheets for each catalog, if you are using more than one catalog or more than one library.
2. For printed indexes, or other sources that come out periodically and do not cumulate, list on each card or sheet what issues of that source you will search:
   a. If you are confining your research to the last five years, for instance, list issues for those five years only;
   b. Check off each issue as you finish reviewing it.
3. For each online and CD-ROM database, list on a card or sheet what period of time is covered:
   a. If the source does not extend its coverage as far into the past as your research requires, note whether a printed index preceded the electronic one, and make a separate card or sheet for that earlier resource;
   b. Note whether the source must be accessed in the library, or if it can be searched from another site on campus or from home.
4. List on each card or sheet the subject headings or keywords under which to search in that particular source:
   a. Remember that there is a wide disparity of indexing terms among catalogs, indexes, abstracts, and databases;
   b. Find out which indexes, abstracts, and databases have their own thesauri or list of subject headings (sometimes called *descriptors)* used in that index. Examine these for useful terms. As you work with each source, add or delete terms, and check them off as you search them;

c. When you look at an actual card catalog, online catalog, or computerized index under the subject headings you have chosen, see if there are additional terms, under which the item is cataloged. They may be at the bottom of the card in a card catalog, or listed as *subject headings* or *descriptors* in an online catalog or index;

d. Use the Library of Congress subject heading lists, or the "Selected Library of Congress Subject Headings in Criminal Justice," printed as Appendix A of this book;

e. Use thesauri, subject heading lists, and subject headings found in library catalogs as the start of your list of keywords for searching online databases. Add or delete terms as you proceed by examining the titles, abstracts, and descriptors of the most relevant citations that you find. Be sure to keep track of what terms you have searched to avoid duplicating your work.

5. When using Internet resources make a card or sheet for each source you want to check:

a. As you find additional resources make another card for each one; be sure to include the URL (Universal Resource Locator) so you, your reader, or your professor can find it again;

b. If you are using a World Wide Web browser on your own computer, you can also bookmark sites or pages to which you want to return.

A Special Caution About Hypertext

You will find that many of the newer computerized research tools use *hypertext* to make the work easier, more enjoyable, or faster for the student or scholar. These tools use *links*, embedded in the text, that can be clicked on with a mouse to bring you to a related item. For example, each bibliographic citation in an online catalog may include a highlighted or numbered list of all the subject headings assigned to the book. The user can just click on the subject heading or type in the number assigned to it to jump directly to a list of all the books in the catalog that have been assigned that subject heading. An online encyclopedia may have particular words or concepts highlighted. Clicking on those words or phrases will bring you to other related articles. A World Wide Web site may list ten other sources of information. Click on any one and you can view it immediately.

Hypertext brings a wonderful feeling of freedom. One or two mouse clicks and you are examining a new subject, never having to pick up a pen to note the subject heading, only to put it down again while keying the words back into the computer. One or two clicks and you can follow your train of thought to the next related encyclopedia article, never having to search for, write down, and look up each one.

Obviously, though, this can wreck havoc with your attempts to organize your research. If you are searching an online catalog under the heading "Wife

Abuse" and the second book listed has also been cataloged under "Abused Wives," resist the urge to jump to "Abused Wives" or you may never examine the twenty other books listed under "Wife Abuse." Instead, use your research record to add "Abused Wives" to the subject headings you must search.

Finish reading that online encyclopedia article and taking notes on it before you jump to the related articles. If the related articles seem too compelling to postpone, note in your research record that you need to check the original source again.

World Wide Web sites, with their myriad links to other sources and their determinedly nonlinear organization, can shatter the plans of the most organized researcher. Use your research record to keep track of which sites you have visited, which were useless, and which you wish to return to. The Internet is often referred to as cyberspace, but it can seem more like quicksand, drawing you in slowly until you have drowned in enticing links, beautiful pictures, and words without substance. Taken seriously, your research record can be your rope back to safety if you get hopelessly lost.

7. BUILD A BIBLIOGRAPHY

When you find items that are useful to you, list the full bibliographic information, either on your cards, on separate notebook sheets, or in a file on your computer. It is vital that bibliographic citations be legible and complete. Most librarians can tell dozens of horror stories about frenzied late-night telephone calls begging for one piece of missing bibliographic information.

At this stage do not attempt to be too evaluative. If the item seems useful, list it. You can discard superfluous materials later. Also, do not be hampered by the suspicion that your library may not have an item. If the library does not own a title, it can often be obtained from another library.

Realize that this is a recursive process, and that you will be building your bibliography throughout the research process. As you begin to read the items on your list, you will find other relevant items listed in their bibliographies.

Allow room for serendipity. When you go to the shelves to look for a book, don't put blinders on; look around at the other books on the shelves in that area. Are they also relevant to your topic? When you locate a periodical article on your list, look over the table of contents in the issue of the journal. Have you stumbled on a special issue of the journal devoted to your topic? Are you lucky enough to be holding in your hand other articles that are useful to your research, or perhaps letters to the editor in subsequent issues supporting or refuting the original article?

Most researchers find at least some of their information simply by accident or by browsing. Allow such accidents to happen to you. Do not, however, waste inordinate amounts of time browsing the titles of hundreds or books or articles. Use your judgment and don't stray too far from your master plan.

8. LOCATE MATERIALS

Locating materials is largely a mechanical procedure, but one that frequently requires more time than the average researcher considers reasonable. Ideally, everything you need can either be borrowed or photocopied. In reality, you will probably hit some snags. Be sure to allow more time than you think you will need.

If you are unable to locate things on the shelves, find out if your library provides a search service for items that appear to be missing. Will the library recall titles you need if they are checked out on long-term loan? Will it accept reserves for items being used by another patron?

Acquaint yourself with services to obtain books and journals that are not in your library. Many libraries now have available, either in print, in microformat, on computer, or over the Internet, catalogs of other libraries to aid you in locating material (see pp. 59–62 for information on searching catalogs over the Internet). Most libraries provide an interlibrary loan service that will obtain needed material for you from other libraries; some belong to local and regional consortia that permit patrons to borrow from any member library.

9. MASTER A CITATION FORMAT

If you look in the subject section of a library catalog under "report writing" or "research" you will find books telling you how to cite, and how to write.

Books that tell you how to cite materials are called style manuals. These began as lists of rules for printers to use in setting type and have evolved into books of rules for writers to use in preparing papers, articles, and books. Take time to study the style manual you will use, where you will find the details of the formats and mechanics for presentation of your research. Pay particular attention to the preparation of footnotes or endnotes and of bibliographies. Master the kinds of information needed for each, and the mechanics of its arrangement, without losing sight of the underlying reason for including citations. Students tend to get obsessive about punctuation when preparing a bibliography and agonize about whether to use a comma or a period. The point of the notes and the bibliography, however, is to tell the reader what sources of information the author used in preparing the article, book, or report, and to give the reader sufficient information so that he or she can find that source and read it. As you are building your bibliography make sure you are collecting all the information you need so that the readers of *your* report can find the sources *you* used. Stick to the main formats; exceptions can be checked later. If you do not purchase a copy of the style manual, or even if you do, make a sample copy of the basic examples to keep with your research record. Such practice assures that you will record complete information in the required format.

Possible style manuals to use include the following:

The Chicago Manual of Style. 14th ed. Chicago: University of Chicago Press, 1993.

Gibaldi, Joseph. *MLA Handbook for Writers of Research Papers.* 4th ed. New York: Modern Language Association of America, 1995.

Li, Xia. *Electronic Styles: A Handbook for Citing Electronic Information.* 2nd ed. Medford, NJ: Information Today, 1996.

Publication Manual of the American Psychological Association. 4th ed. Washington, DC: American Psychological Association, 1994.

Slade, Carole, William Giles Campbell, and Stephen Vaughan Ballou. *Form and Style: Research Papers, Reports, Theses.* 9th ed. Boston: Houghton Mifflin, 1994.

Turabian, Kate L. *A Manual for Writers of Term Papers, Theses, and Dissertations.* 6th ed. Chicago: University of Chicago Press, 1996.

10. CHOOSE AND USE A METHOD FOR TAKING NOTES

For years writing guides have recommended cards for maintaining bibliographic records and for taking notes. Some guides even discuss the relative merits of the various sizes and colors of cards. It is a time-proven method. In the past twenty or thirty years, however, many people have forsaken the taking of notes for the making of photocopies, either of entire articles or of pertinent sections. Commuter students and part-time researchers in particular may need to collect materials in the library and do their reading and evaluation at another time and place.

Many people today also feel it is faster to highlight important paragraphs than to take notes and copy quotes by hand or with a computer. Time saving is their major consideration. Be aware, however, that the very process of note-taking involves analysis of the material, which can then be incorporated directly into your work. Use of photocopying can reduce time spent in the library, but reliance on photocopying to the total exclusion of note-taking can actually make the process of synthesizing information more difficult in the end.

When researchers make extensive use of photocopying, their "notes" end up measuring 8½ by 11 inches. If this is the method of research you use, then it is more efficient for you to list your bibliographic sources on separate sheets of paper that can be interfiled easily with your photocopies, or simply to write the full citation on the photocopy. Always identify the source of your photocopy at the time you make the copy.

If you have a computer at home or have a laptop computer that you can take with you to the library, you may find that you prefer to take notes on your computer. You can use an elaborate file or database management system to sort your notes by topic, or simply use your word processing software to create a file of notes for each source you use. The computer makes it easy to search for key words in your notes, to organize them, and to cut and paste from your notes directly into your first draft when appropriate.

As you collect your notes, be sure that you understand plagiarism. Not only direct quotations, but also paraphrased or summarized information and ideas must be documented. The sources must also be noted for all visual material such as tables or cartoons. Plagiarism is a serious academic offense. If you are unsure of what is considered to be "permissible" use of sources, talk to your professor, or consult one of the style manuals listed above.

Remember that most access tools do not give you qualitative assessment of the resources you have chosen. You must analyze your information, discovering its strengths and weaknesses, and comparing and contrasting ideas for variations and similarities. Research can be defined as a systematic inquiry into a subject in order to discover facts and revise theories.

11. REVISE THE OUTLINE

Having gathered your material, taken notes, and evaluated the substance of your sources, go back to your draft outline to add the extra details you have learned about your topic. Often the material, as you evaluate it, falls into logical segments. Take advantage of such natural divisions. The more detailed the outline you produce at this point, the less rewriting you will have to do.

One final note: Be prepared to discard some of the material you have collected. Not everything that sounded great at one point in your research will be usable now. Padded writing may look impressive, but professors and editors generally like it lean.

12. WRITE THE FIRST DRAFT

If at all possible, use a computer to write your paper. Few people can compose sentences, paragraphs, or chapters in their heads that come out perfectly the first time they appear on paper. A computer allows you to easily change your words as your ideas form, makes major revisions possible, and reduces the pain of the inevitable process of rewriting.

If you have not done much writing recently (or ever) you may want to look at some books that discuss writing techniques. Many guides also offer tips on the methodology of assembling a research paper. With variations, they discuss the sequence of sections, outlining, sentence structure, grammar, and punctuation, and make suggestions to make the job easier. Try one of these titles:

Harbrace College Handbook. 12th ed. Fort Worth: Harcourt Brace Jovanovich, 1994.

Meyer, Michael. *The Little, Brown Guide to Writing Research Papers.* 3rd ed. New York: HarperCollins, 1994.

Runkel, Philip Julian. *A Guide to Usage for Writers and Students in the Social Sciences.* Totowa, NJ: Rowman & Allanheld, 1984.

Strunk, William, Jr., and E. B. White. *The Elements of Style.* 3rd ed. New York: Macmillan, 1979.

Walker, Melissa. *Writing Research Papers: A Norton Guide.* 3rd ed. New York: Norton, 1993.

Williams, Joseph M. *Style: Toward Clarity and Grace.* Chicago: University of Chicago Press, 1990.

Zinsser, William Knowlton. *On Writing Well: An Informal Guide to Writing Nonfiction.* 5th ed. New York: HarperPerennial, 1994.

Writing help is also available online over the Internet. The following site provides handouts on writing research papers, parts of speech, sentence construction, citing sources and other writing concerns, and points to additional sources of online writing help:

The Purdue University Online Writing Lab (OWL). Available [Internet] at http:// owl.english.purdue.edu/

13. REVISE

After you have written your first draft, put your work aside for a day and then reread it. Try to read it as your intended audience will read it. Have you explained unfamiliar ideas? Are your arguments logical? Do you support your thesis?

If you are using a computer to write your paper, you will be more willing to endure editing and rewriting more than once. Multiple passes through your effort are useful because you will find it is easier to correct your grammar and spelling after you are confident that you have expressed your ideas well. Use a spelling checker if you have one.

3

Bibliographic Searching

In Chapter 1 we discussed the information flow in criminal justice. If you did not read that chapter, or did not understand it, go back and read it now. In this chapter we will discuss how to find the information you need using the bibliographic tools available—primarily in computerized form. The paradox of computer use in libraries is that while computers have made it easier for you to find information, they have made it harder to understand the nature of the information you can find.

When computers were nonexistent in libraries or invisible in the backrooms of technical processing departments, library users often found it difficult to use library tools but easy to understand what they were for. Once you understood the concept of information flow and had defined what part of the information flow you needed to access, it was simple to decide which library tools to use. If you were looking for books, you used the library card catalog; for periodical articles, an index or abstract; for a general overview of a topic, an encyclopedia; for statistics, an almanac or special statistical publication. If you located a book or an article through the catalog or an index you would go and read the source in print.

A single networked computer can now substitute for all of these tools—for the card catalog, the printed periodical index, the encyclopedia, the statistical reference book, and even for the printed text of the article or book. The computer makes searching for, and using, the information fast and easy, but to make the best use of the tool, the user must have a more sophisticated knowledge of the nature of information and of how computers store and retrieve it.

WHAT IS A DATABASE?

A *database* is a collection of data, or small pieces of information, organized so that the information can be easily retrieved. Typically the data are organized into *records,* which are further subdivided into *fields.*

In a bibliographic database, a record represents a single book or article. The different types of information that you normally collect for a citation in a bibliography are separate fields in the bibliographic record. A record for a book is likely to contain an author field, a title field, a date field, a field for the place of publication, a publisher field, and fields for each subject heading assigned by a cataloger to the book. Some book records also have fields that list the contents of a book, especially if the book consists of a collection of essays by different authors.

A record for an article in a journal also has an author field, a title field, a date field, and often contains fields for subject headings (though they may be termed descriptors). But instead of fields for place of publication and publisher, it has fields for the name of the journal the article appeared in, for the volume of the journal, and for the specific page numbers the article appeared on. Some records may also have fields for an abstract, or summary, of the article.

A library usually makes many different databases available to its users. The library online catalog is the database that contains the bibliographic records for all the books owned by the library; this will be discussed further in Chapter 5. There are also databases, equivalent to printed indexes and abstracts, that contain records for articles in particular disciplines like psychology, sociology or criminal justice, as you will see in Chapter 7. These different databases may be accessed from the same computer or computer terminal, or from totally separate computer systems.

Once the bibliographic information about a book or article is systematically stored in a computer database in records and fields, it can be transformed onto different computer media (computer tape, CD-ROM, or diskette, for example) and used on different computer systems (for example, mainframe computers, or local area networks). The database does not change, but the *search software* probably does.

SEARCH SOFTWARE

The computer programs that allow you to search a database for the information you want are called *search engines* or *search software*. It is the search software that determines if all words in a field are searchable, and if all fields in a record are searchable or only some. Data records for books, for example, often have fields that contain information about the contents of the book—a very short summary, or perhaps the entire table of contents. Some search engines allow you to search this contents field, and some do not.

The *user interface* part of the search software determines what the user sees on the computer screen and what the user must do to search the database. If you are looking for a book by its title, must you select "title search" from a menu, or do you type the command "t=" followed by the title of the book? Can you search for a combination of fields—the author's last name and the title, for example—or must you search one field at a time? Can you browse a list of titles or subject headings, or look for exact matches only? Can you search for free text, or keywords, that may appear in any field? Can you combine concepts with Boolean logic?

All this is determined by the search software, not by the database. Some commercially produced databases, such as *Psychological Abstracts*, are distributed for use by many different vendors, each of which provides its own search software. They may also be leased to libraries on computer tape to be loaded onto a computer and searched using the same search software as the online catalog. This explains why you can walk into three different libraries and search the same database, but have a different experience in each library. You may get very different results from what you thought was the exact same search. The database has not changed, but the way you search it has.

BIBLIOGRAPHIC SEARCHING

Keyword Searching

If the contents of a particular field in a database—the title field, for example—were simply listed in alphabetical order, the result would be that you would browse through the records very much as if you were browsing through a card catalog or a printed index. *Keyword*, or free text, searching liberates you from the tyranny of the alphabet by granting the ability to search for a word that appears anywhere in a field, not just at the beginning.

Most search software allows for keyword searching, but the fields that are searchable vary greatly from program to program. With some search engines, entering a single word automatically searches every field in every record of the database. With other programs you must specify which field or fields you want to search. Some fields may not be searchable at all. When you start searching in a database, think about the fields in which your word will be searched. In some periodical indexes words in the field containing the title of the journal will be searched. Will this help you find relevant articles, or overwhelm you with erroneous hits?

Boolean Searching

Using a concept called *Boolean logic*, the computer can combine subjects and coordinate concepts. Boolean logic employs the words (or *operators*)

AND, **OR**, and **NOT** (shown in capital letters only for purposes of illustration) in order to build sets of citations. Most search software allows the use of Boolean logic to combine words, either within a field, between fields, or in the entire record.

For example, you plan to write an article comparing and contrasting jails and prisons. By using the **AND** operator you can retrieve those records in the database that have *both* the word **jails** *and* the word **prisons**, as shown in Figure 3.1.

By using the **OR** operator, you can broaden your search and retrieve articles that discuss *either* **jails** *or* **prisons**, as shown in Figure 3.2.

If you want to retrieve articles on jails alone, not those that also include a discussion of prisons, you can eliminate the latter by using the **NOT** operator, as shown in Figure 3.3.

The **NOT** operator is a risky one to use, however, particularly if you are using Boolean logic to search keywords in all fields, including abstracts. Computers are very literal; they do not make judgments. The **NOT** operator in the last example literally instructs the computer to find the word **jails** anywhere it appears in a record; if the word **prisons** also appears in the same record eliminate the record from the results. Using this logic, if the following phrase appeared in an abstract, the citation would be discarded: "the study focuses on conditions in **jails** rather than in **prisons**."

Most search software allows you to search databases with combinations of Boolean operators to allow you to find precisely what you need. To find citations about violence in either prisons or jails you can enter the phrase: **(jails OR prisons) AND violence**, as shown in Figure 3.4. Use parentheses to instruct the computer which operators to apply first, just as if you were writing a mathematical expression.

The most flexible search engines allow you to use Boolean logic and at the same time restrict one or more of your terms to particular fields. You can restrict some of your terms to a subject heading field, for example, or instruct the computer to limit your citations to those within a particular date range. In some cases you can even search for types of material, such as films or reports.

Figure 3.1
Jails AND Prisons

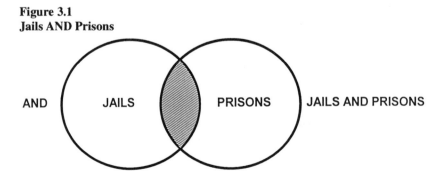

Figure 3.2
Jails OR Prisons

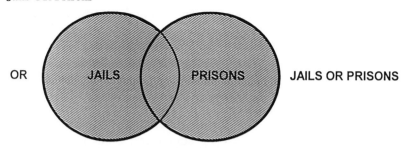

Figure 3.3
Jails NOT Prisons

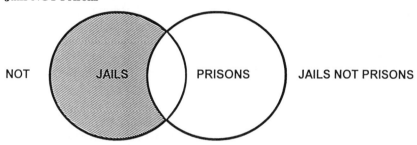

Figure 3.4
(Jails OR Prisons) AND Violence

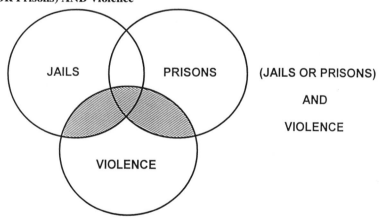

The particular commands that you must use will vary depending on the search software and its user interface, but the concepts remain the same. As always, you must think carefully about what you are trying to find, and then learn how to structure your search for the software you are using.

Phrase Searching

Think about what can happen if you enter two or more words together as a phrase. Each word in the phrase can appear as a separate entity in the database, and the search engine must decide what to do with the combination of words. It can search for the words exactly the way you entered them; that is, the words must appear in a field next to each other and in the exact order you typed. It can search for words that are next to each other but in a different order; for example, finding **abused sexually**, as well as **sexually abused**. Some search engines seek to increase the number of responses by looking for the words in any order as long as they both appear in the same field; for example, finding the phrase "sexually and physically abused." Still another possibility is that, in order to give the user a greater number of hits, the search engine automatically searches for both words appearing anywhere in a record—in effect, a Boolean AND search.

Somewhere, in a help screen or an online tutorial, most search systems explain what happens when keywords are entered into the system without qualification. Particularly flexible search engines allow you to specify exactly how you want words to be related by using *proximity* (sometimes called *relational* or *positional*) *operators* such as ADJ, NEAR, SAME, and WITH. Find out if your computerized systems use these terms and how they define them. Become an efficient searcher by learning what the software does when left to its own devices, and find out how to make it search the fields you want in the manner you want.

Truncation

Yet another technique made possible by computer searching is the ability to truncate a word. The concept of *prison* is expressed by the words **prison**, **prisons**, **prisoner**, or **prisoners**. In most systems it is possible to simply type the word **prison** followed by a truncation symbol—frequently a question mark or an asterisk (e.g., **prison?**)—to search all words which begin with those six letters. With some search engines the same symbol can be used as a *wild card* within a word to search for words that have all of the same letters except for one; for example, **wom?n** can be **woman** or **women**.

WAIS Searching

WAIS is a very different way of searching for information in full-text databases. WAIS (Wide Area Information Server) searching was developed by a company called Thinking Machines in the late 1980s. WAIS uses client–server software in which a specially constructed database is located on a server computer and the search engine is on another client computer. WAIS uses keywords to retrieve documents but does not use standard Boolean operators

(AND, OR, NOT). Instead, WAIS searches for and ranks documents according to the frequency of occurrence of the keywords. WAIS rarely returns an empty set; that is, "no records found." If a WAIS search fails to find records with both words it returns records that contain just one of the words, listing first those records where the word is used most frequently. In Boolean terms, it starts with an AND search and moves to an OR search if necessary. WAIS uses artificial intelligence to try to satisfy a search request in any way possible.

Many WAIS clients also use a tool called *relevance feedback*, where the searcher can identify the most relevant text found so far, and ask for more information similar to those items.

WAIS is widely used to search databases found on the Internet (see Chapter 4). It has also been used, or adapted, to search large, commercially provided full-text databases, where the sheer number of words renders Boolean searching less useful. The Dow Jones/News Retrieval system uses WAIS, and WESTLAW uses a form of WAIS searching in the natural language search it developed for its huge legal database.

FULL-TEXT SEARCHING

As the cost of computer storage has decreased, publishers have increasingly produced the entire text of even large documents in machine-readable form. Legal materials such as laws, cases, and regulations were computerized fairly early by companies like Mead Data Central (LEXIS) and West Publishing (WESTLAW); both because of the need of lawyers to be able to search for materials quickly, thoroughly, and efficiently, and because of the ability of law firms to pay the enormous costs involved in converting the printed documents to machine-readable form, in developing the search software necessary to search such complex databases, and in connecting to mainframe computers via telephone lines. Newspapers like *The New York Times* also appeared full-text in machine-readable form fairly early in the computer revolution, to be used by businesses willing to pay for up-to-date information available instantly. Both LEXIS and WESTLAW (through a connection with DIALOG Information) have expanded to provide access to the full text of thousands of newspapers, magazines, and journals (see Chapter 8).

More recently, the evolution of CD-ROM technology for home computers has led to the development of full-text databases such as encyclopedias and other reference tools.

Full-text databases can often be searched in their entirety using keyword searching and either Boolean or WAIS logic. But the enormity of full-text databases requires extreme care in the user's choice of search words and how they are combined.

Full-text databases can also come with hypertext links embedded in the documents. If an encyclopedia article mentions a concept that is more fully described elsewhere, for example, the user can just use the mouse to click on the concept to read the other article. If a legal decision cites an earlier case, a user can click on the citation for that case to view it instantly.

MEDIATED SEARCHING

When database searching was in its early stages, the databases were housed on mainframe computers. Specially trained librarians acted as mediators between the users and the searching software, and connected to the databases via modem and telephone lines. Computer time was very expensive, and searches were charged by the minute.

This type of searching has not entirely disappeared. There are still many databases, including some in criminal justice and forensic science, that are available only on large mainframe systems maintained by companies like DIALOG and DataStar. The connection to the database now can be made via the Internet rather than a dialup telephone line, but the search software is still too complex for the average user to master.

There are advantages to a mediated search. Although you cannot access the database yourself to experiment with different search strategies, you will be dealing with a librarian or other trained searcher who is experienced both with constructing a search logically and with the search software involved. While you may have to pay for the search, it can be a very efficient use of your time and money.

USING CARD CATALOGS AND PRINTED INDEXES

Libraries today are very different than they were ten or fifteen years ago. They are now filled with rows of personal computers or computer terminals linking the user to multitudes of databases. Not all information has been converted to machine-readable form, however, and print resources should not be neglected.

Manual searching involves looking through cards in a catalog or examining printed volumes of an index. The information you will find—author, title, date, and the like—is similar to what you find in a computerized resource; but the methods of finding the information differ. In a card catalog, keyword searching is not an option. Instead, you must use the printed *Library of Congress Subject Headings* list (or use the list in Appendix A) to find a valid subject heading for your topic. Many library users enjoy browsing through catalog cards. The eye may capture related, or even unrelated, sources of information of use now or at a later date.

With a printed index or abstract you need to examine the introductory information at the front of each volume to find out how the index is arranged and how to search it. Some indexes have a classified arrangement: *Criminology, Penology and Police Science Abstracts*, for example, is divided into broad areas like criminology, deviant behavior, juvenile justice, police, and courts, so that users can browse through abstracts of related articles.

CHOOSING AN INFORMATION SOURCE

The choice of information source must be based on the type of information you need and the resources available to you. Throughout this book we note whether the information sources are available in print, on CD-ROM, online through a paid commercial service, or over the Internet. Decide what type of information you need—where in the information flow you want to "plug in"—and then adapt your search techniques to the tools you must use. The user interfaces, the search engines, and the format of the resources are constantly changing, but if you keep in mind what kind of information you are seeking, you will be able to use different pathways to the same destination.

4

Using the Internet

The Internet has become the buzzword of the mid- to late 1990s. We are constantly being told that the Internet will change the way we live; the Internet will replace newspapers; the Internet will replace libraries; the Internet will replace television. What is the Internet, and how has it changed the life of a criminal justice researcher seeking information?

WHAT IS THE INTERNET?

The Internet is simply a worldwide network of computer networks. It had its origin in 1969 when the U.S. Department of Defense developed an experimental network called the ARPANET to enable computers to talk with one another. The Defense Department computers needed a common language, or *protocol* to communicate, and developed the *Internet Protocol (IP)* of putting computer information into discrete *packets*, or envelopes, of information. All computers on the Internet today use the *TCP/IP* protocol, a further development of IP.

In the late 1980s the National Science Foundation decided to build on the IP protocol to connect academic computers to NSF's new supercomputer centers over telephone lines. NSF encouraged the academic institutions to use the burgeoning network for purposes other than accessing supercomputers. The resulting popularity of the new network led to an overwhelming increase in traffic, and NSF contracted with MERIT (Michigan's educational network), IBM, and MCI to manage the traffic. In 1993 various Internet management services were turned over to the InterNIC, a collaboration between AT&T and Network Solutions, Inc.

For a fuller discussion of the history of the Internet see the following sources:

Krol, Ed, and Ellen Hoffman. *FYI on "What is the Internet?"* Network Working Group. Request for Comments: 1462, FYI:20. May 1993. Available [Internet] at http://rs.internic.net/nic-support/fyi/fyi20.html

Krol, Ed. *The Whole Internet User's Guide and Catalog.* 2nd ed. Sebastopol, CA: O'Reilly & Associates, 1994.

There are several important issues to keep in mind when thinking about the Internet. Most important, the Internet connects computers in real time. BITNET, a popular academic computer network of the 1980s, enabled users to send information, in the form of electronic mail or other computer files, from one computer to another, but the files could arrive seconds, minutes, or hours after they were sent. The exchange of information over the Internet, however, takes place nearly instantaneously, enabling host and client computers to have an actual dialog as easily as a terminal in the same room with a mainframe or a microcomputer on a local area network.

A second critical aspect of the Internet is its anarchic structure. There are many organizations that currently have some responsibility for Internet administration or connections:

- The InterNIC, the organization that manages
    a. *IP addresses*—the unique numbers that identify computers on the Internet; and
    b. Internet *domain names*—the part of the Internet name that links to the IP address and identifies organizations; for example, loc.gov, for the Library of Congress, or umich.edu, for the University of Michigan.
- The Internet Society, a nongovernment international organization for global coordination for the Internet and its internetworking technologies and applications.
- The Internet Engineering Task Force, an international group of network designers, operators, researchers, and vendors that meets to develop networking standards.
- Local, regional, and long distance telephone companies that maintain and manage the telephone lines that connect the computers.
- Internet Service Providers, both national (e.g., AT&T Worldnet, MCI, AOL) and local, that connect schools, businesses, and individuals to the Internet.

But there is *no* Internet governing body to say who can or cannot be connected to the Internet, or what can or cannot be made available. It is unclear to what extent the federal or state governments can attempt to regulate the Internet, considering that the Internet crosses both state and national boundaries.

This lack of regulation has serious criminal justice implications, of course, but it also has implications for information management. The only control over information provided on the Internet is that exerted by the organization represented by the domain name or, more commonly, by the individuals providing the information.

INTERNET TOOLS

As the Internet developed, network engineers developed various tools to enable computers to communicate with one another in this new environment. These tools are constantly changing, with some gaining in popularity as others lose. Some of those you will find most useful are described below.

Telnet

Telnet is a remnant of the days (still with us) of large mainframe computers. Telnet enables a microcomputer to pretend to be a terminal connected to a mainframe or minicomputer. Telnet was an enormous breakthrough because it took advantage of the real-time nature of the Internet. Using telnet, it does not matter whether the computer you are communicating with is in the same room or around the world; the communications protocol, and users' actions, are the same (although, realistically, communicating with computers outside the United States is often much slower).

Telnet is *client–server* software. The user runs a *client* program on his or her own PC which interacts with a related program running on the remote *server* or *host* computer.

There are two types of telnet: non-IBM or *ASCII*, often called vt100 *terminal emulation* because it emulates the popular vt100 terminal; and IBM, often called *tn3270* emulation because it seeks to emulate an IBM 3270 terminal, used to connect to an IBM mainframe. Often, ASCII emulation is simply called *telnet* and the IBM-type emulation is called *tn3270*.

Telnet is now probably most often used to connect to online library catalogs, one of the earliest, and still one of the most important, information resources available on the Internet. They will be discussed further in Chapter 5.

FTP

FTP, or *file transfer protocol*, as its name implies, enables the transfer of computer files from one computer to another. The files transferred can be text files, data files, multimedia, or computer programs. Most World Wide Web (discussed below) browsers have ftp built in, and the user need not even be aware that he or she is using ftp.

E-mail

Electronic mail, better known as *e-mail*, is simply a form of file transfer, with the file being a personal message. It need not take place in real-time (occasionally, bottlenecks develop in Internet traffic and mail is delayed for hours); in fact, e-mail does not require the Internet at all. E-mail was thriving when BITNET was the most common network used by colleges and universities. With the growth of the Internet and of online services such as America Online that reached into people's homes, e-mail has become a form of communication that rivals the post office.

E-mail has had a tremendous impact on scholarly communications, as we saw earlier in Chapter 1. It is easier and faster for scholars to exchange ideas, information, drafts of papers, or even angry words through e-mail than through the postal service.

Discussion Lists

Discussion lists, sometimes called *LISTSERV*s after one of the more popular programs used to manage discussion lists, are an extension of e-mail. Discussion list software resides on one computer and manages a mailing list of all the individuals who have subscribed to the discussion. An e-mail message sent to the list is distributed to all members of the list, who are then free to comment on the message. Discussion lists can be open or closed. Anyone can subscribe to an open list. With a closed list, individuals must apply to a listowner, who will accept or reject the application. Lists may be closed because they are set up for individuals in an organization, department, or even college class, to communicate with each other.

Discussion lists can also be moderated or unmoderated. On a moderated list, messages are first screened by the moderator, who discards or returns those postings that are either sent to the wrong address, are irrelevant, or are inflammatory—depending on the guidelines for the particular list.

Some lists are archived, in which case it is possible, though not usually easy, to search through old messages to find information on a particular topic. When you subscribe to a discussion list you are usually informed who the listowner is and whether the list is moderated or archived.

The content of the discussions on these lists varies with the individuals subscribed and the declared subject matter. Some mathematical and scientific lists are like ongoing academic conferences, whose electronic conferees float ideas and theories so they can be supported or shot down. Many library science discussion lists focus on the practical aspects of finding information or managing resources. Criminal justice lists vary enormously in content from day to day. There, students and experienced researchers search for information, while ideologues of all political persuasions seek to convince others of their beliefs.

Three of the most widely used criminal justice discussion lists are these:

CJUST-L—Sponsored by the Lloyd Sealy Library of John Jay College of Criminal Justice, this is an open list on all aspects of criminal justice with a slant toward academic issues. To subscribe to CJUST-L, send e-mail with the message: SUB CJUST-L FirstName LastName to CJUST-L-REQUEST@CUNYVM.CUNY.EDU

POLICE-L—Also sponsored by the Lloyd Sealy Library of John Jay College of Criminal Justice, this is a closed list restricted to sworn law enforcement officers. To subscribe to POLICE-L, send e-mail with the message: SUB POLICE-L FirstName LastName to POLICE-L-REQUEST@CUNYVM.CUNY.EDU

UNCJIN-L—Sponsored by the United Nations Crime and Justice Information Network, UNCJIN-L was set up for the international exchange and dissemination of information on crime prevention and criminal justice issues. To subscribe to UNCJIN-L, send e-mail with the message: SUB UNCJIN-L FirstName LastName to LISTSERV@LSERV.UN.OR.AT

Network News

When you subscribe to a discussion list, the amount of e-mail you receive on your computer increases at a sometimes alarming rate, and much of it will turn out to be irrelevant to your interests. When you subscribe to a *newsgroup* maintained by a network news service, the news articles reside not on your computer but on a special newsserver computer, to which you typically have access through your own newsreader software (sometimes part of your World Wide Web browser) and your Internet Service Provider. You can read posted messages and reply to them. You can also browse through newsgroups to which you are not subscribed, searching for information in past messages, which typically remain online for relatively brief (one to two weeks) periods of time. The most widely used network news service is called USENET (sometimes known as NETNEWS) and is often included as a information resource by Internet search services.

Gopher

Gopher was developed in 1991 at the University of Minnesota. Gopher, like telnet and network news, is client-server software: the user runs a client program on his or her PC that can communicate with server software on the host computer. With gopher, the host computer provides a series of menus which leads to information, usually in simple ASCII or plain text, either on that computer or on another computer via an automatic link. Gopher was the first program to make the Internet user-friendly. The gopher client software requires very little in the way of power from the user's PC or speed from the Internet connection. It is not especially suitable for graphics or other media, however.

Many academic and government sites still operate gopher servers to accommodate users with older computers or slower Internet connections who need to view text-based information. However, the real boom in Internet usage occurred with the development of faster, more powerful personal computers, higher-speed modems and Internet connections, and the World Wide Web.

World Wide Web

The *World Wide Web* (WWW or just the Web) was developed by the CERN High-Energy Physics laboratories in Geneva, Switzerland, and introduced to the scientific world in 1991. WWW, like gopher, is client–server software. Rather than a series of menus, however, the Web is based on *hypertext*, a method of linking computer files nonlinearly at relevant points within the document. While gopher is text-based, Web links can be to text, graphics, sound, movies, or even computer programs.

The Web can easily interface with older Internet tools, such as telnet, gopher, or ftp and with newer applications just being developed. The Web is accessed through client software called "browsers," such as Netscape and Microsoft's Internet Explorer. Both enable you to read text, see graphics, hear sound, and use related Internet applications. Because of a lack of standards, however, Web sites created with one browser in mind may appear quite different, in terms of color and general page display, when viewed with another browser.

One important piece of software is rapidly becoming a Web standard, however. Adobe, a company famous for developing computer fonts and the software to display and print them, has produced Acrobat® software that enables a publisher to display on a computer an exact replica of the printed page. Adobe is distributing its Acrobat® Reader free of charge over the Internet, to be used in conjunction with WWW browsers. With the free reader, Internet users can view and print the pages of a document exactly as they appear in print. The files that can be viewed this way have the file extension *PDF* (*portable document format*). As you will see in Chapter 9, many government documents are available over the Internet in only this format.

The Web requires fast personal, preferably multimedia, computers and speedy Internet connections. Even if you use top-of-the-line equipment, however, the traffic on the Internet can cause frustratingly slow response time.

Most users feel that slow response time is a cheap price to pay for the attractive, easy-to-use, often entertaining information available over the Web. The Web has become so popular with the general public that most companies now feel compelled to maintain some sort of presence on the Web, whether to advertise their projects, to provide technical information, or just to appear *au courant*. More important for readers of this book, the Web is a mine of information on all subjects. In the field of criminal justice, one of the major sources of information is the U.S. government, which has undertaken to make an astounding number of its publications available over the Web.

INTERNET ADDRESSES

Throughout this book, whenever a resource is available on the Web, it will be noted, and its Internet location will be given. Fortunately, Internet locations have been standardized in the form of a *Uniform Resource Locator*, or *URL*. URLs which begin *gopher://* refer to gopher servers, those which begin *ftp://* refer to ftp servers, and those which begin *http://* refer to those sites that use *hypertext transfer protocol*; in other words, World Wide Web sites. The double slash is followed by the name of the server where the information can be found, sometimes followed by the *path* of the particular document. For example, the following is the URL for the home page for the U.S. Department of Justice, Bureau of Justice Statistics:

http://www.ojp.usdoj.gov/bjs/welcome.html

www.ojp.usdoj.gov is the name of the computer which stores WWW information for the Office of Justice Programs of the U.S. Department of Justice; it corresponds to an IP numeric address assigned by the InterNIC. **bjs** is the directory in which this particular file is found (probably the main directory for the Bureau of Justice Statistics files), and **welcome.html** is the name of the individual computer file which displays as a Web page. The **html** extension in the file name indicates that this file is in *hypertext markup language* (or *HTML*), the format for Web pages (on computers that use only three character file extensions, you will see this as **htm**). A Web page is simply what is displayed by an **html** or **htm** file. The "page" can be much larger than a computer screen, and can print as a great many paper pages.

The naming conventions for servers are interesting and provide information about the site to which you are linked, for example:

thomas.loc.gov

Thomas is the name given by the Library of Congress to one of its web servers. **loc.gov** is the *domain name* (or official Internet name) for the Library of Congress. When you type in or link to an Internet address, the domain name is found by one of many computers on the Internet that act as *domain name servers* by matching the name to the IP address of the physical computer and then routing your request to the correct machine. **gov** at the end of the domain name indicates that this is a government site. Other common domain name endings in the United States are **edu** for educational institutions, **com** for commercial or profit-making organizations, and **org** for non-profit organizations.

Outside the United States the domain names end in a two-character abbreviation for the name of the country; **uk** for United Kingdom, for example. **www.gu.edu.au** is the address of the server at Griffiths University in Australia, where domain names contain both **edu** to identify an educational institution and **au** to identify the country. Government agencies in the United States, particularly state government agencies, are also beginning to use domain names that end in **us**, so that **http://criminaljustice.state.ny.us** is the address of the New York State Division of Criminal Justice Services Web site.

It is important to pay attention to the domain name when viewing a site on the Internet. Often it is one of the few clues you will have to judge who is responsible for the site.

FINDING THINGS ON THE INTERNET

As the Internet has grown, so has the problem of locating information on "the Net." If the Internet can be likened to a vast library of information (and it often is) then, as some pundit once put it, it is like a library where the card catalog drawers have been opened and the cards scattered on the ground.

Fortunately, almost as fast as information is being added to the Internet, individuals and organizations have been working to organize the information and make it more easily available. There are a few Web sites that are providing an estimable service by listing and categorizing links to criminal justice resources on the Internet. These are an excellent place to begin an information search.

Justice Information Center: A Service of the National Criminal Justice Reference Service. Available [Internet] at http://www.ncjrs.org/

The *Justice Information Center*, perhaps the premier criminal justice site, will be discussed further in future chapters. It provides access to full-text government documents and pointers to other Web sites in corrections, courts, crime prevention, criminal justice statistics, drugs and crime, international criminal justice, juvenile justice, law enforcement, research and evaluation, and victims.

Greek, Cecil. *Criminal Justice Links*. Available [Internet] at http://www.fsu.edu/~crimdo/cj.html

Cecil Greek attempts to list every criminal justice-related WWW resource on this well-known Web site.

Criminal Justice Information Technology Institute. *Links to Criminal Justice Sites*. Available [Internet] at http://www.mitretek.org/justice/cjlinks/

The nonprofit Criminal Justice Information Technology Institute's primary mission is to provide technical support to state and local agencies and organizations for the acquisition of modern criminal justice information systems. It also maintains a well-organized, thorough collection of links to federal agencies, international agencies, and state and local agencies; and to Web sites dealing with prisons and corrections, courts and the law, and criminal justice education.

In addition, numerous general-purpose searching and organizing tools have been developed to try to replace that metaphorical card catalog. In the early period of Internet expansion the major users of the Net were computer scientists, who were eager to share programs, and occasionally text files, through ftp sites. *Archie* is a tool that was developed to allow users to search the numerous ftp sites for the name of a particular file. With the growth of gopher sites in the early 1990s, *Veronica* was born to search for menu items listed on the gophers. (*Jughead* also made a brief appearance as a local search engine for gopher sites.) The major finding tools now, of course, focus on the World Wide Web.

Perhaps the single best guide to using the Web and the many search tools and directories that can be found there is provided by the Internet Scout, a project of the InterNIC (a cooperative activity between the National Science Foundation, Network Solutions, Inc., and AT&T). You will find this guide particularly useful when your research departs from strictly criminal justice concerns:

Internet Scout. *Scout Toolkit.* Available [Internet] at http://scout.cs.wisc.edu/scout/ toolkit/

The *Scout Toolkit* provides many services in one place. It has intelligent, clear discussions of search indexes, directories, subject catalogs and subject guides, with links to some of the best. It provides a listing of Web tools (browsers, plugins, etc.), with links to the sites where they can be downloaded. It has reviews of the most important online magazines found on and devoted to the Internet. Perhaps most important is the section called "Scout Select Bookmarks," an annotated listing of meta-sites—those sites that try to organize Internet resources. The meta-sites listed here were very selectively chosen for their quality and depth of resources as the best Internet starting points for academics and researchers.

World Wide Web Search Indexes

One obvious way to search the World Wide Web is through a search index. Search indexes like *Alta Vista*, *Lycos*, and *InfoSeek* send out robots that automatically search the Web, maintain a database of Web sites (and often USENET news groups as well) and provide a search engine to search the database. They provide access to millions of Web pages and are constantly updated.

Web search indexes are powerful tools, but they differ from traditional printed or online indexes in a number of significant ways. First, as we discussed in Chapter 3, indexes can have a controlled vocabulary (subject headings) or rely totally on free text. Web search indexes have no controlled vocabulary. Users must rely for access strictly on the words contained in the Web pages themselves or on keywords provided as hidden codes by the Web page designers.

Second, the universe of a traditional printed or online index is small when compared to the Internet. Traditional indexes focus on only the articles published in a particular field or in a particular set of journals. Web indexes attempt to index the entire universe of Web pages, covering all subjects, and all types of information from personal Web pages to online journals.

Web indexes differ from each other both in how they build their databases of information and how users search them. The same search can result in amazingly different results depending on which search index is chosen and how it is searched. Some indexes search the words "criminal justice" assuming they are a phrase (two words next to each other in that order) in a Web page. Other indexes search for them as two words, contiguous or not, both of which must appear somewhere in a Web page (i.e., connected with a Boolean AND). Still other indexes search for them as two words, either of which may be in a page (i.e., connected with a Boolean OR). Some indexes perform a type of WAIS searching that uses relevance ranking, based on how often the words are used, or how near they are to the beginning of the page; others do not. When using a search index you need to spend some time determining how it works and how it searches.

Even with a basic understanding of the particular search index you are using, you may find that searching a phrase like "criminal justice" can yield over 40,000 hits. As you can imagine, this is not a very effective way to look for information on a general subject.

Search indexes can be very effective, however, when you are looking for something specific, such as whether a particular organization has a Web page, or technical information on a specific product. An excellent guide to Web search indexes is provided by

Internet Scout. *Scout Toolkit: Searching the Internet.* Available [Internet] at http://scout.cs.wisc.edu/scout/toolkit/index.html

This clear, well-written guide provides descriptions of the major Web search indexes and provides links to them, along with general discussions of different searching techniques, such as Boolean searching, and proximity searching. Other pages on this site discuss Web directories and subject guides.

Some of the major search indexes are

Alta Vista. Available [Internet] at http://altavista.digital.com/

Excite. Available [Internet] at http://www.excite.com/

InfoSeek. Available [Internet] at http://www.infoseek.com/

Lycos. Available [Internet] at http://www.lycos.com/

World Wide Web Directories

WWW directories such as *Yahoo* and *Magellan* arrange Web sites into subject categories. There is some human intervention involved both in the selection and arrangement of the sites, resulting in fewer false hits (irrelevant listings). These directories can usually be browsed via a subject tree or searched using search engines similar to those discussed above. The advantage of using a directory is that only a selected group of sites is included and much of the "noise" of the Web is eliminated.

The *Scout Toolkit: Searching the Internet*, described above, also discusses various Web directories and subject guides.

Some of the better known directories are

Yahoo. Available [Internet] at http://www.yahoo.com. *Yahoo* was one of the first and is certainly one of the best known of the Internet Directories. It is so comprehensive that many users view it and use it as a search index.

Magellan. Available [Internet] at http://www.mckinley.com. Magellan reviews the sites that it includes and rates them with up to thirty points. It includes Web sites, ftp and gopher servers, newsgroups, and Telnet sessions.

BUBL Information Service. Available [Internet] at http://bubl.ac.uk/link. *BUBL* was started by librarians in England as the Bulletin Board for Librarians. It arranges Internet sites, both WWW and gopher, into a subject tree based on the Dewey Decimal Classification. An alphabetical listing by subject and a search form are also available.

INFOMINE: Scholarly Internet Resource Collections. Available [Internet] at http://lib-www.ucr.edu/ *Infomine* may be the most valuable of these directories for academics and scholars. A service of the library at the University of California, Riverside, it provides links to over 10,000 academically valuable Internet sites, including databases, electronic journals, electronic books, bulletin boards, listservs, online library card catalogs, articles, and directories of researchers. The links can be browsed by subject or searched by keyword; most have extensive annotations.

Other Strategies to Locate Information

Other strategies to locate information on the Internet may be even more effective. One of your best options is to start from the Web page of your college or research library. Many libraries are now maintaining Web sites with the dual purpose of providing information about the library and pointing their users to particularly worthwhile sites. The Web pages listed there often lead you to other sources of information which you can bookmark or note for later exploration and use. Web pages from libraries or colleges with a criminal justice specialty are

Lloyd Sealy Library of John Jay College of Criminal Justice. Available [Internet] at http://www.lib.jjay.cuny.edu

State University of New York. University at Albany. School of Criminal Justice. Available [Internet] at http://www.albany.edu/scj/

Cambridge University. Institute of Criminology. Available [Internet] at http://www.law.cam.ac.uk/crim/iochpg.htm

Many librarians and Internet explorers have been writing subject guides to Internet resources since the years when telnet and ftp were the only options. These subject guides (constantly updated, of course) are available in two collections:

Argus Clearinghouse (formerly University of Michigan *Clearinghouse for Subject Oriented Guides*). Available [Internet] at http://www.clearinghouse.net/

Arranged into broad subject areas, Argus can be a difficult source to use, but the authors of the guides are identified and the sites are rated.

World Wide Web Virtual Library. "By Subject" available [Internet] at http://www.w3.org/ pub/DataSources/bySubject/Overview.html "By Category Subtree" available [Internet] at http://www.w3.org/pub/DataSources/bySubject/Overview2.html

Finally, use the sites mentioned in this book. They have all been examined for content, relevance, and authority and many will lead you to other, newer or more relevant, sites.

EVALUATING THE INFORMATION ON THE INTERNET

A major problem with the Internet is the lack of formal review and evaluation of the information found there. Information found in libraries has been judged and evaluated in several ways. First, a publisher has judged the information worthy of publication. In the case of a book, the publisher may have sent the manuscript to independent or inhouse reviewers to evaluate quality and marketability. In the case of a journal article, either the editors of the journal or independent reviewers have read and evaluated the article for suitability of publication. Second, a librarian has reviewed the title of the journal or book and, based on knowledge of the reputation of the publisher and needs of the library users, has decided to purchase the journal or book. Often, there is a third layer of judgment—either book reviews or inclusion in a periodical index.

None of these traditional means of "vetting" a publication exist on the Internet. Extremists at all points of the political compass are free to make their arguments with as much or as little truth as they please. Those who know nothing about a subject are as free to put out information as those who have been studying it for years. It takes only a few hours and a few dollars for a subscription to an Internet Service Provider to "publish" on the Internet.

It falls heavily on the user to judge the quality of the information he or she finds, but there are some techniques which can help to form judgments.

First, think about how you found the site. Was it a direct link from a library Web page or that of a government agency? Has the library or agency stated that it recommends the site? If that is the case then the library or agency has already done some evaluation for you.

Second, carefully examine the authorship of the page or site. Is it clear what individual or agency is responsible for it? Web pages with no known author should be viewed as suspect. If the author is stated, who is it? Is it an individual or organization that you know of personally or by reputation? Are the purposes of the organization clearly stated? Is it possible to verify its legitimacy? Is there an address where the individual or organization can be reached?

Third, can you judge if the information presented is accurate and objective? If statistics are presented, is the source given? Do the facts presented agree or disagree with what you know from other sources? Does there seem to be a bias in the presentation?

Fourth, is the page current? Is there an indication of the date it was last updated? Many organizations and individuals write Web pages and then abandon them. The Web changes so quickly that any links found on a page can be quickly outdated.

Fifth, is the information likely to remain online for any length of time? Libraries make a commitment to maintain indefinitely the materials they acquire, but there is no such commitment on the Internet. Remember, professors or other scholars reading your work need to be able to verify and examine your sources—hence the importance placed on communication and information flow in Chapter 1. Will they be able to do this if information on the Internet is moved or removed? This is a problem that will loom larger as computer drives fill with aging information, and managers of Web sites and other Internet resources must decide whether to keep the older material, delete it, or archive it in some manner. Unfortunately, many Webmasters are unaware of the needs of scholarly communication or of the potential significance of their decisions.

USING THE INTERNET EFFECTIVELY

The preceding sections are so full of caveats and cautions that you may be wondering whether it is worth using the Internet to find criminal justice information at all. The answer, of course, is that it is extremely useful for some things and worthless for others.

The Internet does not substitute for commercially published books or journals. Academics continue to publish their works in traditional forms because that is how their reputations are built. Publishers continue to publish in print because most people still prefer to read in print, and only in that format can they be assured of a return on their investment. Nevertheless, there is a small, gradual move toward the publishing of journals on the Internet. Some of these are available at no cost from academic institutions and some are available by subscription from commercial publishers.

Newspapers and newsletters are often available on the Internet with the same or similar content as the print version. For the most part, however, there is no indexing and there are no back files.

On the other hand, the wealth of information available from organizations and agencies that do not need to make a profit from the documents they produce is truly astonishing. Federal, state, regional, and international organizations, eager to raise their public profile, anxious to fulfill their mandates of providing information to the public, and finding that publishing on the Internet is often cheaper than publishing in print, are rushing to the Internet with high-quality, authoritative material. Research reports, statistics, laws, law cases, and regulations are all important to the criminal justice researcher and they are available on the Internet.

Throughout this book we have noted worthwhile resources that are accessible through the Internet. In most cases, these are available both in print and over the Net. Researchers should use whichever is most convenient. Some sources, however, can only be found on the Internet. If you do not have Internet access from home, your local academic or public library should be able to connect you.

Part II

LOCATING INFORMATION

5

The Library Catalog

You are undoubtedly familiar with the single most important tool in the library: the catalog. Regardless of its form the modern library catalog enables you to know (1) whether the library owns a particular book; (2) all the books the library owns by a particular author; and (3) all the books the library owns about a particular subject. For purposes of this discussion we will assume that the catalog includes only books, but documents, recordings, tapes, items in microform, and titles of periodicals may also be included.

SOME HISTORY

Libraries have always attempted to maintain records of what they own. The earliest such records were not catalogs in the sense that we know that term, but were just lists, sometimes arranged in broad subject areas, sometimes by the order in which the books were received, but most commonly by author or by title.

By the nineteenth century most of these lists were kept in large ledger-books with separate sections for each letter of the alphabet. Because the books were entered over a period of time, the ledgers were only roughly alphabetical. Later in the century, a system evolved of putting information about the books onto individual cards so that new acquisitions could easily be put in proper alphabetical order and a semblance of order was achieved.

Until the twentieth century, authors were the only element which were consistently listed in library catalogs; titles were included only occasionally, and subjects not at all. Because the quantity of material available was so much more limited than today, scholars were able to work successfully within these limitations.

The earliest attempts to provide information about the subjects of books came in the form of entering the book in the ledger by catchword title, with the "informative" word first, such as "Convicts, the value of solitary confinement for," or "Prisoners, the isolation of." These examples—one listed under "C," the other under "P"—make clear the problems involved in the "Catchword title" approach. The type of consistent subject approach with which we are now familiar did not become feasible until after the publication of uniform lists of subject headings by the Library of Congress early in this century. Until then, library users looking for books on a subject had to hope that they had access to the book stacks themselves, and that the books were arranged on the shelves in some sort of classified order.

CATALOGING RULES

Authors

The development of cataloging rules, arcane as so many of them seem to noncatalogers, brought consistency to the catalog, and was a tremendous boon to the researcher. *Uniformity of entry* for authors means that all the books by Thomas A. Jones will be listed together in one place, whether he chose to sign his name as Thomas Jones, Thomas A. Jones or Thomas Arthur Jones.

Uniformity of entry also means that when an organization—a corporation, or a private or government agency—is considered to be responsible for the work, rather than the individual or individuals who did the actual writing, then the name of the organization is always entered the same way in the catalog. Authors such as the Subcommittee on the Judiciary, the Police Foundation, or the New York Police Department are often referred to by many different names. It is the cataloger's job to decide on one official name, so that works produced by the same organization can be found together.

Subjects

The development of uniform lists of subject headings was a revolutionary change in libraries. Now users could expect to find all books about prisoners listed together whether they are referred to as prisoners, convicts, cons, or jailbirds. Most libraries in the United States use the subject heading lists established by the catalogers at the Library of Congress (*Library of Congress Subject Headings*). Library of Congress subject heading rules emphasize specificity; a book is entered under the most specific subject applicable—for example, "Jails" rather than "Correctional Institutions."

A further refinement is the subdividing of subjects by geographic divisions (Prisoners—Texas) or by subject subdivision (Prisoners—Education). Of course, an obvious problem that arises is what to do with a book on the education of prisoners in Texas. Is it listed in the catalog under "Prisoners—Texas—Education" or "Prisoners—Education—Texas"? The distressing truth is that the answer has changed over time and place; in some libraries where old cataloging records are not corrected, you can still find similar books under both headings. Fortunately, the development of online library catalogs has ameliorated this problem.

THE CATALOG CARD

As we have seen, the development of a card system for catalogs meant that information about the books in the library could be kept in a logical sequence. As cataloging rules developed, librarians devised the idea of a "unit card." Those of you who still use or who have used a card catalog have seen this card. It lists in the following order (when all elements are present): author, title, imprint (place of publication, publisher and date); number of pages; size of the book; presence of a bibliography; and sometimes a list of the chapters, essays, or stories included in a collection.

The unit card also lists, at the bottom, all the headings under which the book should be found in the catalog: joint authors, variant titles, and every subject heading that has been assigned to the book. This same unit card is then reproduced several times, each time with a different heading across the top, to be filed into a different part of the catalog.

If you are using a library with a card catalog, either as its only catalog or as the catalog for older books, you will be able to find a book in as many different ways as there are headings assigned to the book. In libraries with a *divided catalog* the cards with the author's name at the top will be filed separately from the cards with subjects listed at the top; or there may be an author and title catalog kept separate from a subject catalog. In a *dictionary catalog* all of the cards are filed together in one alphabet, but very sophisticated filing rules are used to arrange the cards so that works *by* an author, for example, are not intermingled with works *about* the author.

THE ONLINE CATALOG

Almost all major research libraries, and most college and university libraries, have abandoned the card catalog in favor of the *online public access catalog* (sometimes called *OPAC*). The online catalog has caused as great a change in libraries as the development of cataloging rules and catalog cards. Instead of separate headings typed on a unit card, libraries now put the same information into author, title, or subject *fields* in a bibliographic *record*. All of these records make up the catalog, which has become a large, complex *database* (see Chapter 3).

While the form of the catalog is dramatically different, the rules of uniformity of entry still apply. This means that all the books by an author can still be found together, as well as all the books on a particular subject. Of course, the books are no longer found by flipping through cards but by searching a computer, so the "how" of finding books in a catalog is dramatically different.

Using an Online Catalog

Whereas card catalogs basically come in two types—divided and dictionary—online catalogs come in as many different flavors as there are companies that sell OPAC software (more, actually, since some companies market several different versions of their OPAC). Some online catalogs feature plain screens on simple terminals; others have beautifully designed graphical user interfaces (GUIs) with icons and pictures. Some catalogs present you with menus of choices; others expect you to type in commands that may or may not be displayed to you on the screen. As we saw in Chapter 3, the database—the catalog—is separate from the search engine and user interface.

Get to know how to search the catalog in your own local academic or research library. Most libraries offer demonstrations or short courses covering how to search the catalog, and provide written handouts or other documentation describing its use. Most catalogs also offer online help. As always, ask a librarian if you need help. He or she can help you find the most efficient path to the information you need and can often reveal shortcuts that can save you time and effort.

Online catalogs can be searched in three basic ways, although there are hybrids and exceptions to this rule. A *browse* search is most like searching the old card catalog. You enter a word or the beginning of a word into the computer and you are presented with a display listing entries that appear alphabetically before and after that word. Normally you can choose which field or index you wish to search; the effect is like flipping through cards in a divided catalog. If you do a browse search of a combined index of all fields, it is like browsing in a dictionary catalog. A browse search never returns the phrase "No entries found" because it always puts you in the part of the index nearest to what you typed.

An *exact match* search looks for the word or phrase that you typed in and tries to match it with an author, title, or subject to find the exact entry you want. If you know precisely what you are looking for, this is the most efficient way to find a book. If you are a poor speller or typist, however, you will see the dreaded "No entries found." Most catalogs that search for exact matches assume automatic truncation at the end of what you type, so that if you only type the first word of a title, for example, you will see a list of all titles beginning with that word.

A *keyword* search is the most powerful search; the type that really differentiates an online catalog from a card catalog. A keyword search looks for a word anywhere it may appear in a field, not just at the beginning. The OPAC software and decisions made by your library determine how keyword searching works in the catalog you use. Sometimes you must select which field or fields you want searched—just the title field, for example, or just the subject field. Sometimes the search engine is set up to search only the title field for a keyword search, or only the title and subject fields. Other OPACs automatically search all fields for a keyword, including fields that list the table of contents or other notes. Read the catalog screens carefully, or ask a librarian, to find out which fields a keyword search examines in the catalog you use.

When keyword searching is combined with Boolean searching (using AND, OR, and NOT, for example) the online catalog becomes a very powerful tool, enabling you to find books more efficiently and more comprehensively than you ever could with a card catalog.

Finding a Known Item

If you know the exact book you are looking for, you should have a very easy time whether the catalog is on cards or on a computer. The fastest way to find a book is to search under the title, unless the title is very common (*Introduction to Criminal Justice*, for example). If the title is very common, or you know the author and are unsure of the title, or you want to find all the works of a particular author, then search by the author's last name. Some online catalogs have a very fast author/title search whereby you can search under the author's last name and part of the title.

When the title you are seeking is a common word (*Report*, for example) and the author is an organization with a complicated or variable name, then try to do a keyword search for author using words from the name of the organization; or, if possible, do a general keyword search using words from the name of the organization and from the title. For example, if you are searching for the annual report of the New Jersey State Police, a title search under "Annual Report" is likely to yield hundreds, or even thousands of entries. An author search under "New Jersey State Police" may find nothing, since the official name of the organization, as found in most library catalogs, is "New Jersey. Division of State Police." The most efficient search would be the following keyword search:

annual report AND new jersey AND state police

Finding books by authors with Spanish surnames can be a similarly daunting task. The Puerto Rican sociologist Luis Nieves Falcon is listed in the catalog not as "Falcon, Luis Nieves" but as "Nieves Falcon, Luis." A keyword search of the author field for **Nieves** AND **Falcon** should find books by this author regardless of the official form of entry.

Finding a Book by Subject

Finding what books a library owns on a particular subject is a challenge, but a few simple tricks can save you time and greatly improve the quality of your library research. The online catalog has made it possible to find information in a book that was formerly known to only those who had already examined it.

First, think about whether you already know of a good book on the subject—perhaps one recommended to you by a professor or colleague, or one you have discovered through a specialized encyclopedia. Look up that book in the catalog by its title or author and check to see what subject headings have been assigned to the book. Even in these days of online catalogs, subject headings still serve the function of bringing together under one standardized term all the books the library owns on a subject. Then do a subject search using the subject heading or headings closest to your topic.

If you do not know of any particular book on your topic, use the subject heading lists in Appendix A of this book to try to locate an appropriate subject heading, or use the printed *Library of Congress Subject Headings*.

Try doing a keyword search using the word or words from the subject headings you have identified. If your online catalog searches many different fields together (title, subject, and contents fields, for example), you may locate additional books with chapters or essays on your topic, but where the entire book is not about the subject.

A keyword search using subject headings can be particularly helpful when there are subject subdivisions involved, and illustrates how powerful online catalogs can be. If you are interested in attitudes of police officers, then the appropriate subject heading to search is "Police—Attitudes," which is "Police" followed by the subject subdivision "Attitudes." Consider the searches shown in Table 5.1, however, all done recently in one library's online catalog.

As you can see, keyword searching, even with just two words, can be a very powerful tool. Some OPACs allow very sophisticated keyword searches using positional and Boolean operators in nested searches. If you are interested in comparing crime prevention programs in Canada and Australia, for example, you could use the search

crime WITH prevention AND (Canada OR Australia)

to find books with the phrases **crime prevention** or **prevention of crime**, and the words **Canada** or **Australia**. Find out if your library's OPAC allows these type of searches, and what commands or search screens are necessary.

Supercatalogs

The same software used to search the library catalog database can also be used to search a periodical index database. Many libraries use the same hardware and the same software to search the catalog and one or more periodical indexes in a sort of supercatalog. The databases are still separate; you will not find periodical articles when searching the library catalog or vice versa, but you must be careful to pick the database that has the information you want. If you walk up to a computer screen in your library and it provides you with a choice of the library catalog or several periodical indexes, remember the information flow in criminal justice and, before you select a database, think about where you want to plug into that information flow.

Table 5.1
Some Examples of Word Searches

Search Terms	Number of Hits
s = police--attitudes (a *subject* search for the subject heading **police** followed by the subheading **attitudes**)	78
s = police--United States--attitudes (a *subject* search for the subject heading **police** followed by the geographic subdivision **United States** followed by the subject subdivision **attitudes**)	35 (includes books on attitudes of police in the U.S. as a whole; does not duplicate the 78 books found above)
k = police.su. AND attitudes.su. (a *keyword* search for both the word **police** in a subject field AND the word **attitudes** in a subject field)	283 (includes books on the attitudes of police in different countries and different states)
k = police AND attitudes (a *keyword* search for the word **police** and the word **attitudes** found anywhere in the record: author fields, titles, subjects, contents, etc.)	410 (includes all of the above, plus books on citizens' attitudes toward police, books with chapters on police attitudes, and a number of totally irrelevant books)

Online Catalogs of Other Libraries

Library card catalogs are huge, immutable objects. Except for those few that have been published as book catalogs, they have to be consulted in the library to which they belong. Online catalogs and computer networks have made it possible for library catalogs to become virtual catalogs; users can dial up their local library catalogs from home using telephone lines, and an online catalog on the Internet can be searched from anywhere in the world.

Library catalogs were developed to describe the books held in a particular building. Why should researchers be interested in the holdings of a library far out of commuting distance?

First of all, if you are looking for a particular book that your own library doesn't own, do not try checking the catalog of every library you can think of to see where you can find it. It makes sense to look at the catalogs of libraries to which you have immediate access; but beyond that, use one of the online union catalogs listed below or, better, let your interlibrary loan department track down books for you; it can borrow from other libraries as well as locate the material.

Many researchers check the catalog of a library they are planning to visit in the future, both to save time and to see what the library's collection is like in a particular subject. Students thinking of pursuing a graduate degree, or faculty thinking about a job change or a temporary haven for a research project, may want to see if the library of the institution they are considering supports their research.

All libraries have different collections; even those that claim to be strong in criminal justice have strengths in different areas. Collections are built by librarians to satisfy the needs of their public: citizens, faculty, students. What is added to the library depends on the geographic area—libraries in Texas are likely to have more information on police in Texas than a library in Oregon—and on the courses being taught or the research needs of the faculty. In many ways the catalog of a library with a strong collection in a subject is like a good bibliography that can lead you to important resources.

Most libraries share standardized, usually Library of Congress-produced, cataloging records through online bibliographic utilities like OCLC or RLIN to eliminate expensive original cataloging of every book they purchase. Some libraries, however, add subject headings beyond what the Library of Congress has assigned, to assist scholars in particular fields; or they may add contents notes to illuminate an aspect of a book that might otherwise go unnoticed.

Finally, remember the discussion about different search engines and different user interfaces. If your local library's OPAC does not search all fields in a book's record—particularly if it does not search contents notes—or if it does not allow keyword and Boolean searching, then searching another catalog may actually be helpful in finding books that your local library owns.

Some catalogs you may want to search are

John Jay College of Criminal Justice (New York, NY)
> *Note*: The John Jay Library catalog is part of CUNY+, the OPAC of the City University of New York.
> tn3270 to cunyvm.cuny.edu
> at VM/ESA screen, <Tab> twice to COMMAND==>
> type **dial vtam**
> at VTAM menu, type **cunyplus**

at CICS screen, clear the screen
at blank screen, type **lnav**
at Database Selection screen, type **dpac** to search the OPAC

Sam Houston State University (Huntsville, TX)
telnet to niord.shsu.edu
at Username:, type **saminfo**
at Selection prompt, type **a** for Newton Gresham Library
at Selection prompt, type **d** for Library Catalog

State University of New York at Albany
telnet to library.albany.edu
at login prompt, type **opac**

University of Illinois at Chicago
http://www.uic.edu/htbin/libcat
or tn3270 to uicvm.uic.edu
at logo, <Tab> twice to Command==>
type **uiccat**
at Welcome to LUIS screen, press <Enter>

University of Toronto
telnet to library.utoronto.ca
at Username:, type **utlink**
at Password:, press <Enter>

University of Toronto Criminology Library Crimdoc Database
Note: This database is the catalog for the government documents, reports, working
papers, and so forth, in the Criminology Library.
http://www.library.utoronto.ca/htbin/crimdoc

Cambridge University Radzinowicz Library (Cambridge, England)
telnet to ul.cam.ac.uk
at first menu, select **3** for Union Catalogue of Departmental Libraries
at Union Catalogue menu, type **6** to select a preferred library
at list of preferred libraries, type **33** for Criminology (Radzinowicz) Library
at Union Catalogue menu again, try **5** (Keyword search) first unless you are searching for a known title

University of Tubingen, Germany
telnet to opac.ub.uni-tuebingen.de
at login: prompt, type **opac**
at Password:, type **opac**

Griffiths University, Australia
telnet to library.itc.gu.edu.au
at login: prompt, type **library**

The National Libraries of the United States, the United Kingdom, and other
countries are also available for searching over the Internet:

Library of Congress Catalogs
WWW access at http://lcweb.loc.gov/catalog/

or telnet (or tn3270) to locis.loc.gov

at LOCIS menu, select **1** for Library of Congress Catalog

British Library: *OPAC 97*

WWW access at http://opac97.bl.uk/

East, John. *National Library Catalogues Worldwide*. Available [Internet] at http://www.uq.edu.au/~mljeast/

Provides telnet links and instructions for accessing national library catalogs around the world.

• • •

Other online catalogs can be found using the following sources:

Nelson, Bonnie R. *OPAC Directory 1997*. Medford, NJ: Information Today, 1997.

The 1997 edition of the *OPAC Directory* lists 1,400 library catalogs available over the Internet or by dialing up, with access and searching instructions, and information about subject strengths and significant publicly available online resources. There are geographic, subject, and database indexes.

HYTELNET on the World Wide Web. Available [Internet] at http://library.usask.ca/hytelnet/

Provides WWW access to a database of library catalogs available over the Internet, with Internet addresses and logon instructions.

Union Catalogs

There are two online union catalogs that are worth consulting if your library subscribes to them. They provide access to the cataloging records of thousands of libraries in one search. They may not, however, provide access to local subject headings or locally input contents notes, and they are heavily weighted towards libraries in the United States and Canada.

WorldCat. Available online from OCLC (EPIC and FirstSearch).

WorldCat is the OCLC Online Union Catalog, containing more than 33 million bibliographic records describing over 550 million items owned by over 22,000 libraries around the world. Each record provides information on which libraries own an item.

RLIN Bibliographic Database. Available online from RLIN.

A union catalog of 75 million items held in comprehensive research libraries and special libraries that belong to the Research Libraries Group, plus over 100 additional law, technical, and corporate libraries that catalog their materials using RLIN (the Research Libraries Information Network).

PUBLISHED BOOK CATALOGS OF OTHER LIBRARIES

Many of the card catalogs of major research libraries were reproduced in book format in the 1960s and 1970s. They remain useful for historic purposes. Two book catalogs of particular interest are

Cambridge University. Institute of Criminology. *The Catalogue of the Radzinowicz Library.* 6 vols. Boston: G. K. Hall, 1979.

The arrangement of this catalog is different from those familiar to most Americans. Reduced-size reproductions of cards from the card catalog of this famous criminology library are arranged according to the Bliss classification scheme. The emphasis is on British police and crime, and the catalog is not limited to books, it also includes pamphlets, reports, and particularly for the earlier periods, individual periodical articles.

Los Angeles Public Library. Municipal Reference Library. *Catalog of the Police Library of the Los Angeles Public Library.* 2 vols. Boston: G. K. Hall, 1972. *Supplement.* 2 vols. 1980.

This catalog of one of the oldest police libraries in the United States includes reports, pamphlets, and individual periodical articles as well as books. The inclusion of periodical articles for the period prior to the publication of standard periodical indexes for police material makes this source particularly important for historical work.

6

Encyclopedias, Dictionaries, and Annual Reviews

Encyclopedias have suffered from bad press: They are frequently thought of as primarily for children, as unscholarly, and as unsuitable sources for the serious student or researcher. This reputation is unfortunate and usually inaccurate.

Despite the popular conception of what should be contained in an encyclopedia or dictionary, those who compile and edit such books are a very diverse group and, accordingly, the range of information contained within them is surprisingly varied. A glance at Chart D suggests the breadth of features in some of the encyclopedias and dictionaries discussed in this chapter.

The distinction between encyclopedias and dictionaries is fairly clear to the average person. A dictionary has definitions; an encyclopedia has articles. Somehow this clear distinction has been muddled by publishers, leading to multivolume "dictionaries" containing long articles and single-volume "encyclopedias" containing only definitions. As a practical matter, the distinction in the title is insignificant; what is important is knowing where to look for what kind of information.

Annual reviews are included in this chapter because they provide overviews of a subject limited to the current research and ideas on the topic.

ENCYCLOPEDIAS

In Chapter 1 we discussed encyclopedias as frequently representing the last stage in the information flow. After an idea or fact has circulated and has been accepted in the scholarly community, it finds its way into those forms of secondary literature designed to cumulate, synthesize, and summarize the information of the field. Foremost among these are encyclopedias.

Chart D
Selected Encyclopedias and Dictionaries: Summary of Features

Feature	Encyclopedia of Crime and Justice	Crime and the Justice System in Amer.	Criminological Thought	Cops, Crooks, and Criminologists	Encyclopedia of Police Science	Dictionary of American Penology	Encyclopedia of American Prisons	Guide to American Law	Encyc. of the Amer. Constitution	Encyclopedia of World Crime	Sifakas, Encyc. of American Crime	Rush, Dictionary of Criminal Justice	DeSola, Crime Dictionary
Biographies, extensive	A	●	●	●		●	●	●	●	●			
Biographies, short	A	●		●		●		●	●		●		
Biographies of criminals	A								●	●			
Specific crimes	●			B					●	●			
Organizations and societies	●					●		●		●		●	●
Government agencies						●		●		●			
Judicial decisions discussed	●	●			C		E	●	●		I		
Large number of case citations	●	●						●	●				
Case name index	●				●			●	●				
Statutes cited and discussed	●							●			●		
Statute index	●							●					
Bibliographies	●	●	●			●	●	●	●	●	F		
Illustrations								●		●	●		
Other special features						D				G	H	J	K

A. No separate biographies, but substantial biographical information within articles; names listed in index.

B. Under names of criminals.

C. Short synopsis of important decision in article on Supreme Court.

D. Appendixes have addresses of prison systems and prison reform organizations and many statistical tables.

E. Discusses large number of judicial decisions and provides lists of case citations in the article called "Legal Issues."

F. Extensive bibliography in the index volume.

G. Indexes by type of crime.

H. Broad classified index for types and locations of crimes, wrongful convictions, and the like.

I. Large appendix discusses Supreme Court cases by topic.

J. Useful appendixes include forensic agencies and organizations, as well as lists of refereed journals.

K. Large number of appreviations and acronyms. Appendixes have foreign terms and "Place-Name Nicknames."

What Encyclopedias Can Do for You

Here are some of the problems encyclopedias can help solve:

- You need to write or speak on probation but do not know enough about the problem to narrow the topic. The series of articles called "Probation and Parole" in the *Encyclopedia of Crime and Justice* will help.

- Sutherland is one of the great names in criminology; a fast way to get a basic outline of his ideas is through his biography in the *International Encyclopedia of the Social Sciences*; a thorough examination of the man and his theories can be found in *Criminological Thought: Pioneers Past and Present*.

- Your professor has been talking about the "military model" of policing but you are not sure you understand what it is. The article in the *Encyclopedia of Police Science* gives you the historical and theoretical background you need.

- You are a sociologist studying child abuse and need an overview of the problems involved in police search-and-seizure restrictions. You can get it from reading the article on "Search and Seizure" in either the *Guide to American Law* or *American Jurisprudence, 2nd*.

- The book about gangs that you are reading mentions the Swamp Angels, and you want to know who they are; you need to know when Willie Sutton died or what *omerta* is; all of these can be found in *The Encyclopedia of American Crime*, by Carl Sifakis.

History of Encyclopedias

Encyclopedias, conceived of as total compendia of all knowledge, are more than 2,000 years old. The most famous of the early compendia is the work of the mid-eighteenth-century group of French thinkers called the Encyclopedists, who worked largely under the editorship of Denis Diderot. Probably the first truly modern encyclopedia, their thirty-five-volume work, with articles contributed by most of the leading thinkers of the period, was an attempt to encompass all the ideas and intellectual ferment of that era.

Following the pattern established by the Encyclopedists, the late eighteenth and nineteenth centuries continued to produce attempts at truly universal scholarly encyclopedias. One of the last such efforts, started in Germany in 1818, issued 167 volumes, completing only about half the alphabet before suspending publication in 1889.

The *Encyclopaedia Britannica*, inspired by Diderot's great French *Encyclopédie*, first appeared in Scotland in 1768. From that time until its eleventh edition, published in 1910–1911, it too was an attempt at a scholarly compendium written for the highly educated minority. But with the increasing information flow from the newer fields in science, technology, and the social sciences, as well as the growth of scholarship in the more traditional subjects, it became clear to publishers that to encompass on a scholarly level all that was known about everything was an unattainable ideal.

Thus, today, the *Britannica*, the *Americana, Colliers*, their online and CD-ROM counterparts, and other encyclopedias with which you are familiar, rather than being compendia of all that is known about the world, attempt only brief summaries of the highlights. In addition, in response to rising rates of education and literacy, these encyclopedias are now written for the average adult rather than the scholar, with simpler versions such as the *World Book Encyclopedia* and *Britannica Junior* prepared especially for children. General encyclopedias continue to be useful in providing background information in areas that are unfamiliar. There is no better way to quickly pick up enough knowledge about a foreign country or a historical period and the criminal justice system in that place or time.

Nevertheless, encyclopedias written for the serious student and scholar still exist. As publishers realized that it was impossible to include all that was known about everything in one set of books, they also realized that encyclopedias could be produced containing all that was most important about a single subject.

Probably the first such single-subject encyclopedia in English dealing with the social sciences was *The Encyclopedia of Social Reform, Including Political Economy, Political Science, Sociology, and Statistics, Covering Anarchism, Charities, Civil Service, Currency, Land and Legislation Reform, Penology, Socialism, Social Purity, Trades Unions, Woman Suffrage, Etc.* One thick volume, whose contributors included most of the leading social reformers of the day, it was first published in 1897.

The first large-scale modern encyclopedic treatment of the social sciences was the fifteen-volume *Encyclopedia of the Social Sciences*, published between 1930 and 1935. It was viewed universally as an outstanding scholarly achievement and was updated in 1968 as the seventeen-volume *International Encyclopedia of the Social Sciences*.

As earlier scholars found it necessary to divide universal knowledge into specializations, so by the mid-twentieth century it became necessary to divide specializations into subspecialities. Thus we now have separate encyclopedias for the various branches of the social sciences.

USEFUL ENCYCLOPEDIAS FOR THE
CRIMINAL JUSTICE RESEARCHER

Criminal Justice Encyclopedias

General

Encyclopedia of Crime and Justice. 4 vols. New York: Macmillan, 1983.

Students and researchers are fortunate to have this set available. Although now over fourteen years old, it still provides thorough background information on criminal justice concepts, institutions, and history.

Articles are well written, authoritative, and frequently of substantial length. They discuss the history and development of ideas and movements in all areas of criminal justice, as well as their current status. In an effort to include developmental, historical, and comparative aspects of the topics, many major areas are covered by a series of articles written by several experts. The value of the articles is further enhanced by considerable attention to legal precedent, citations to statutes and other legal documents, good bibliographies, and a very fine general subject index. There are no separate biographies, although there is considerable information about people within the articles.

No encyclopedia is designed to be read from cover to cover. This set, however, makes good browsing for those interested in criminal justice.

Crime and the Justice System in America: An Encyclopedia. Ed. Frank Schmalleger with Gordon M. Armstrong. Westport, CT: Greenwood Press, 1997.

The focus of this one-volume encyclopedia is on contemporary criminal justice in the United States. Unlike the long, in-depth articles of the *Encyclopedia of Crime and Justice*, articles are short, describing specific terms or concepts ranging from the Code of Hammurabi to DNA Profiling. Many of the entries are for significant criminal justice-related Supreme Court cases, and other cases are mentioned within appropriate articles. There are also articles on individuals who have significance to contemporary criminal justice, including Supreme Court justices and defendants and victims such as Bernhard Goetz, Larry Davis, and Rodney King. Articles are signed by the experts who wrote them. Most have short bibliographies and, in addition, there is a bibliographic essay at the end of the volume.

Johnson, Elmer H., ed. *Handbook on Crime and Delinquency Prevention.* New York: Greenwood Press, 1987.

Although this is not, strictly speaking, an encyclopedia, it is intended as a general resource for studying crime prevention and prevention of juvenile delinquency. There are fourteen signed articles on different aspects of prevention, each with accompanying bibliography.

Martin, Randy, Robert J. Mutchnick, and W. Timothy Austin. *Criminological Thought: Pioneers Past and Present.* New York: Macmillan, 1990.

This fascinating book discusses the development of criminological thought from the perspective of the individuals who helped shape the discipline. Each chapter deals with one of fifteen pioneers of criminological theory, providing a biographical sketch, descriptions of basic assumptions held by contemporaries, key ideas developed by the theorist, and later critiques. Works by and about each individual are listed at the end of each chapter. Interestingly, there are two tables of contents: one lists the subject of each chapter chronologically, the other by theoretical school.

Police and Law Enforcement

Cops, Crooks, and Criminologists: An International Biographical Dictionary of Law Enforcement. New York: Facts on File, 1996.

Biographical dictionaries contain short biographies of individuals who meet the criteria for inclusion—in this case, people who have been involved with any aspect of law enforcement. Famous criminals and lawmen are included, of course, but also profiles of forensic scientists such as Alec Jeffreys, a pioneer in DNA "fingerprinting"; crime reporters like Ben Hecht; and some of the founding fathers of criminology. Several articles have suggestions for further reading, and a detailed (though incomplete) index leads to the biographies of individuals involved with particular organizations, types of crimes, publications, and so on.

Encyclopedia of Police Science. 2nd ed. New York: Garland, 1995.

This encyclopedia is truly worthy of the name. The signed articles were written by notable practitioners and scholars of criminal justice and are often quite lengthy, delving into the historical and theoretical backgrounds of such topics as the "military model" of policing and the police academy. Of particular note are the articles on "Police History" and "Police Brutality." Excellent bibliographies follow most of the articles. Since articles tend to be long and detailed, use the index to find specific topics. The volume concludes with a "Bibliography of Police History" and an index of legal cases.

Corrections

Encyclopedia of American Prisons. Ed. Marilyn D. McShane and Frank P. Williams III. New York: Garland, 1996.

This very useful work has long, detailed articles signed by academics, with bibliographies at the end. It includes biographies of individuals important in the history of corrections, articles about important prisons, and lengthy articles about subjects such as correctional officers, crowding, and legal issues. A number of the articles contain extensive references to significant court cases.

Williams, Vergil L. *Dictionary of American Penology.* Rev. ed. Westport, CT: Greenwood Press, 1996.

More properly termed an encyclopedia, this one-volume compendium contains short articles on administrative and security problems, rehabilitative approaches, and significant historical trends and events. Particularly useful are the articles on the prison systems of each state. The 1996 edition has been thoroughly revised with updated statistics and references (which appear at the end of each article). Also included in the new edition are over 200 pages of statistical tables on corrections and public attitudes toward criminal justice, from the U.S. Bureau of Justice Statistics. Other appendixes contain addresses of prison systems and of prison reform organizations.

Terrorism

Mickolus, Edward F. *Transnational Terrorism: A Chronology of Events, 1968–1979.* Westport, CT: Greenwood Press, 1980.

Mickolus, Edward F., Todd Sandler, and Jean M. Murdock. *International Terrorism in the 1980s: A Chronology of Events.* Ames, IA: Iowa State University Press, 1989. 2 vols. Vol. 1, 1980–1983; Vol. 2, 1984–1987.

Mickolus, Edward F. *Terrorism, 1988–1991: A Chronology of Events and a Selectively Annotated Bibliography.* Westport, CT: Greenwood Press, 1993.

These three works offer comprehensive coverage of terrorist incidents over a twenty-five-year period. The chronological arrangement is awkward and unhelpful in finding out about the aims or history of terrorist organizations or the responses to terrorism in different countries, but in the first two works there are, at least, indexes by name of terrorist group, location of attack, and type of attack. The last of the three works lacks these indexes but does include a fairly comprehensive bibliography. The bibliographies that accompany the earlier works are discussed in Chapter 11 (p. 141).

Shafritz, Jay M., E. F. Gibbons, Jr., and Gregory E. J. Scott. *Almanac of Modern Terrorism.* New York: Facts on File, 1991.

Contains a chronology of terrorism from 1946 to 1990 and an encyclopedic section with entries for terrorist groups, government organizations, countries, and related topics.

Thackrah, John Richard. *Encyclopedia of Terrorism and Political Violence.* London: Routledge and Kegan Paul, 1987.

Easier to use than the other works on terrorism listed here, this slim volume provides short articles on individuals, groups, and countries involved with terrorist activities.

Security

Fay, John J., ed. *Encyclopedia of Security Management: Techniques and Technology.* Boston: Butterworth-Heinemann, 1993.

This one-volume (nearly 800-page) encyclopedia covers the field of security from "Access Control" to "Zero-Base Budgeting" discussing the many facets of a security manager's responsibilities. Articles signed by experts describe different types of security situations (e.g., hospital security, museum security), security problems (e.g., fire safety, internal theft), and responses (e.g., alarms, questioning techniques). Many of the articles are quite long and detailed; some have short bibliographies. There are no cross-references within the articles but there is a subject index at the end of the volume.

Fennelly, Lawrence J., ed. *Handbook of Loss Prevention and Crime Prevention.* 3rd ed. Boston: Butterworth-Heinemann, 1996.

The *Handbook* contains forty-one chapters on crime prevention and security, covering homes, businesses, specialized problems like hospital security, and different physical methods of crime prevention. Articles are written and signed by different experts in the field. Some chapters have bibliographies; others contain various appendixes. The third edition includes contemporary concerns such as workplace violence and computer hacking. There is a subject index.

Protection of Assets Manual. 4 vols. (looseleaf) Santa Monica, CA: Merritt Company, 1983– .

Although intended as a manual for the security professional, this looseleaf work provides encyclopedic coverage of the protection field. Articles cover the whole range of issues in security management, including alarms and communications, fraud and computer crimes, terrorism, security law, and alcoholism. The detailed subject index appears in the first volume immediately after the table of contents.

Social Science Encyclopedias

International Encyclopedia of the Social Sciences. 17 vols. New York: Macmillan and The Free Press, 1968. *Biographical Supplement.* Vol. 18. 1979.

Since publication, this work has been viewed as a model subject encyclopedia, the single most important and encompassing publication for the social sciences. Written by acknowledged experts, it gives authoritative coverage to the fields of anthropology, economics, geography, history, law, political science, psychiatry, psychology, sociology, and statistics. Also included are approximately 600 biographies.

Published by the same firm that later produced the *Encyclopedia of Crime and Justice*, it is similar in format and approach. Because its emphasis is on the developmental aspects of the social sciences, it is still considered one of the most valuable sources for overviews and orientation to the social sciences, even though it is now somewhat dated.

An eighteenth volume of 215 supplementary biographies was added in 1979.

Encyclopedia of the Social Sciences. 15 vols. New York: Macmillan, 1930–1935.

Predecessor to the *International Encyclopedia of the Social Sciences*, this historic set is still valuable for the researcher, especially one interested in early developments in the social sciences.

✓*Encyclopedia of Sociology.* 4 vols. New York: Macmillan, 1992.

This four-volume set contains 370 major articles, including a significant number on crime, criminology, the criminal justice system, and social problems. All articles are signed and many have significant bibliographies.

✓*Encyclopedia of Psychology.* 2nd ed. 4 vols. New York: John Wiley & Sons, 1994.

This is an excellent place to find short articles on the psychological aspects of criminal justice from "Deviance" to "Correctional Institutions." Articles are signed and contain bibliographical references to the major works on the subject described. Volume 4 contains short biographical articles, a full bibliography, and a name and subject index.

✓*Encyclopedia of Drugs and Alcohol.* 4 vols. New York: Macmillan, 1995.

Both long overview articles and short pieces on specific drugs and substance abuse topics are included. Volume 4 contains appendixes listing various drug abuse organizations, a fascinating timeline showing federal involvement in drug control efforts, and the U.S. Schedules of Controlled Substances.

✓*Encyclopedia of American Social History.* 3 vols. New York: Scribner, 1993.

Of particular interest is Part 12: Social Problems, Social Control, and Social Protest, which includes articles on "Crime and Punishment" and "Police and Fire Protection," as well as articles on long-standing social problems like prostitution and alcoholism. This work is useful in putting American criminal justice issues in historical perspective.

✓Levinson, David. *Aggression and Conflict: A Cross-Cultural Encyclopedia.* Santa Barbara, CA: ABC-CLIO, 1994.

The author uses worldwide, cross-cultural surveys and several hundred ethnographies to provide a broad appraisal of aggression and conflict around the world. The various articles provide the American criminal justice researcher with alternate ways of viewing such common transgressions as rape, homicide, and family violence, as well as crime in general. Most articles have cross references and a short bibliography.

Encyclopedia of Bioethics. Rev. ed. 5 vols. New York: Macmillan, 1995.

The revised edition of this well-respected encyclopedia pays added attention to ethical issues surrounding topics of interest in criminal justice, such as prostitution, abuse (of children, the elderly, and domestic partners), and the death penalty. Articles are lengthy, signed by the experts who wrote them, and have substantial bibliographies.

Encyclopedias in Law

/*Guide to American Law: Everyone's Legal Encyclopedia.* 12 vols. St. Paul, MN: West Publishing Co., 1983–1985. Supplements, 1990– .

This multivolume encyclopedia of legal information is written for the lay person. The articles are accurate and well written, although there is variation in the depth of coverage. Some articles are limited to definitions of terms; others are the short, fact-summary type usually found in general encyclopedias; still others are long, analytical articles that could be very helpful in providing detailed background information on legal topics. The unusual arrangement of the encyclopedia may be somewhat confusing, as the long, analytical articles are printed on buff pages that interfile with the white pages of the rest of the encyclopedia, and may duplicate topics covered in less detail in the white pages. The long articles include useful bibliographies.

Those who do not have ready access to a law library, or who want a completely nontechnical discussion of a legal topic, will find this source useful. But they should be sure to check the buff pages as well as the white. The *Guide* is kept up to date by bound, one-volume supplements, issued irregularly.

American Jurisprudence, 2nd. Rochester, NY: Lawyers Co-op, 1962– . Updated by replacement volumes and pocket parts.
Corpus Juris Secundum. St. Paul, MN: West Publishing Co., 1957– . Updated by replacement volumes and pocket parts.

These are the two standard legal encyclopedias. In appearance both sets can be intimidating to the unfamiliar user, but most criminal justice students find these helpful sources well within their capabilities. Hints for their use are given in Chapter 12, "Research in Legal Resources" (pp. 166–167).

Encyclopedia of the American Judicial System: Studies of the Principal Institutions and Processes of Law. 3 vols. New York: Scribner, 1987.

The three volumes are organized into six major sections—Legal History, Substantive Law, Institutions and Personnel, Process and Behavior, Constitutional Law and Issues, and Methodology—each with extensive, signed essays on different aspects of the general topic. Of particular interest to criminal justice students are articles on "Criminal Law," "The Criminal Justice System," "The Police," "Plea Bargaining," "Sentence Alternatives," and "Criminal Procedure." The excellent index leads you to many other fascinating articles. Unfortunately, there are no supplements to keep this work current.

Encyclopedia of the American Constitution. 4 vols. New York: Macmillan, 1986. *Supplement I,* 1992.

This comprehensive encyclopedia was issued to commemorate the bicentennial of the Constitutional Convention. The signed articles range from major overviews of historical periods and themes to short entries on minor topics or cases. There are biographical sketches of Supreme Court justices and other important figures in constitutional history, and thorough discussions of landmark cases and of each constitutional amendment. The longer articles include short bibliographies. The Case, Name, and Subject indexes in Supplement I are cumulative and refer to articles in the main volumes as well as in the supplement.

Popular Crime Encyclopedias

The following sources were written not for the criminal justice researcher, but for the general public. Often filled with lurid details, they make very interesting reading. On a more practical note, they are excellent sources for finding out the particulars of famous crimes that are still discussed and studied, or for identifying crimes of a particular nature that could be used for illustrative purposes or for further, more scholarly, study.

Gaute, J. H. H., and Robin Odell. *The New Murderers' Who's Who*. London: Harrap, 1989.

Contains an interesting classified index with entries such as "Blunt instrument" or "Unsolved crimes."

Kohn, George C. *Dictionary of Culprits and Criminals*. 2nd ed. Lanham, MD: Scarecrow Press, 1995.

This small dictionary provides brief information on over 1,200 lawbreakers. The appendix provides a classified listing of criminals by type of culprit.

Nash, Jay Robert. *Encyclopedia of World Crime*. 6 vols. Wilmette, IL: CrimeBooks, Inc., 1989.

This six-volume set primarily offers popularized, even sensationalized accounts of crimes and criminals. Volume 4 contains some interesting supplements that are mostly chronological lists of major crimes like arson, lootings, and skyjackings. Volume 5 is a dictionary and Volume 6 an index to the set.

Nash, Jay Robert. *World Encyclopedia of 20th Century Murder*. New York: Paragon House, 1992.

Condensed from *Encyclopedia of World Crime*.

Nash, Jay Robert. *World Encyclopedia of Organized Crime*. New York: Paragon House, 1992.

Condensed from *Encyclopedia of World Crime*.

Sifakis, Carl. *Encyclopedia of American Crime*. 2nd ed. New York: Smithmark, 1992.

This one-volume encyclopedia is largely concerned with crime and criminals in the United States, although there are some short general articles on criminal justice topics such as plea bargaining and arrest procedures. A useful feature is the index, which contains lists of articles under broad subject categories such as gangs, labor and labor rackets, lynchings, wrongful convictions, types of crimes, and geographic headings.

Sifakis, Carl. *Encyclopedia of Assassinations*. New York: Facts on File, 1991.

Alphabetically arranged by the name of the victim, or intended victim, of the assassination.

DICTIONARIES

A specialized dictionary defines a word in relation to a specific body of knowledge. Although a word may have multiple meanings, the special dictionary takes it from its broader context and defines it in terms of a particular field. Changing nuances in the use of the word may be described, along with broader or narrower terms which help achieve an internal consistency of terminology within the field.

In addition to definitions, some specialized dictionaries include the type of information customarily found in encyclopedias: brief biographies, explanations of acronyms and abbreviations, and information about organizations and places.

Conversely, the *Encyclopedia of Crime and Justice*, discussed above, includes a lengthy and very useful glossary of legal and criminal justice terminology.

Below is a selection of specialized dictionaries that are most useful to criminal justice researchers. There are others that deal more specifically with law, social science, drug use and abuse, psychology, and public administration. Ask your librarian to make a suggestion if you need one of these.

Black, Henry Campbell. *Black's Law Dictionary*. 6th ed. St. Paul, MN: West Publishing Co., 1990.

The standard legal dictionary.

D'Auria, Michael M. *Legal Terms and Concepts in Criminal Justice*. Wayne, NJ: Avery Publishing Group, 1983.

Limited to legal terminology, this may be easier to use than a full legal dictionary.

De Sola, Ralph. *Crime Dictionary*. Rev. ed. New York: Facts on File, 1988.

While this dictionary does not include many legal or sociological terms, it does include foreign terms, abbreviations and acronyms, names of terrorist organizations, and a great many drug-related terms. Definitions are clear and informative.

Fay, John J. *The Police Dictionary and Encyclopedia.* Springfield, IL: Charles C. Thomas, 1988.

In spite of its title this work is much more a dictionary than an encyclopedia. The author's aim is to cover everything an entry-level police officer might need to know, and the words included run the gamut from legal terms to forensic terms to police slang.

Ferdico, John N. *Ferdico's Criminal Law and Justice Dictionary.* St. Paul, MN: West Publishing Co., 1992.

Designed to be used by criminal justice professionals without a formal legal education, this dictionary defines criminal justice terms in lay language. Its clear explanations and multiple cross references should make it particularly useful for students.

National Criminal Justice Thesaurus: Descriptors for Indexing Law Enforcement and Criminal Justice Information. Washington, DC: U.S. Department of Justice, National Institute of Justice, 1994.

This work contains listings of descriptors—terms used to index literature—in the National Institute of Justice/NCJRS database. A thesaurus rather than a dictionary, it includes synonyms and broader and narrower terms for the entry word. It can be particularly helpful in compiling lists of terms to search in library catalogs or periodical indexes and abstracts.

Rush, George E. *The Dictionary of Criminal Justice.* 3rd ed. Guilford, CT.: Dushkin Publishing Group, 1991.

This is the most generally useful of the special dictionaries in criminal justice because it reflects the multidisciplinary nature of the field. The third edition also includes useful, concise summaries of Supreme Court cases affecting criminal justice, organized by constitutional issue.

ANNUAL REVIEWS

Like encyclopedias, annual reviews provide overviews, but rather than synthesizing what is already known, they highlight the best in current research. Annual reviews may contain specially commissioned articles or a selection of recently published articles. They may attempt to cover many subjects in each issue or limit each to a single topic. Regardless of their scope, however, annual reviews are always good sources for quality, up-to-date bibliographies.

Annual Review of Sociology. Palo Alto, CA: Annual Reviews, Inc., 1975– .

This annual review seeks to reflect the depth and diversity of sociology. Specialists are invited to write critical articles reviewing significant recent developments in the field. Crime, poverty, drug abuse, and related topics have all been discussed in recent years. An online index to titles, names, and abstracts—beginning with Volume 10—is available without charge on the World Wide Web at http://www.annurev.org/soc/home.htm. Full-text articles may be ordered here as well.

/ *Crime and Justice: An Annual Review of Research.* Chicago: University of Chicago Press, 1979– .

Commissioned essays discussing current research in all areas of criminal justice are contained here, along with extensive bibliographies. Some of the volumes focus on particular themes such as family violence, drugs and crime, modern policing, or crime prevention.

Criminal Justice History: An International Annual. Westport, CT: Greenwood Press, 1980– .

Publishes research, research notes, essays, conference assessments, and book reviews in the field of criminal justice history.

Criminal Law Review. New York: Clark Boardman, 1979– .

This anthology includes some of the most significant articles published during the preceding year. Each volume incudes selections in the four areas of substantive criminal law, constitutional rights and remedies, trial and sentencing, and professional responsibility. Each year there is a very useful introductory survery of significant court decisions dealing with criminal law.

Sage Criminal Justice System Annuals. Beverly Hills, CA: Sage Publications, 1972–.

Different topics are covered each year. Samples are "Drug Treatment and Criminal Justice," "The Juvenile Justice System," "White Collar Crime," "Legal Rights of Prisoners."

7

Indexes and Abstracts

What is an index? What is an abstract? Traditionally, an index is an alphabetical list of names, places, or topics discussed in a publication. Indexes can appear in the backs of books to help you find information in the book. An abstract is a summary of the important points of a document.

Periodical indexes and abstracts, often called indexing and abstracting services, provide access to individual articles in periodicals in the same way an index in the back of a book provides access to the information in the book. In the past, indexing and abstracting services appeared in print and usually were published several times a year, with annual cumulations, to provide up-to-date access to recent issues of the periodicals. Today, most of them appear in computerized form as well as in print, providing all the advantages of computerized searching that were discussed in Chapter 3. Many of these services are not limited to the indexing of periodicals, but also cover reports, documents, dissertations, and even chapters in books. Some services index so many different types of material and come out so infrequently that they are closer to the bibliographies that will be discussed in Chapter 11 and, in fact, a few are mentioned here.

You will recall the location of articles in the information flow discussed in Chapter 1. Indexes and abstracts provide the earliest truly systematic access to information as it is published in current literature.

VARIETIES OF PERIODICALS AND INDEXES

In the discussion of information flow, a distinction was made between three kinds of information sources: those designed for popular consumption, those designed for the professional, and those designed for the scholar. You may, at times, want to use periodicals designed for any one of these target audiences; much depends on the nature of your research. If you are writing on the methodology of community policing, you may well use professional journals; on the public's reaction to it, popular magazines; on the concept and theory of community policing, scholarly journals. Remember to read all of these critically and to keep in mind the source of the information when judging its accuracy or reliability.

Even though indexes devoted to criminal justice will be your primary resources, since this is an interdisciplinary field, indexes designed for related areas must also be considered. Business indexes will lead to articles about personnel research, psychology indexes to articles about deviant behavior, education indexes to articles about juvenile delinquency, public affairs indexes to articles on political responses to crime.

Indexes may reference popular, scholarly, or professional journals, or a combination of these. They may be limited to a particular discipline or cover multiple subject areas. They may list articles in a classified subject arrangement, as books are arranged on the shelves of a library; or they may list articles under different *descriptors*, using a controlled vocabulary similar to the subject headings in a library catalog.

Computerization and increased competition in the indexing and abstracting industry has lead to a greater number of journals being indexed, new multidisciplinary mega-indexes, and the merging of previously separate indexes. In the past, there were indexes which clearly were meant for a popular audience, and others which covered academic and professional literature of specific fields. These clear distinctions between indexes are blurring. It is up to you, the researcher, to make a judgment based on the information you find in the index or sometimes in the article itself. Refer back to Chapter 1 on information flow and review the difference between popular, scholarly, and professional literature.

USING INDEXES AND ABSTRACTS

Periodical indexes in print have been available since the nineteenth century; computerized indexes made their appearances in the early 1970s. These first online indexes were loaded on large mainframe computers that were accessed over telephone lines by trained searchers. Computer time was very expensive and the search software required knowledge of arcane commands. These online systems, managed by database vendors like DIALOG and DataStar, still exist. Generally, they charge fees based on minutes of connect time and number of citations viewed or printed. They usually are not freely available to students or researchers, but require the use of a librarian as an intermediary. Many libraries, if they offer access to such online services, charge their users for the cost of the search. However, indexes on these systems are often more current than those available elsewhere and they provide access to thousands of databases, many more than an individual library could subscribe to.

To make these online indexes (or databases) more accessible, some companies have developed user-friendly interfaces to allow untrained users to search the databases directly. They may charge the user a direct fee through a credit card, or they may contract with libraries to provide limited or unlimited searching of databases by the library's patrons. For example, OCLC, an organization founded to provide computerized cataloging services for librarians, now also offers EPIC, a traditional online service searched by librarian intermediaries, as well as FirstSearch, an end-user search service designed for use by library patrons themselves. RLIN, another cataloging service developed by research libraries, offers CitaDel, a collection of periodical indexes and other databases accessed through EUREKA, its end-user search interface.

With the advent of personal computers and CD-ROMs, many computerized indexes have become available for direct use by library patrons, and for at-home or in-office use by individuals. Libraries now often network their computers and CD-ROM drives to provide their patrons with access to many indexes (databases) from the same personal computer workstation. As we saw in Chapter 3, if these CD-ROM indexes are purchased or leased from different companies, the search software and user interface will be quite different. At the same time, with the development of online public access catalogs (OPACs), libraries are now able to use the OPAC search software to access indexes received on CD-ROMs, received on magnetic tape and loaded onto an OPAC computer, or even loaded onto another library's OPAC computer and shared through the Internet.

The same index may appear in libraries in an almost bewildering variety of formats. *Psychological Abstracts* is one of the most extreme examples, appearing as the following:

- A printed index, appearing since 1927, published monthly.
- A CD-ROM database, called PsycLIT, available from at least three different vendors (SilverPlatter, EBSCO, and Ovid Technologies), usually indexing articles back to 1974, updated quarterly.
- An online database, called PsycINFO, searched through intermediaries, available from at least four different online search services (DataStar, DIALOG, Ovid Technologies, and OCLC's EPIC), usually containing citations back to 1967, updated monthly.
- An online database searchable by end-users from OCLC's First Search, or CompuServe's Knowlege Index, with coverage from 1967, updated monthly.
- A database available through a local library OPAC, covering as many years as the library chooses to purchase on magnetic tape.

A research library may have *Psychological Abstracts* in any one or more of these forms and the search software and the user interface will vary depending on which company is providing the database or which company's OPAC is being used to search it.

It is no longer possible, therefore, to predict what a particular index will look like in any one library or how to use it. Most online indexes have built-in help files or are presented with printed instructions for use. Read the instructions and, as always, ask the librarians for help if you need it.

To further complicate matters, huge mega-indexes have appeared. In some cases these are the result of various computerized indexes being merged. The H. W. Wilson company, for example, which produces *Readers' Guide to Periodical Literature*, *Social Sciences Index*, *Education Index* and others, offers its indexes to libraries on magnetic tape, to be loaded onto local OPACs. Libraries have a choice of buying one, or many, of these databases, and keeping them as separate indexes or loading them as one large merged index, to be called "The Wilson Indexes," or "Periodical Index," or whatever the library chooses to call it. This merged index covers many different subjects in the social sciences, sciences and/or humanities, and covers both scholarly and popular periodicals.

In other cases, information companies have chosen to simply scan into computers the tables of contents of hundreds or thousands of the most common periodicals, sometimes adding subject headings and abstracts and sometimes not. In some instances these periodical indexes or abstracts are combined with the full text of the articles, which are available online for searching or delivered separately on CD-ROM, via fax or over the Internet. The competition among information companies is great, and new products are emerging monthly.

When using an index, whether in print or on computer, keep these issues in mind:

1. What years does it cover? How current is it?
2. What discipline, or disciplines, does it cover?
3. Does it have a controlled vocabulary of subject headings or descriptors, or rely only on keywords?

CRIMINAL JUSTICE INDEXES AND ABSTRACTS

Criminal Justice Abstracts. (Formerly *Abstracts on Crime and Delinquency* and *Crime and Delinquency Literature.*) Monsey, NY: Willow Tree Press, 1968– . Quarterly. Also available on CD-ROM from SilverPlatter, updated annually or quarterly; and online from WESTLAW, updated quarterly.

Criminal Justice Abstracts offers comprehensive coverage of the main journals in criminal justice as well as broad coverage of new books, dissertations, and reports of research institutions, government agencies, and private organizations. The descriptive abstracts include summaries of findings, methodology, and conclusions.

More so than most indexes, there are a number of differences between the print and computerized versions of *Criminal Justice Abstracts.*

The printed index is arranged by large general classifications: "Crime, the Offender, and the Victim," "Juvenile Justice and Delinquency," "Police,"

"Courts and the Legal Process," "Adult Corrections," and "Crime Prevention and Control Strategies." It also has excellent subject and geographic indexes. Some issues of the printed index contain literature reviews, which are not found in the computerized forms.

The CD-ROM and online versions have author, title and keyword access only; although the CD-ROM version comes with a list of suggested search terms. Both the CD-ROM and online versions can be searched using classification codes, equivalent to the general classifications in the print version. While there are no separate geographic search terms, it is easy to use keyword searching to find countries and other geographic entities. Finally, both the CD-ROM and online versions of the index contain abstracts that were not published in the print version.

Many of the reports and documents indexed in *Criminal Justice Abstracts* are available from the Criminal Justice/NCCD Collection of Rutgers University. Older documents may be available as part of the microfiche NCCD Collection, *Crime and Juvenile Delinquency* (see pp. 116–117). Libraries with strong criminal justice collections may also have acquired these documents, which may then be accessible through the library's catalog.

Criminal Justice Periodical Index. Ann Arbor, MI: University Microfilms International, 1975– . Three issues per year. Also available online from DIALOG, updated monthly.

General criminal justice coverage, including security, appears in this alphabetical, printed index to more than 150 journals and newsletters. The subject index is loosely based on Library of Congress subject headings, supplemented by special topics and cross references. Some of the subject headings are overly broad, and there is poor indexing of gender and ethnic issues, with the single subject heading "Blacks," for example, sufficing to cover all indexing about African-Americans. Nevertheless, the inclusion of professional newsletters enhances its value for charting current developments. Unique subject entries list book, film, and periodical reviews and there is a separate author index.

Criminology, Penology and Police Science Abstracts. Amsterdam: Kugler Publications, 1992– .

This scholarly abstracting service was formed from the merger of *Criminology and Penology Abstracts* (1961–1991) and *Police Science Abstracts* (1973–1991). Published in the Netherlands, it is international in scope, "covering the etiology of crime and juvenile delinquency, the control and treatment of offenders, criminal procedure, the administration of justice and police science." Entries tend to stress the theoretical and conceptual treatment of subjects. The arrangement is classified, but there are excellent subject and author indexes that cumulate in the last issue of the year. There is, as yet, no computerized version.

Law, Crime and Penology. San Diego, CA: Sociological Abstracts, 1986– . Updated bimonthly. Available [Internet] at http://www.accessinn.com/socabs/html/lcpdesc.htm

Law, Crime and Penology is a subset of *Sociological Abstracts* (see below) that is available for searching over the Internet by subscription. It is intended for individuals, who can subscribe online or by telephone with a credit card. As of July 1997, the database included over 11,000 records for journal articles, books, book chapters, and conference papers covering crime, correctional problems, family violence, and child abuse.

National Criminal Justice Reference Service (NCJRS) Document Data Base. Rockville, MD: NCJRS, 1972– . Annual. CD-ROM. Also available online from DIALOG, updated quarterly.

NCJRS is an index to the National Criminal Justice Reference Service, the research library of the Department of Justice. A previous version of this online index was the barely usable *Document Retrieval Index,* published on microfiche only. *NCJRS* contains more than 140,000 citations, with abstracts of books, book chapters, journal articles, conference papers, popular magazines, and government documents. Subjects covered include all aspects of criminal justice, including law enforcement, crime prevention, security, juvenile justice, dispute resolution, victim and witness services, and arson. This database is particularly good for comparative studies of criminal justice in other countries. Many of the documents bear the note that they are available on microfiche from NCJRS. These documents can be found in the NCJRS microfiche collection (in those libraries that have bought it) or ordered directly from NCJRS in Rockville, MD (Tel: 1–800–851–3420 or 301–251–5500).

OTHER INDEXES IN THE SOCIAL SCIENCES
AND RELATED FIELDS

General

Social Sciences Index and *Social Sciences Abstracts.* (Formerly *International Index to Periodicals*, 1907–1965; *Social Sciences and Humanities Index*, 1965–1973.) New York: H. W. Wilson, 1974– . Quarterly. Also available on CD-ROM from WILSONDISC, SilverPlatter and Ovid Technologies, 1983– , updated monthly; online from WILSONLINE, DataStar, DIALOG, OCLC (FirstSearch and Ovid), 1983– , updating varies; and on magnetic tape.

Social Sciences Index and *Social Sciences Abstracts* are the same index, but *Social Sciences Abstracts* contains, in addition to citations, abstracts beginning in 1994. Both publications contain more than 393,000 citations to articles and book reviews in some 415 English-language periodicals in the social sciences: sociology, anthropology, geography, economics, political science, and law. H. W. Wilson indexes in general are known for their careful indexing and choice of journals to be indexed and *Social Sciences Index* has long been known as the standard index in the social sciences. Libraries may sometimes combine *Social Sciences Index* in its online form with other H. W. Wilson indexes into a general online periodical index.

Social Sciences Citation Index (SSCI). Philadelphia, PA: Institute for Scientific Information, 1969– . Triennial. Also available on CD-ROM from ISI, 1981– , updated quarterly; online (*Social SciSearch*) from DataStar, DIALOG, and Ovid Technologies, 1972– , updated weekly; and on magnetic tape, 1972– , updated weekly.

Citation indexes were designed for a unique purpose. They do not index the subjects covered in a periodical article; rather they index the references, or citations, mentioned in the article. Researchers have long used the bibliographies in relevant articles and books to find related works, but such bibliographies can refer only to works older than themselves. With a citation index you can search under the name of an author who wrote a significant article at any time in the past, and find out what articles, written since, cite the earlier article in their bibliographies.

Social Sciences Citation Index (SSCI) began in 1969 as a very difficult-to-use index in many volumes with tiny print. It currently contains complete bibliographic data and citations to significant articles from 1,400 social sciences journals worldwide, and social sciences articles from 3,200 journals in the natural, physical, and biomedical sciences. It now appears in various computer media, as well as in print. The CD-ROM versions of the index are certainly easier to use than the print (at the very least, they are easier on the eyes), but they are more complex than most indexes. In addition to allowing you to search for cited references and to list the bibliographies of every article indexed, *SSCI* also enables you to search for related records; that is, those articles whose bibliographies have at least one reference in common.

The easiest way to use *SSCI* is simply to search for keywords. Some versions of *SSCI on CD-ROM* include abstracts, enabling you to search more than just the words that appear in the title. Since there are no added subject headings or descriptors in this index, it is easy to miss important articles that employ terminology different from yours. *SSCI* is most effectively used when you have salient articles to search for.

The CD-ROM and print versions have only annual cumulations, so a complete citation search for an article published several years in the past, or a thorough keyword search across several years, can still be a tedious job of searching multiple volumes or databases. If possible, try to access this source in a library that has mounted the database from tape back to 1981 on a local OPAC, or arrange to have a librarian do a computer search on DIALOG or one of the other database vendors.

Dissertation Abstracts. Ann Arbor, MI: UMI, 1861– . Monthly. Also available on CD-ROM from Ovid Technologies, updated quarterly; and from UMI Ondisc, updated semiannually; online from Ovid Technologies, OCLC (FirstSearch and

EPIC), DataStar, STN International, and RLIN (CitaDel), updated monthly; and on magnetic tape.

This is an essential source for anyone writing a doctoral dissertation or for serious researchers. *Dissertation Abstracts* contains more than 1.1 million citations, with abstracts since 1980, to dissertations accepted for doctoral degrees by accredited North American institutions and more than 200 institutions elsewhere. The various computerized versions are much easier to use than the printed version. If your library has only the printed volumes, then look for the cumulated indexes, where you can search many years at once. Doctoral dissertations can provide reports of cutting-edge research complete with thorough literature reviews, but most libraries do not routinely purchase them. They are available for order, however, from UMI.

Current Contents/Social & Behavioral Sciences. Philadelphia, PA: Institute for Scientific Information, 1969– . Weekly in print and on diskette. Also available on CD-ROM from ISI, updated weekly; online from Ovid Technologies, DIALOG, and DataStar, 1990– , updated weekly; and on magnetic tape.

The *Current Contents* series of indexes began by simply reproducing the tables of contents of various journals in order to provide a current awareness service for scholars in the field. When the information was computerized and became accessible for keyword searching, however, it became usable as a general index. *Current Contents/Social and Behavioral Sciences* contains the complete tables of contents of approximately 1,300 journals in the social and behavioral sciences. Some of the online versions also now contain abstracts. Subject access is by keyword only. The value of *Current Contents* lies in its timeliness and its broad range of coverage. The print and diskette versions do not cumulate but contain only the current week's information. The CD-ROM version includes one year's worth of citations.

Sociology and Related Disciplines

Sociological Abstracts. San Diego, CA: Sociological Abstracts, 1952– . Five issues a year. Also available on CD-ROM (*sociofile*) from EBSCO and SilverPlatter, 1974– , updated three or four times a year; and online from Ovid Technologies, DIALOG, CompuServe (Knowledge Index), DataStar, DIMDI, and OCLC (FirstSearch and EPIC), 1963– , updated bimonthly.

Sociological Abstracts in print was always notoriously difficult to use, but its appearance on CD-ROM has enabled researchers to discover the many strengths of this index. It is one of the best sources for finding information on criminology, the sociology of law, and the many social problems related to crime. *Sociological Abstracts* also covers social policy and social welfare, and provides good coverage of police and corrections. There is excellent cross-cultural coverage, as more than 2,000 journals in thirty languages from fifty-five countries are indexed. Books, book reviews, dissertations, and conference papers are also indexed. A thesaurus of subject descriptors, supplementary identifiers, and long abstracts make it easy to do a thorough search of the online index.

International Bibliography of the Social Sciences: International Bibliography of Sociology. London: Tavistock; Chicago: Aldine, 1952– . Annual.

This is a multilanguage classified listing of scholarly books, chapters in books, pamphlets, articles, and official publications, with a subject index. There are no annotations. Although this is a difficult source to use and is always published several years after the date of articles it indexes, its coverage of international sources is excellent. Unfortunately, there is no index by country, rendering this most useful as a source for obtaining "balance" or for finding sources to help avoid a total U.S. bias in your research.

Social Work Abstracts (formerly *Abstracts for Social Workers*, 1965–1977 and *Social Work Research & Abstracts*, 1977–1993). Washington, DC: National Association of Social Workers, 1994– . Quarterly. Also available on CD-ROM (*Social Work Abstracts Plus*) from SilverPlatter, 1977– , updated semiannually.

Social Work Abstracts contains more than 30,000 citations, with abstracts, to journal articles, doctoral dissertations, and other materials on social work and related fields. Since social workers are, of course, concerned with problems of crime and delinquency, substance abuse, and poverty, this index provides a rich source of articles for researchers in criminal justice.

Anthropological Literature. Cambridge, MA: Tozzer Library, 1979– . Annual. Also available on CD-ROM, updated quarterly; and online from RLIN (CitaDel), 1984– , updated quarterly.

Harvard University's Tozzer Library produces this index of articles in more than 800 scholarly journals, as well as essays from books, from the fields of anthropology and archaeology. Works may be in English or European languages. For criminal justice researchers, this index is chiefly useful for cross-cultural studies of crime, violence, and deviance. The computer versions contain more than 87,000 citations. There are no abstracts.

Violence and Abuse Abstracts. Thousand Oaks, CA: Sage Publications, 1995– . Quarterly.

Indexes and abstracts journal articles and books dealing with interpersonal violence.

Psychology

Psychological Abstracts. Washington, DC: American Psychological Association, 1927– . Monthly. Also available on CD-ROM (*PsycLIT*) from SilverPlatter, EBSCO, Ovid Technologies, 1974– , updated quarterly; online (*PsycINFO*) from Ovid Technologies, DataStar, DIALOG, CompuServe (Knowledge Index), DIMDI, OCLC (FirstSearch and EPIC), 1967– ; and on magnetic tape.

Since 1927, *Psychological Abstracts*, under the guidance of the American Psychological Association, has been *the* abstracting service for the ever-growing field of psychology. *PsycLIT*, the CD-ROM version of the index, now contains over 700,000 citations to periodical articles and more than 66,000 citations to books and relevant book chapters. The computerized versions are much easier to use than the print and, beginning with 1980, they contain more citations. More than 1,300 periodicals in twenty-seven languages are indexed worldwide in all areas of psychology and the behavioral sciences, as well as related fields such as law, business, sociology, psychiatry, anthropology, and medicine. A *Thesaurus of Psychological Index Terms* with added identifiers provides excellent subject coverage. Be sure to use this index if you are doing serious research in the causes and effects of criminal behavior, rehabilitation and prison psychology, job stress, personnel and training issues, or any subject that relates to human behavior.

Law

Current Law Index. Foster City, CA: Information Access Company (IAC), 1980– . Sponsored by the American Association of Law Libraries.
Legal Resources Index (LRI). Foster City, CA: Information Access Company (IAC), 1980– . Monthly. CD-ROM (*LegalTrac*). Also available online from CARL, DataStar, DIALOG, LEXIS-NEXIS, and WESTLAW, updated monthly; and on magnetic tape.

A committee of law librarians selects the more than 900 key law journals, bar association publications, and legal newspapers from the United States, Canada, England, Australia, and New Zealand that are covered here. All versions of the index have standard author, title, and subject searching. The printed *Current Law Index* has a separate index to cases. *LegalTrac* and *Legal Resources Index*, the CD-ROM and online versions, can be searched by keyword, of course, but also by case name or citation and by statute citation. The online versions also index additional legal newsletters and newspapers beyond what is found in the print version.

Index to Legal Periodicals and Books (Previously *Index to Legal Periodicals*, 1908–1993). New York: H. W. Wilson, 1994– . Monthly. Also available on CD-ROM (*Index to Legal Periodicals and Books*) from WILSONDISC, SilverPlatter, Ovid Technologies, 1981– , updated monthly; online from WILSONLINE, LEXIS, WESTLAW, Ovid Technologies, OCLC (FirstSearch and EPIC), 1981– , updating varies; and on magnetic tape.

The print version of the index is very easy to use and has great historical coverage. A salient feature, since 1917, is the "Table of Cases Referred to in Articles." Also included are statutes tables and separate indexes to book reviews. The various computerized versions contain more than 200,000 citations to articles selected from more than 620 legal periodicals, including journals, yearbooks, and annual reviews.

Public Administration and Public Affairs

/ *PAIS International in Print* (formed from merger of *PAIS Bulletin*, 1915–1990 and *PAIS Foreign Language Index*, 1972–1990). New York: Public Affairs Information Service, 1991– . Monthly. Also available on CD-ROM (*PAIS*) from PAIS, EBSCO, SilverPlatter, 1972– , updated quarterly; and online (*PAIS International*) from DataStar, DIALOG, OCLC (FirstSearch and EPIC), RLIN (CitaDel), 1972– , updated monthly.

PAIS is valuable for information on criminal justice administration, public policy, current issues, municipal functions, and comparative studies of public issues such as legalization of drugs, as well as for locating government documents. The computerized versions currently contain more than 400,000 citations, with brief abstracts, to articles and reports in six languages (English, French, German, Italian, Portuguese, and Spanish). *PAIS* indexes over 1,200 journals as well as books, government publications, statistical compilations, committee reports, and reports of public, intergovernmental, and private organizations.

Sage Public Administration Abstracts. Thousand Oaks, CA: Sage Publications, 1974– . Quarterly.

This traditional abstracting service with annual cumulated index is a good place to check for articles, books, and essays in books on general administration and personnel issues.

Sage Urban Studies Abstracts. Thousand Oaks, CA: Sage Publications, 1973– . Quarterly.

Books, articles, pamphlets, government publications, speeches, and research studies are abstracted here. Each issue has a section on "Crime and Criminal Justice," but this index is also valuable for bringing together abstracts of articles on transportation, urban economics, social issues, and other topics of importance to the study of criminal justice in urban areas.

Urban Affairs Abstracts. Washington, DC: National League of Cities, 1971–1994.

Before this index ceased in 1994, it provided extensive coverage of newsletters, journals, and government documents that focused on urban issues and were often indexed nowhere else. Public safety was a major focus.

ABC Pol Sci. (*Advanced Bibliography of Contents: Political Science and Government*). Santa Barbara, CA: ABC-CLIO, 1969– . Five issues per year. Also available on CD-ROM from ABC-CLIO, 1984– , three times per year.

ABC Pol Sci. lists and indexes the tables of contents of over 300 journals, published worldwide, in political science and government.

Business

Business indexes are good places to search for information on white-collar crime, private security, and the economics of crime. They also provide alternative views of some pressing criminal justice issues. A recent search on the phrase "police brutality" in *Business Periodicals Index*, for example, turned up several articles in insurance journals on the liability costs of police brutality.

√ *ABI/Iinform*. Louisville, KY: UMI, 1971– . CD-ROM (*ABI/INFORM Global*) from UMI Ondisc. Updated monthly. Also available online from Ovid Technologies, DataStar, DIALOG, CARL, STN International, RLIN (CitaDel), OCLC (FirstSearch and EPIC), LEXIS-NEXIS, updated weekly; and on magnetic tape.

This business database concentrates on administration and management, including public administration. As such it provides valuable leads to substantive journal articles and is surprisingly effective for criminal justice topics. It contains more than 790,000 citations, with abstracts, to articles appearing in approximately 1,400 international periodicals covering business and management and related functional areas. Since 1991, it has also included the complete text of selected articles from 550 publications.

Business Index. Foster City, CA: Information Access Company (IAC). CD-ROM (current 4 years) updated monthly. Also available online from CARL, 1988– , updated monthly; and on magnetic tape.

Contains more than 3 million citations, with some abstracts, to articles in more than 800 specialized business, management, and trade journals, and to business-related articles in additional newspapers and magazines.

） *Business Periodicals Index* and *Wilson Business Abstracts*. New York: H. W. Wilson, 1958– . Monthly. Also available on CD-ROM from WILSONDISC and SilverPlatter, 1982– , updated monthly; online from WILSONLINE and OCLC (FirstSearch and EPIC), updating varies; and on magnetic tape.

Particularly good for security, this resource covers major security journals as well as business trade publications with security interests. Also valuable for white-collar crime, administration, personnel, and management issues, it is easy to use in print or by computer. *Wilson Business Abstracts*, with coverage back to 1982, includes abstracts beginning with 1990.

Management Contents. Foster City, CA: Information Access, 1974– . Online from DIALOG and DataStar, updated monthly.

This database contains nearly 300,000 abstracts from 130 management journals specializing in group and organizational theory, human resources, and public relations. It is useful for management and personnel issues, which can be similar across all public and private fields.

Education

✓ *ERIC*. Rockville, MD: ERIC Processing and Reference Facility, 1966– . Monthly. Also available on CD-ROM from DIALOG, Ovid Technologies, EBSCO, National Information Services Corporation (NISC), U.S. Department of Education, and SilverPlatter, updated quarterly; online from Ovid Technologies, OCLC (FirstSearch and EPIC), CompuServe (Knowledge Index), CARL, DataStar, updated monthly; on magnetic tape; and [Internet], 1989– at http://ericir.syr.edu/ Eric/

ERIC is a government-sponsored index to journal articles and report literature in education and education-related areas. It is especially good for delinquency, crime and the schools, and correctional education. The print version of ERIC consists of two titles, *Current Index to Journals in Education* (*CIJE*), which is a periodical index; and *Resources in Education* (*RIE*), an index to unpublished documents and research reports that are available on microfiche in the ERIC microfiche collection. The database currently contains more than 850,000 citations, with lengthy abstracts. ERIC documents may be ordered over the Internet from the ERIC Document Reproduction Service at http:// edrs.com/.

✓ *Education Index* and *Wilson Education Abstracts*. New York: H. W. Wilson, 1929– . Monthly. Also available on CD-ROM from SilverPlatter and WILSONDISC, 1983– ; online from OCLC (FirstSearch and EPIC) and WILSONLINE, 1983– ; and on magnetic tape.

Easy-to-use index to more than 400 journals in education. *Wilson Education Abstracts,* with coverage back to 1983, includes abstracts beginning with 1994.

History

America: History and Life. Santa Barbara, CA: ABC-CLIO, 1964– . Three issues a year. Also available on CD-ROM (*America: History and Life on Disc*) from ABC-CLIO, 1969– , updated three times a year; and online from DIALOG and CompuServe (Knowledge Index), 1964– , updated quarterly.

This source is especially good for the history of crime and criminal justice in the United States and Canada, but it also includes many articles about recent, almost contemporary, times viewed from the scholarly perspective of the historian. It contains citations, with abstracts, to social science and humanities literature on all aspects of U.S. and Canadian history, culture, and current affairs from prehistoric times to the present. It covers books, dissertations, and articles from approximately 2,400 journals published worldwide in 40 languages, but all abstracts are in English. Since 1988, it also provides reviews of films and video projects.

INDEXES FOR SPECIFIC GROUPS

Child Abuse and Neglect. Washington, DC: U.S. National Clearinghouse on Child Abuse and Neglect Information, 1967– . CD-ROM. Yearly. Also available [Internet] at http://www.calib.com/nccanch/database.htm

Contains more than 17,000 citations with abstracts to materials concerned with the definition, identification, prevention, and treatment of child abuse and neglect. Materials include books, articles in books and journals, final reports from federally funded grants, conference papers, unpublished papers, state annual reports, court cases, letters to the editor, and excerpts of some current state statutes.

Sage Family Studies Abstracts. Thousand Oaks, CA: Sage Publications, 1979– . Quarterly.

A useful resource for articles on domestic violence.

Sage Race Relations Abstracts. Thousand Oaks, CA: Sage Publications, 1975– . Quarterly.

Published on behalf of the Institute of Race Relations, London, this index covers articles on discrimination, education, employment, health, politics, and law and legislation in the area of race relations.

Women Studies Abstracts. Rush, NY: Rush Publishing Co., 1972– .

Excellent coverage of women as victims of crimes; less so as perpetrators.

INDEXES TO POPULAR MATERIAL

Popular periodicals contain information about notorious crimes, police scandals, political responses to crime, public attitudes towards crime and law enforcement, recent statistics, and a host of other topics of interest to the criminal justice researcher. Besides the indexes listed here, popular periodicals are also indexed in most of the mega-indexes listed in the last section below.

Readers' Guide to Periodical Literature and *Readers' Guide Abstracts.* New York: H. W. Wilson, 1900– . Semimonthly. Also available on CD-ROM from WILSON-DISC and SilverPlatter, 1983– , updated monthly; online from DIALOG, WILSONLINE, OCLC (FirstSearch and OPIC), Ovid Technologies, 1983– , updates vary; and on magnetic tape.

Readers' Guide contains citations to articles appearing in approximately forty of the most popular English-language, general-interest periodicals published in the United States and Canada. Excellent for examining current and historical criminal justice "hot topics" in the popular press, and for finding reports about famous crimes. *Readers' Guide Abstracts*, with coverage back to 1984, also includes abstracts of the articles.

Magazine Index. Foster City, CA: Information Access Company (IAC), 1980– . Monthly. CD-ROM. Also available online from DIALOG; and on magnetic tape.

This general interest database contains more than 2.1 million citations, with abstracts of articles published in more than 450 popular magazines published in the United States and Canada, as well as from *The New York Times*. Approximately half of the articles indexed are available in full text, from LEXIS-NEXIS and DIALOG. Citations are retrospective to 1959; full-text begins in 1983.

Magazine ASAP. Foster City, CA: Information Access Company (IAC), 1992– . CD-ROM. Also available online from DIALOG.

Contains citations, with abstracts, and the complete text of more than 380,000 articles published in more than 100 selected general-interest periodicals indexed in *Magazine Index*.

MEGA-INDEXES

The indexes listed here differ in the number of periodicals they index, the period of time they cover, and the quality of the indexing, but they all cover many of the same journals and can often be used in the same way. Libraries that subscribe to one of these general indexes usually will not subscribe to another, so you will probably use whichever your library has made available. They are often offered as databases available through local online public access catalog (OPAC) systems, or increasingly through the Web.

Academic Index. Foster City, CA: Information Access Co. (IAC), 1989– . CD-ROM. Also available [Internet] by subscription (SearchBank).

IAC offers several different forms of *Academic Index*. All provide indexing and abstracting of general interest periodicals and scholarly journals in the humanities, social sciences, and science and technology. *General Academic Index* indexes 350 journals and newspapers going back to 1989, and is available on CD-ROM. *Expanded Academic Index ASAP* indexes over 1,500 periodicals and provides full-text articles for 500 of them. It is available online over the Internet by subscription through IAC's SearchBank service.

ArticleFirst. Dublin, OH: OCLC, Inc. Online from OCLC (EPIC and FirstSearch). Coverage from 1990 for most journals, updated daily.

Like *Current Contents*, *ArticleFirst* is basically an index to the tables of contents of journals. More than 13,000 journals in the sciences, social sciences, humanities, and popular press are indexed. There are no subject headings or other descriptors added to the database, so users must think carefully to select multiple keywords for the same concept.

ArticleFirst has a companion database, *ContentsFirst*, which searches not for individual articles, but for individual issues of journals, and then lists the tables of contents for those issues.

Masterfile. Ipswich, MA: EBSCO. Available on CD-ROM, online from EBSCOHost, or on magnetic tape.

Like *Academic Index*, *Masterfile* comes in several different varieties from EBSCO, ranging from simple indexing and abstracting of about 400 periodicals, to searchable full-text of 1,500 journals. Dates of coverage vary by subscription.

Periodical Abstracts. Ann Arbor, MI: UMI, 1986– . On CD-ROM, updated monthly. Also available online from CARL, DIALOG, LEXIS-NEXIS, RLIN (CitaDel), and OCLC (FirstSearch and EPIC), updated weekly; and on magnetic tape, updated weekly.

Periodical Abstracts offers comprehensive indexing, with brief abstracts, of over 1,700 general-interest periodicals from the United States, Canada and the United Kingdom, from 1986 to the present. Coverage includes the arts, consumer issues, current events, education, health, history, literature, politics, psychology, sociology and sports in periodicals ranging from news magazines to professional journals and newsletters. It is also available with full-text articles as *ProQuest*.

ProQuest. Ann Arbor, MI: UMI, 1990– . CD-ROM. Also available [Internet] by subscription (*ProQuest Direct*).

ProQuest combines a periodical index of over 4,000 scholarly journals and popular magazines with the full text of articles on CD-ROM, to make finding articles exceptionally easy. There are many forms of *ProQuest* that libraries can subscribe to and that cover various ranges and kinds of periodicals. *ProQuest* is now also available over the Internet to subscribing libraries.

UnCover. Denver: CO: The UnCover Co., 1989– . Updated daily. Available [Internet] at http://uncweb.carl.org or telnet://database.carl.org

UnCover provides access to the tables of contents pages of over 17,000 English-language periodicals and is available for searching over the Internet at no charge. Searching is by author or by keyword from journal titles, article titles, and article summaries (if they appear on the contents page). Articles are available for a fee—chargeable to a credit card—and are delivered by fax. While this database is easily available to anyone with an Internet connection, it does not provide the sophisticated access methods (e.g., subject headings and Boolean searching) found on most indexes in libraries. The ability to receive articles quickly by fax, however, makes this source almost irresistable to anyone who has a home or office fax and can afford the charges.

8

Newsletters, Newspapers, and News Broadcasts

All newsletters, newspapers, and radio and television news broadcasts perform the same general function. They provide the latest news to a target audience.

NEWSLETTERS

Newsletters are published primarily to convey current information to a group of readers with a common interest. Professional associations, corporations, government agencies, nonprofit organizations, and private publishers are among the groups that frequently publish newsletters.

Information contained in newsletters varies considerably: biographies of important people in the profession, notices of appointments to new jobs, employment listings, book reviews, notes on new or pending legislation and on recently decided cases, editorials, articles about recently awarded grants, research studies projected or currently under way, and notices of interim or final research reports. Most newsletter articles are brief.

We have seen in Chapter 1 how newsletters, although not generally viewed by their publishers as research tools, can be important for the researcher. Not only do they contain information about the newest ideas and projects, but they have a more lasting value in those instances when a particular idea or study was not carried forward into a journal article or book.

Criminal Justice Periodical Index (*CJPI*) is the key to locating information in many of the newsletters of the criminal justice profession. It is an easy-to-use, straightforward, alphabetical subject index. Available online as well as in print form, it is discussed in detail in Chapter 7 (p. 83). Many valuable newsletters, however, are not included in *Criminal Justice Periodical Index*. The careful researcher may want to browse through some of these omissions on a regular basis.

Because newsletters are designed for current awareness and not for research, some libraries do not subscribe to them; others keep only the current issues. Where they are not available in a local library, they can be obtained on interlibrary loan.

Below is a list of newsletters selected to show the breadth of information and the variety of sources available.

General Criminal Justice Newsletters

Crime Control Digest: A Comprehensive and Independent News Summary for the Law Enforcement Professional. Washington, DC: Washington Crime News Service, 3918 Prosperity Ave., Suite 318, Fairfax, VA 22031–3334. 1967– . Weekly.

News items survey criminal justice developments on the local and national levels and track developments in Congress and the courts. Indexed: *CJPI*.

Criminal Justice Newsletter: An Independent Report on Issues in Criminal Justice Policy and Administration. PaceCom Incorporated, 1900 L Street, NW, Suite 312, Washington, DC 20036. Formerly published by the National Council on Crime and Delinquency. 1970– . Twice monthly.

Includes brief news notes; longer articles of summary and analysis; and regular announcements of conferences, training opportunities, and printed and online resources. Indexed: *CJPI, Current Law Index, Legal Resource Index*.

State Capitals: Public Safety and Justice Policies (formerly *From the State Capitals: Public Safety and Justice Policies*). Wakeman/Walworth Inc., 300 North Washington St., Alexandria, VA 22314. 1984– . Weekly.

Focuses on criminal justice issues—police, corrections, juvenile justice, gun control—throughout the United States. Not indexed.

Police

FBI Law Enforcement Bulletin. Washington, DC: Federal Bureau of Investigation, 1935– . Monthly. Also available online [Internet] at http://www.fbi.gov/leb/leb.htm

Not as scholarly as a journal, but with more information than the typical newsletter, the *FBI Law Enforcement Bulletin* contains articles written by practitioners for practitioners. Current issues are available through the FBI's World Wide Web site; back issues (to December 1989) may be downloaded as compressed files. Indexed: *CJPI, Abstracts in Criminology and Penology, Criminal Justice Abstracts*.

Law Enforcement News. John Jay College of Criminal Justice, 899 Tenth Ave., New
   York, NY 10019. 1975– . Twice monthly.

A newspaper for law enforcement professionals, with lengthier, more in-
depth articles than most newsletters, this publication includes a regular "Around
the Nation" survey of current news as well as announcements of upcoming
events. Summaries of recent issues and some full-text articles are available
through the John Jay College Library Web site at http://www.lib.jjay.cuny.edu/
len. Indexed: *CJPI.*

Law Officer's Bulletin. Bureau of National Affairs, 1231 25th St., NW, Washington,
   DC 20037. 1976– .

Discussions of recent federal and state legal decisions affecting law officers. Indexed: *CJPI.*

CJ Management and Training Digest. Washington, DC: Washington Crime News Service, 3918 Prosperity Ave., Suite 318, Fairfax, VA 22031–3334. 1995– . Twice
   monthly.

Short news articles focus on management and training of law enforcement
personnel. Indexed: *CJPI.*

Search and Seizure Bulletin. Quinlan Publishing, 23 Drydock Ave., Boston, MA 02210–
   0048. 1964– . Monthly.

Summaries and comments on federal and state court cases related to search
and seizure. Indexed: *CJPI.*

Corrections

Jail & Prisoner Law Bulletin. Americans for Effective Law Enforcement (AELE),
   5519 N. Cumberland Ave., #1008, Chicago, IL 60656–1498. 1972– . Monthly.

Summaries and short discussions of pertinent federal and state court decisions. Not indexed.

The Keepers' Voice. International Association of Correctional Officers, 133 S. Wabash,
   Box 53, Chicago, IL 60605. 1980– . Quarterly. Recent issues also available
   [Internet] at http://www.acsp.uic.edu/iaco/about.htm

This association newsletter, published in cooperation with the Office of International Criminal Justice at The University of Illinois in Chicago, focuses on
practical issues of training, resources, job notices, and the like. Not indexed.

On the Line. American Correctional Association, 4380 Forbes Blvd., Lanham, MD
   20706–4322. 1977– . Five times a year.

Newsletter of the Association. Not indexed.

Overcrowded Times. Edna McConnell Clark Foundation, P.O. Box 110, Castine, ME
04421. 1990– . Six times a year.

Short articles on current trends in corrections; some international coverage. Indexed: *CJPI.*

Security

Security Letter. Security Letter, 166 East 96th St., New York, NY 10128, 1971– .
Semimonthly.

Very short news briefs on public and private security in the United States
and abroad. Indexed: *CJPI.*

*Corporate Security with Technology Alert: Biweekly Intelligence Tracking Cutting-
edge Practices, Trends and New Technologies for Security Executives.* Warren,
Gorham & Lamont, 31 St. James Ave., Boston, MA 02116. 1981– . Biweekly.

Articles focus on current problems of private security executives. Indexed:
CJPI.

Security Law Newsletter. Crime Control Research Corporation, 1063 Thomas Jefferson
St., NW, Washington, DC 20007. 1981– . Monthly.

Summaries, with comments, on recent court decisions affecting private
security. Indexed: *CJPI.*

NEWSPAPERS

Newspapers are valuable sources of information for the criminal justice
researcher. They are often the first place and sometimes the only place reports of local and even national crime statistics, or reports of commissions
can be found. Newspapers can be used to study events or attitudes in a single
locality or to compare reactions to similar problems in different localities.
Regardless of the research topic, however, newspapers must always be used
with great care. Although frequently described as objective and cited as primary sources, newspapers always have a degree of selectivity and subjectivity in the information presented. Someone decides which story to write, what
to emphasize in the description of an event, whom to interview, and what
parts of the interview to print. Simply by deciding how much coverage to
give to local crimes, newspapers can influence the public perception of the
pervasiveness of crime in a community.

With the above in mind, the criminal justice researcher can look to newspapers for a variety of information:

• Newspapers, like newsletters, contain announcements of research studies. Agencies
  anxious to publicize their activities may send press releases or hold press confer-

ences to announce receipt of a grant, the start of a project, or the publication of an interim or final report.

- Newspapers reflect community attitudes. They are an outstanding source of information and opinion on topics such as police and community relations, public pressures for court reform, community response to placement of penal institutions, and political pressures on the criminal justice system.

- Newspapers contain descriptions of events. They report what happened at the scene of a crime; who said what at the end of a trial or at a city council meeting; eyewitness reports of a riot; and interviews with citizens, politicians, and police officials.

In the past, the back issues of only a few newspapers of national importance, such as *The New York Times* and *The Wall Street Journal*, were easily available in libraries, primarily on microfilm. Increasingly, however, more and more newspapers are becoming available in microfilm, on CD-ROM, and online.

Newspapers Online

The full-text of many newspapers is now available online from many sources, both free and fee-based. DIALOG, the online database provider, now offers access to the full-text of over fifty newspapers from around the country, with coverage in some cases back to 1983. LEXIS-NEXIS provides the searchable full text of more than 3,600 magazines and journals, and over 800 newspapers. Some college and university libraries have subscriptions to LEXIS-NEXIS, allowing for unlimited searching by their students.

As we noted in Chapter 3 (pp. 33–34), you need to be careful when searching full-text databases, because the magnitude of words accessible for searching increases the likelihood of finding irrelevant articles. You need to spend some time learning about the system you are using. Check with your librarian to find out if you have access to the full-text of newspapers through one of these fee-based services and whether any training is offered.

The fee-based systems are generally more complete, have much greater historical depth, and are easier to use than the newspapers found on the Internet. Internet-accessible newspapers, however, do have the advantage of being free and widely available. For the most part, these newspapers are accessible using World Wide Web browsers. The contents of the newspaper WWW sites vary tremendously. Some sites offer complete full-text of the current day's paper plus back issues; some offer additional articles not found in print; some merely tell you what is in the printed papers; others provide local community information and nothing from the printed paper. The lack of archival information limits the value for the researcher of most of these local online newspapers. The fact that the contents are likely to disappear each day also makes citing these sources problematic.

Newspapers of national importance that are available over the Internet include the following:

Chicago Tribune. http://www.chicago.tribune.com/

The online version of the *Chicago Tribune* provides the stories from the current issue of the newspaper, "Between Editions" articles, and special Internet features. The paper's archives are searchable online back to 1985, but there is a fee to download the full-text of articles found in back issues.

The Christian Science Monitor Electronic Edition. http://www.csmonitor.com/

The *Christian Science Monitor's* motive is "to injure no man, but to bless all mankind," and its "spin" on the news is a more positive view of the world. The electronic edition contains the full text of the daily newspaper, as well as special multimedia features. A useful feature of the news stories is the inclusion of WWW links to background material about the story. To its credit, the *Christian Science Monitor Electronic Edition* allows for full-text searching and display of its entire paper back to 1980.

Los Angeles Times. http://www.latimes.com/HOME

At this site you can find the news stories from the current day's edition of the *Los Angeles Times*, as well as general community information. Back issues of the *Los Angeles Times* to 1990 can be searched and the headlines displayed at no charge; there is a charge to display or download the full article.

The New York Times. http://www.nytimes.com

You can find the current day's edition of *The New York Times* here. Registration is required for a "subscription" but is free to U.S. subscribers. The online version of *The New York Times* is updated several times a day and contains some articles not found in the printed version. Selected older articles are also available on the site, and can be located through keyword searching.

The Washington Post. http://www.washingtonpost.com/

Contains the current day's text of *The Washington Post*, plus selected features including a weekly "Crime Watch" for Washington-area neighborhoods.

Washington Times. http://www.washtimes.com/

Full-text articles from the current front page plus other selected articles are available.

USA Today. http://www.usatoday.com/

Updated constantly throughout the day, but no back issues are available, nor is it possible to search an online index for anything but the current day's articles.

Directories of Internet Newspapers

Editor and Publisher Online Newspapers. Available at [Internet] http://www.mediainfo.
    com/ephome/npaper/nphtm/online.htm

Editor and Publisher magazine maintains an online directory of online newspapers, which can be searched by name of newspaper or browsed by geographical area. As of July 1997, the site listed over 1,700 newspapers. The directory entries include annotations and live links to the newspapers.

AJR Newslink. Available at [Internet] http://www.newslink.org/news.html

American Journalism Review offers a useful directory of newspapers available online, with indexes of newspapers by region and by genre (metropolitan papers, campus, and alternative).

Newspaper Indexes: Computerized

Newspaper indexes were developed to keep the researcher from growing old or going blind while looking for information in newspapers. A wide range of commercially prepared indexes is now available online through commercial services, local online public access catalogs, and CD-ROM, as well as in print. Your decision about which to use should be based on coverage, ease of use, and availability; by all means first use whatever online source your library is offering.

The online commercial services that provide full text of newspapers, such as LEXIS-NEXIS and DIALOG also, of course, act as indexing services. Additional computer indexes are the following:

National Newspaper Index. Foster City, CA: Information Access, 1979– (1982– for
    the *Los Angeles Times* and *The Washington Post*). CD-ROM. Also available
    online through DIALOG; over the Internet (subscription only) as part of InfoTrac
    SearchBank; and on magnetic tape.

Provides complete indexing of the *Christian Science Monitor*, the *Los Angeles Times*, *The New York Times*, the *Wall Street Journal*, and *The Washington Post*.

Newspaper Abstracts. Ann Arbor, MI: UMI. Dates of coverage vary. CD-ROM as part
    of *ProQuest*. Also available online from DIALOG, OCLC (FirstSearch and
    EPIC), and RLIN (CitaDel); over the Internet with a subscription to ProQuest
    Direct; and on magnetic tape.

Indexing and abstracting twenty-six of the nation's most important newspapers, this database is available in many forms and, depending on the library's subscription, full-text of newspaper articles may be available either on CD-ROM or via fax or mail.

Newsbank Electronic Information System. New Canaan, CT: NewsBank, Inc., 1980– .
    Monthly. CD-ROM.

Indexes 2 million articles selected from U.S. newspapers and periodicals.
Accompanying microfiche collection contains copies of the articles.

Newspaper Indexes: In Print

The New York Times Index. New York: New York Times, 1851– . Semimonthly.
Personal Name Index to the "New York Times Index," 1851–1975, with *Supplements*
    to 1993. Verdi, NV: Roxbury Data Interface, 1977– .

Although a New York City newspaper, coverage in *The New York Times*
has always been national in scope. Generally considered one of the nation's
best newspapers, both microform copies of the paper and its various printed
and online indexes are readily available. Printed indexes have been made for
the paper back to the first issues in 1851.

The *Personal Name Index to "The New York Times Index"* lists, in one
alphabet, all personal names in *The New York Times Index*, from 1851 to 1975,
with supplements to 1993. This index is particularly useful in searching for
information that predates the online indexes. It is much faster to search the
cumulative *Personal Name Index* than to look through *The New York Times
Index* itself year by year. Use this if you are looking for information about a
criminal or a criminal justice personality, or for articles on a criminal justice
topic that is associated with individuals whose names you know. Remember,
the *Personal Name Index* is an index to an index—it refers you to the appropriate volume and page of *The New York Times Index* where the actual citation to the newspaper article can be found.

Washington Post Index. Ann Arbor, MI: UMI, 1972– .

The first ten years of the published indexes to the *Washington Post* are somewhat difficult to use; but since 1982 typography has improved, and very useful
geographical subdivisions have been added for most subjects. The *Washington Post* is also indexed in all of the general online newspaper indexes.

Wall Street Journal Index. New York: Dow Jones, 1958– .

The *Wall Street Journal* covers news of economic importance nationally
and internationally. While you will not find articles about local crimes, you
will certainly find articles about the economic impact of crime.

NEWS BROADCASTS

Much of today's news is communicated through broadcast media rather
than newsprint. Anyone who regularly watches network news programs knows

how much coverage is given to topics of interest to criminal justice researchers. Fortunately these broadcasts do not disappear after they are shown but are archived in a variety of ways.

Television News Index and Abstracts. Nashville, TN: Vanderbilt University Library, 1968– . Also available [Internet] at http://tvnews.vanderbilt.edu/

The Television News Archive is a unique institution. Realizing that network news broadcasts have the same historical research value as the major daily newspapers, it has recorded, abstracted, and indexed national television newscasts since August 5, 1968. Included in the Archive are videotapes of the evening news programs of ABC, CBS, and NBC, the nightly news show "Nightline" (since 1988), and CNN PrimeNews (since 1989). The Archive also tapes and indexes special reports and news-related special programs. You may request, for a fee, the loan of a videotape of a broadcast, or request the compilation of a series of items from several different broadcasts.

Television News Index and Abstracts has been published monthly since the inception of the archive. The abstracts are fairly detailed, specifying what was shown as well as what was said, and include the names of people who can be heard as well as seen. There are indexes to names, places, and subjects.

The Television News Archive maintains an excellent Web site, with the complete *Index and Abstracts* browsable by date or searchable using a WAIS index.

CNN Interactive. Available [Internet] at http://www.cnn.com

The Cable News Network broadcasts news reports and related interviews and commentary twenty-four hours a day. Its Web site provides the latest news in stories written for the site, and also maintains archival copies of past Web stories, transcripts of news broadcasts and, in some cases, video clips. Many of the stories include pictures. The full text of the online archives is searchable (look for the "Search" button on the home page) but voluminous enough that care must be taken in formulating a search. When searching a phrase be sure to use quotes around the phrase (e.g., "capital punishment") to ensure that the words appear together and do not come from two different news stories reported in one broadcast.

AJR Newslink. Available at [Internet] http://www.newslink.org/broad.html

American Journalism Review's World Wide Web site provides links to the WWW pages of radio and television networks and broadcast stations. Information found at individual sites varies tremendously.

9

Documents, Reports, and Conference Proceedings

Reports, government documents, and conference proceedings are grouped together in this chapter because they share several common characteristics. They tend to appear early in the information flow, they are generally written for a small audience of specialists, and they are difficult to find and to find out about. Libraries frequently do not buy reports, documents, and conference proceedings individually but may acquire them as part of a collection, and the individual items in the collection may not appear in the library catalog. Different search techniques are needed both to discover that they exist and to locate them.

Government documents are publications issued or authorized by any office of a legally organized government. Reports are records of (1) an organization or group, (2) research results, (3) research in progress, or (4) other technical studies. Conference proceedings are collections of reports and papers presented at conferences. In actuality, a government document can be a report and a report can be a government document. The main concern is not in the definition but rather in locating the specific document or report that best contributes to your research. Most sources discussed in this chapter will not deal exclusively with criminal justice subjects; they are, however, important sources of criminal justice information.

GOVERNMENT DOCUMENTS

Documents can be issued by governments at any level: federal, state, regional, county, municipal, intergovernmental, or international. They may appear in print, in microform, on CD-ROM, on computer tape, or online over the Internet. Access to them is as varied as the sources from which they emerge and the media in which they appear.

Federal Documents

Federal documents are found at every level in the information flow, from the raw statistical data issued by the Bureau of the Census or the Bureau of Justice Statistics, to the summary volumes and recommendations issued by national criminal justice commissions. Documents containing raw data are considered primary sources; documents interpreting that data are secondary sources. In a single year, the U.S. Government Printing Office publishes thousands of titles in paper, microform, CD-ROM, and online formats. To assure that this wealth of data is available to its citizens, the Superintendent of Documents sends free copies of these items to almost 1,400 depository libraries throughout the country. Other libraries buy just the items they need. The Government Printing Office also maintains a Web site on the Internet and provides access to its online offerings to all libraries and individuals with Internet access.

Not all federal documents are published by the Government Printing Office, and most depository libraries choose not to accept all documents made available by the Superintendent of Documents. Having access to a depository library, therefore, does not mean that you will be able to find everything published by every federal agency. Thousands of technical reports are available only through the National Technical Information Service (see the section on Reports, below), for example, and some agencies issue reports that they do not consider "published" and so are not available through the Government Printing Office. To further add complications, almost every federal agency now has a presence on the Web, and may or may not make some of its documents directly available to the public through that medium.

Early in your research you should consider whether government documents may provide some of the information you need, and you should become familiar with the intricacies of finding and accessing these documents. The sheer mass of material emanating from the variety of federal agencies assures coverage of a broad spectrum of topics. Business, economics, political science, social science, public administration, law, criminal justice, statistics, and psychology are all subjects within the purview of federal documents.

Libraries include government documents in their collections in several ways: (1) they catalog them and integrate them into the regular collection; (2) they catalog them but put them in a separate section of the library; (3) they do not catalog them at all but keep them in a separate section with their own access tools. In recent years, with the availability of computerized bibliographic records for government documents, it has become common to find more recent government documents in the catalog, while older ones remain accessible only through specialized access tools. Ask a librarian how your library handles government documents.

If a library catalogs some or all of its government documents, you should be able to find those through the library's catalog. Performing a subject or keyword search in the catalog will very likely yield many government documents, complete with information on where the document is located in the library. If you are trying to find out if your library owns a particular government document, try to search for it by title; the author of a government document is usually considered to be the department or agency that issued it, and library catalog rules about government authors are so complicated, and change so frequently, that even experienced librarians often throw up their hands when asked to find a government agency in the catalog. If you have trouble finding the document by title, then try a keyword search if that is available, or ask a librarian to help you.

In libraries that have a separate government documents section, you find items arranged on the shelves by the Superintendent of Documents (SuDocs) system rather than the Dewey or LC classification systems. SuDocs call numbers group documents by the agency that issues them. Thus, items on the same subject are not necessarily shelved together. Studies on violence done by a presidential commission, for instance, will be shelved with the commission's publications. Studies on violence completed by the National Institute of Justice will be in an entirely different location.

Finding Federal Documents

The federal government and its agencies, which for the most part do not need to show a profit from their publications, have embraced the Internet wholeheartedly as a cost-effective method of distributing information to constituents. The Department of Justice, in particular, appears to be publishing all its documents on the Web, which is rapidly becoming the first place to look for criminal justice documents, as the following site demonstrates:

Justice Information Center: A Service of the National Criminal Justice Reference Service (NCJRS). Available [Internet] at http://www.ncjrs.org

Judged by content, this may well be the single most significant criminal justice site on the Internet. Hundreds, possibly thousands, of criminal justice government documents are available here in full-text in both ASCII and Adobe Acrobat (PDF) format. The entire site, except for the PDF documents, is keyword searchable, yielding an enormous full-text database of criminal justice reports and documents.

The National Criminal Justice Reference Service acts as a clearinghouse for information to support all bureaus of the U.S. Department of Justice, Office of Justice Programs: the National Institute of Justice, the Office of Juvenile Justice and Delinquency Prevention, the Bureau of Justice Statistics, the Bureau of Justice Assistance, the Office for Victims of Crime, and the OJP Program Offices. It also supports the Office of National Drug Control Policy. Recent documents and reports of all these agencies are available here.

The site is divided into criminal justice topics—Corrections, Courts, Crime Prevention, Criminal Justice Statistics, Drugs and Crime, International, Juvenile Justice, Law Enforcement, Research and Evaluation, and Victims—and both documents and additional Internet resources are listed for each one. Unfortunately, the lists of full-text documents contain only titles; in most cases, it is necessary to click on the Adobe Acrobat link, not just to read the entire document, but to find out the agency responsible for it, its publication date, and its length.

As a research library which collects books, journals, and documents on criminal justice and provides an index to them on CD-ROM, NCJRS is further discussed under the section "Reports."

This site also provides links to other criminal justice WWW and gopher sites, and descriptions of criminal justice discussion lists with subscription instructions.

• • •

The following publications will help you understand the organization of the federal government and help you find publications issued by one of its branches.

The United States Government Manual. Washington, DC: U.S. Government Printing Office, 1935– . Annual. Also available [Internet] at http://www.access.gpo.gov/ nara/nara001.html (GPO Access); and at http://www.gpo.ucop.edu/catalog/ 96_govman.html (University of California GPO Gate)

If the plethora of federal government agencies tends to discourage or confuse you, take time out to look at this manual. It provides succinct descriptions of the agencies of all three branches of the government. Published annually, it relates the history and clarifies the structure of each agency, and delineates the interaction among agencies. The WWW versions of the *Government Manual* are difficult to use; the GPO Access version cannot be browsed, but only searched via keywords; the University of California version provides table of contents access to chapters in both ASCII and PDF form.

Monthly Catalog of United States Publications. Washington, DC: U.S. Government Printing Office, 1895– . Monthly. Also available online from OCLC (FirstSearch and EPIC), July 1976– .
MOCAT. 1994– . Available [Internet] at http://www.access.gpo.gov/su_docs/dpos/ adpos400.html

The nasty stories you may have heard about the printed *Monthly Catalog* are no longer true. This monthly guide to federal government documents now has multiple indexes: author, title, subject, key words from titles, series/reports and stock numbers. Monthly indexes are cumulated semiannually and annually. From all the access points you can find the entry number for the item you need and then its call number. The indexes prior to 1974 may be intimidating; ask for assistance.

MOCAT, the *Monthly Catalog* on the World Wide Web, is a wonderfully helpful tool. It contains cataloging records for items published in the *Monthly*

Catalog since January 1994 and is updated daily. The full-text of each record is searchable with a WAIS search engine that returns citations in ranked order to yield the most relevant items first. Read the instructions; if two words are entered with no intervening operator then a Boolean OR is assumed (a citation is considered relevant if either of the two words is found). To search a phrase, enclose the phrase in quotation marks.

This database has some unique features that take thorough advantage of the World Wide Web. Some documents are listed in *MOCAT* with hypertext links to WWW versions. In addition, you can find out which depository libraries in your area have chosen to receive that document.

It is important to remember that the *Monthly Catalog* is primarily an index to documents available through the federal depository program, and that the depository program does not include all government documents.

Cumulative Subject Index to the Monthly Catalog of United States Government Publications, 1900–1971. 15 vols. Washington, DC: Carrollton Press, 1973.
Cumulative Title Index to United States Public Documents, 1789–1976. 16 vols. Arlington, VA: U.S. Historical Documents Institute, 1982.

These two cumulations can save hours of work in finding older government documents.

CIS/Index to Publications of the U.S. Congress. Washington, DC: Congressional Information Service, 1970– . Monthly.
Congressional Masterfile 1: 1789–1969. Washington, DC: Congressional Information Service. CD-ROM.
Congressional Masterfile 2: 1970–Present. Washington, DC: Congressional Information Service, 1970– . CD-ROM.

Rare indeed is a subject or issue that is not, sooner or later, discussed in Congress. These excellent resources index all publications of the U.S. Congress except the *Congressional Record.* Hearings, prints, documents, reports, and public laws are all indexed and described in detailed abstracts. Testimony and supporting documents supplied by witnesses at hearings are included. So detailed are the abstracts that they not only summarize the document, but also actually index its contents, giving you page numbers on which specific information appears.

The printed *CIS Annual* comes in two volumes, an index volume and an abstract volume. You search the index volume under subjects, names, or other access points to find an abstract number and use that number to locate the full abstract in the abstract volume. The CD-ROM versions are, of course, much faster to use; many years are searched together and the indexes are linked directly to the abstracts.

Congressional Information Service also sells a microfiche set that provides copies of all the documents indexed in their Congressional indexes. If your library subscribes to the microfiche set with indexes you will find that using Congressional documents can be even easier than finding books. If your library does not subscribe to the microfiche set, you can use the information in the abstract volume to find the document in a local depository library.

American Statistics Index. Washington, DC: Congressional Information Service, 1974– .
    Also available on CD-ROM as part of *Statistical Masterfile.*

ASI works very much like CIS, but it indexes all government publications that have significant statistical content. Since so many documents contain statistics, this index is an excellent way to find documents on particular subjects, even if you are not primarily interested in the statistics themselves. For further details see Chapter 10 (pp. 131–132).

Congressional Compass. Washington, DC: Congressional Information Service, 1996– .
    Available [Internet] by subscription.

Congressional Information Service, the company that publishes the products listed above, has joined with LEXIS-NEXIS to provide online access to the full-text of almost all Congressional publications, including committee reports beginning with the 101st Congress and hearing transcripts beginning with the 104th Congress. Documents are accessible by many controlled indexes as well as by keyword, full-text searching. For researchers whose libraries subscribe to this service, this should be, by far, the easiest method of accessing Congressional publications.

U.S. Government Periodicals Index (formerly *Index to U.S. Government Periodicals,*
    1970–1987). Congressional Information Service, 1992– . Also available on CD-
    ROM, and online through RLIN (CitaDel), 1993– .

While the *Monthly Catalog* gives you titles of government periodicals, this tool indexes substantive articles of lasting research and reference value appearing in approximately 180 periodicals published by the U.S. government.

PAIS International in Print (formed from merger of *PAIS Bulletin,* 1915–1990 and
    PAIS Foreign Language Index, 1972–1990). New York: Public Affairs Infor-
    mation Service, 1991– . Monthly. Also available on CD-ROM *(PAIS)* from
    PAIS, EBSCO, SilverPlatter, 1972– , updated quarterly; and online *(PAIS In-*
    ternational) from DataStar, DIALOG, OCLC (FirstSearch and EPIC), RLIN
    (CitaDel), 1972– , updated monthly.

PAIS, discussed in detail in Chapter 7 (p. 89), is known for its indexing of selected government documents and reports.

Berens, John F. *Criminal Justice Documents: A Selective, Annotated Bibliography of U.S.*
    Government Publications Since 1975. Westport, CT: Greenwood Press, 1987.

An annotated guide to 1,098 U.S. government documents published between 1975 and October 1986 in the criminal justice system; crime and criminals, law enforcement, the courts, corrections, juvenile justice, and security are all covered. It covers only eleven years, but it represents a time of prolific government research and reporting on criminal justice.

• • •

Only if you need to do exhaustive or retrospective research in federal documents will you use these additional tools. Ask your librarian for help with the following standard sources:

Poore, Ben Perley. *A Descriptive Catalog of the Government Publications of the United States.* Washington, DC: U.S. Government Printing Office, 1885. Reprint. New York: Johnson Reprint, 1970.

Covers September 5, 1774 to March 4, 1881.

Ames, John Griffith. *Comprehensive Index to the Publications of the United States Government, 1881 to 1893.* 1905. Reprint. New York: Johnson Reprints, 1962.
Documents Catalog. Washington, DC: U.S. Government Printing Office, 1896–1945. Reprint. New York: Johnson Reprint, 1963.

Together, these cover 1893 to 1940. Overlaps *Monthly Catalog.*

Guide to U.S. Government Publications. McLean, VA: Documents Index, 1973– .

Compendium of lists of serials, periodicals, and irregular publications issued by government agencies. Valuable for tracing agency changes; contains elusive titles.

Selected Federal Government World Wide Web Sites

University of Michigan Documents Center. *Federal Government Resources on the Web.* Available [Internet] at http://www.lib.umich.edu/libhome/Documents. center/federal.html

This is one of the most comprehensive of the nongovernment directories of federal government information, and is easier to use than many of the "official" federal sites. A particularly nice feature is "Documents in the News"—links to documents that report on headline-making news or have become the topics of headlines.

GPO Access. Available [Internet] at http://www.access.gpo.gov/su_docs

The Superintendent of Documents is continuing the practice of providing free public access to U.S. government documents by maintaining this Government Printing Office World Wide Web site. Users with direct WWW access can connect to the site at the above address; others can view *GPO Access* from depository libraries. Through this site users can search the *U.S. Government Manual,* the *Monthly Catalog,* the *Congressional Directory,* the *Congressional Record, General Accounting Office Reports,* the U.S. *Budget,* and many other standard government publications. In addition, *GPO Access* allows the user to search GILS, the government information locator service, a difficult-to-use database that indexes government information available on the Internet.

Library of Congress World Wide Web site. Available [Internet] at http://www.loc.gov/

The Library of Congress's World Wide Web site provides access to *Thomas*, a legislative information system (described on page 155); the Global Legal Information System (described on page 204); the Library of Congress *Marvel* gopher system, which attempts to organize some of the text-based information on the Internet; links to **WWW** sites of government agencies; subject guides to Internet resources; and a variety of other services. The American Memory project of the Library of Congress is particularly interesting. It provides text and reproductions of documents, pictures, sound files, and moving images from the collections of the Library of Congress that are intended to be the beginning of a National Digital Library.

Justice Information Center: A Service of the National Criminal Justice Reference Service (NCJRS). Available [Internet] at http://www.ncjrs.org

Already discussed earlier in this chapter, this site should be the first place you check for federal criminal justice documents.

United States. Department of Justice World Wide Web site. Available [Internet] at http://www.usdoj.gov/

Many agencies within the Department of Justice maintain **WWW** or gopher sites to provide information to the public. All such agencies can be found here alphabetically by name, by organization chart, or by topic. Under the topic "Law Enforcement," for example, can be found **WWW** sites for the Federal Bureau of Investigation, the Drug Enforcement Administration, the United States Marshals Service, and the Federal Bureau of Prisons.

Bureau of Justice Statistics World Wide Web site. Available [Internet] at http://www. ojp.usdoj.gov/bjs/

Most of the recent publications of the Bureau of Justice Statistics are available in full-text here. For further discussions of the Bureau of Justice Statistics see Chapter 10.

International Documents

Access to international documents is discussed in Chapter 15.

State Documents

Access to state documents is much more problematic than access to federal documents. No exhaustive index exists to help you find publications by state, county, or local government. Within each state a state library may serve as the depository for state and local documents. If so, a visit to that library will enable you to assess its potential for research. Many state libraries have made their catalogs available for searching over the Internet. Some state libraries or state historical societies also produce indexes to their state's publications. The fastest way to find out if your state's publications are indexed is to check with your librarian. Many state government agencies, like their federal counterparts, are finding that the Internet is an effective means of making documents accessible, and these documents are consequently more easily available than ever before. Still, persistence is an asset in tracking down documents issued below the federal government level. The following Web sites and publications should be helpful:

Statistical Reference Index (SRI). Washington, DC: Congressional Information Service, 1980– . Monthly. Also available on CD-ROM as part of *Statistical Masterfile.*

This should be your first stop when searching for state documents, because it includes many reports at the state level. Even if you are interested in discussion and not statistics, remember that most documents contain some statistics. Those which do, even if mainly narrative, are included here. This index is most easily used in its CD-ROM form, as part of the *Statistical Masterfile.* See Chapter 10 (pp. 131–132) for further information.

State and Local Government on the Net. Piper Resources. Available [Internet] at http://www.piperinfo.com/state/states.html

This Web site is possibly the best guide on the Internet to official state and local Internet resources. Users can browse an index by state or do a quick keyword search across states on a topic. Many of the listings have annotations explaining what an agency is or does. This site is updated frequently.

StateSearch. Available [Internet] at http://www.nasire.org/ss/index.html

StateSearch is a WWW service of the National Association of State Information Resource Executives and is designed to serve as a topical clearinghouse to state government information on the Internet. Information is arranged by categories; selecting "criminal justice" links you to a Web page with connections to the criminal justice information offered by different states. The information made available by the states varies a great deal in utility—from press releases describing the state attorney general's office to edifying statistics on crime and corrections.

State and Local Governments: A Library of Congress Internet Resource Page. Available [Internet] at http://lcweb.loc.gov/global/state/ or http://lcweb.loc.gov/global/state/stategov.html

Maintained by the Library of Congress, this Web page provides links to state government information pages, as well as connections to "Meta-Indexes for State and Local Government Information," and "State Maps," maintained by other information services.

The Monthly Checklist of State Publications. Library of Congress. Washington, DC:
    U.S. Government Printing Office, 1910–1994.

Now mostly of historic interest, the *Checklist* was maintained and published
by the Library of Congress up to 1994. It lists and indexes all state publications
sent to the Library of Congress by state governments or agencies. Each issue is
arranged by state, with a subject index. Beginning with 1987, a separately
published subject index for each volume appeared the following year. Coverage of criminal justice issues is excellent for the period of time covered.

State Government Research Checklist. Lexington, KY: Council of State Governments,
    1947– . Bimonthly.

This newspaper-like publication lists and briefly abstracts research reports
issued at the state level, whether by legislative service agencies, state study
commissions and committees, or intergovernmental groups. The Council of
State Governments maintains a searchable database of the documents listed
in the *Checklist* that is available to state government officials and CSG associates. It is particularly useful for topics of concern to state legislators, such
as sex crimes or criminal justice information systems.

State Libraries

State libraries usually try to maintain comprehensive holdings of all government documents produced by the state. Searching the state library catalog is an
excellent way to find state government documents on criminal justice issues.
Many state libraries have automated their catalogs and made them available
over the Internet. Check the following sources to find out if an online public
access catalog is available for the state library you are interested in. Ask your
local library for help in obtaining any useful documents you may find.

State Libraries. United States. Library of Congress. Available [Internet] at http://
    lcweb.loc.gov/global/library/statelib.html

This Web page was developed by the Library of Congress in cooperation
with the American Library Association and the Chief Officers of State Library Agencies (COSLA). It brings together links to the WWW sites of the
state library, state library agency, state library network, or state library commission of most states in the United States. Many of the state library web
pages provide connections to the library's online catalog.

The State Library Web Listing. Available [Internet] at http://www.state.wi.us/agen-
    cies/dpi/www/statelib.html

Maintained by the Wisconsin Division for Libraries and Community Learning, this is a listing by state of state library WWW pages, many of which have
direct WWW or telnet links to their state library catalogs.

County and Municipal Documents

Surprisingly, county and municipal documents are the easiest government documents to identify and locate, thanks to the following:

Index to Current Urban Documents. Westport, CT: Greenwood Press, 1972– . Quarterly.
Urban Documents Microfiche Collection. Westport, CT: Greenwood Press, 1972– .

The *Index* is an easy-to-use access tool for documents from almost three hundred cities or counties. It includes hundreds of police department annual reports and special reports on particular problems such as riot control, public relations, rape, police ethics, and violence. Subject and geographic indexes, cumulated annually, note the documents, most of which are available in the *Urban Documents Microfiche Collection.* If your library does not purchase the microfiche set, use interlibrary loan.

• • •

The World Wide Web site, *State and Local Government on the Net* from Piper Resources (http://www.piperinfo.com/state/states.html), already discussed under State Documents, is also just as useful for local government information.

Local Libraries

If your area has a county, municipal, or regional reference library, be sure to use it. The library may be part of a public library or may be in a governmental office. Call ahead to make an appointment, since the contact person may need time to pull together the items or information you need.

The public libraries of many cities and counties try to maintain collections of local documents. Use the following source to locate online catalogs for larger libraries:

Library Catalogs: USA: By State (HYTELNET). Available [Internet] at http://library.usask.ca/hytelnet/usa/usa.html

Maintained by Peter Scott, this Web site offers a fairly comprehensive listing of online public access catalogs available over the Internet.

Regional and Intergovernmental Documents

You may find documents from regional and intergovernmental agencies in any one of the indexes discussed throughout this chapter. If the federal government is involved, check the federal sources. If local government is involved, check the tools that index state, county, or municipal sources. *PAIS International* is a particularly good source for these regional and intergovernmental items. Be aware that such documents tend to be missed by indexing sources. Piper Resource's *State and Local Government on the Net* (http://www.piperinfo.com/state/states.html), mentioned earlier, also maintains links to sites of regional and intergovernmental organizations. Still, a call or visit to the regional or intergovernmental agency may be the most effective research avenue.

Major Criminal Justice Commission Reports

Special mention should be made of reports generated by government commissions established to investigate a specific aspect of criminal justice. These are indexed by the *Monthly Catalog* at the federal level and by the various sources mentioned at other government levels. Major commission reports are noted in Appendix C.

REPORTS

When we look at our definition of reports, we can certainly anticipate a problem in accessing them. We said that reports are records of an organization or group, of research results, of research in progress, or of other technical studies. As such, they can fall within every stage of the information flow and within any format—from an unpublished manuscript to a bound book or a multivolume set. Reports can be primary sources if they present findings, or secondary sources if they interpret the findings. Reports cover a broad spectrum of topics from methodology to statistics to evaluation.

Note that many sources that index reports recognize the difficulty of obtaining the documents once you have identified them. Hence, these companies or agencies not only index reports but also make available the actual documents, usually on microfiche but occasionally online. As you work, take note of these sources.

We have already discussed some excellent leads to reports: *Monthly Catalog of United States Government Publications, American Statistics Index*, and *Statistical Reference Index*. There are other sources to explore. Be reminded again: many of these do not deal exclusively with criminal justice subjects, but are viable sources of criminal justice information. Note that in some cases these are organizations that provide information and not just access tools.

Criminal Justice/NCCD. John Cotton Dana Library, Rutgers University, 15 Washington St., Newark, NJ 07102.

Crime and Juvenile Delinquency. Glen Rock, NJ: Microfilming Corporation of America, 1960–1990.

Crime and Juvenile Delinquency: A Bibliographic Guide to the Basic Microform Collection. Glen Rock, NJ: Microfilming Corp. of America, 1977.

Crime and Juvenile Delinquency: A Bibliographic Guide to the Documents. Sanford, NC: Microfilming Corp. of America, 1976– .

Criminal Justice Abstracts. Monsey, NY: Willow Tree Press, 1968– . Quarterly. Also available on CD-ROM from SilverPlatter; and online from WESTLAW.

Rutgers University acquired the library of the National Council on Crime and Delinquency (NCCD), renaming it the Criminal Justice/NCCD Collection. Founded in 1909, the nonprofit NCCD concerned itself with all manifestations of crime. Its library grew over the years to include periodicals, newspaper clippings, state and federal documents, dissertations, studies, monographs, and published and unpublished reports.

The reports in this collection are probably its most valuable contribution, since they are less likely to be available through other sources. Thousands of these noncopyrighted items, including many subfederal government reports, have been microfilmed by the Microfilming Corporation of America and indexed by the printed guides *Crime and Juvenile Delinquency*. Check with your librarian to find out if your library owns the microfiche set of documents. Some libraries which own the set have entered the bibliographic records for the documents into the library's online catalog, eliminating the need to use the rather cumbersome *Bibliographic Guide*.

The most recent reports are indexed in the printed and CD-ROM index, *Criminal Justice Abstracts* (see pp. 83–83 for further information on this index). Additions to the microfiche collection have not appeared for several years, but the Criminal Justice/NCCD Collection will provide interlibrary loan for any documents not available in your own library.

National Criminal Justice Reference Service (NCJRS) Library, Box 6000, Rockville, MD 20849–6000. (Telephone: 1–800–851–3420.)
NCJRS Document Data Base. Rockville, MD: NCJRS. CD-ROM. Updated annually. Also available online from DIALOG, updated monthly.

NCJRS has been discussed earlier in this chapter (p. 107) as a provider of federal criminal justice information resources over the Internet, and in Chapter 7 (p.84) as the source of a major criminal justice index. NCJRS maintains a database of over 140,000 reports, books, documents, audiovisual resources, and journal articles from its collection. It is the reports and document segment of this database that is of primary interest here. This database should always be examined when doing research on criminal justice subjects. Arson, prison crowding, crime prevention, victim services, organized crime, and crime among immigrants are only a handful of the topics included.

A national and international clearinghouse, NCJRS disperses its criminal justice information by means of interlibrary loan and document distribution in both paper copy and on microfiche. About 25 percent of the collection is available on microfiche, free in limited quantities, otherwise by purchase. Again, check with your librarian to find out if your library owns the microfiche collection, or for help in obtaining documents from NCJRS.

The Rand Corporation. 1700 Main Street, Santa Monica, CA 90401–3297 (Telephone: 310-393-0411). WWW page available [Internet] at http://www.rand.org/
Selected Rand Abstracts: A Quarterly Guide to Publications of the Rand Corporation. Santa Monica, CA: Rand, 1963– . Quarterly. Comparable database available for searching [Internet] at http://www.rand.org/Abstracts/abstracts.html
Criminality, Justice, and Public Safety: A Bibliography of Selected Rand publications. Santa Monica, CA: Rand, June 1996. Also available [Internet] at http://www.rand.org/areas/biblio.html

Rand is a nonprofit institution that aims to improve public policy through research and analysis. It is one of the primary research centers in the country and has been studying criminal justice issues since the late 1960s. Its Criminal Justice Program, established in 1976 to consolidate this work, conducts systematic, multidisciplinary research in law enforcement and crime control, career criminals and criminal careers, juvenile offenders, drug problems, prosecution and sentencing, corrections and prison management, probation and parole, effectiveness and equity of the criminal justice system, and drug policy.

Rand research findings are reported in journal articles, commercially published books, and reports published by Rand. Most of the nonclassified publications are indexed in the printed *Selected Rand Abstracts* and the online database of Rand Abstracts available on the World Wide Web. The printed *Abstracts* has subject and author indexes; the online database may be searched by author, title, words in abstract, or document number. Both information sources provide detailed abstracts. Many of the documents are free and most of them can be ordered online. Ask your library first to find out whether the documents are already owned or can be ordered through interlibrary loan.

The printed bibliography, *Criminality, Justice, and Public Safety*, lists Rand reports on criminal justice issues back to 1970, with detailed abstracts and subject and author indexes.

Some of the more recent Rand reports are available in their entirety through Rand's World Wide Web site. In addition, Rand Research Briefs, policy-oriented summaries of some of the more importance documents, are available online beginning with 1995.

National Technical Information Service (NTIS). Springfield, VA 22161.
Government Reports Announcements & Index. Springfield, VA: National Technical
    Information Service, 1964– . Semimonthly.
NTIS Database. Available online through Canada Institute for Scientific and Techni-
    cal Information, DataStar, DIALOG, ESA/IRS (in Italy), Questel-Orbit, Inc,
    Ovid Technologies, SilverPlatter, and STN International.
NTIS Order Now (products added to the NTIS collection within the last 90 days).
    Available [Internet] at http://chaos.fedworld.gov/ordernow

The word "technical" can be misleading. Many of the almost 3 million reports dispersed by NTIS are in the field of behavioral and social sciences. Government-sponsored research mushroomed during the post–World War II era. Since these particular research reports were not published by the federal government, they did not usually find their way into the pages of the *Monthly Catalog*. In 1970, the National Technical Information Service was established to distribute on a cost recovery basis, in either paper or microfiche, the federally sponsored research reports of federal agencies, their contractors, and their grantees. NTIS has since also become a central source of federally generated, machine-processable data files. Online searches and prepackaged bibliographies, titled "Published Searches," have been added to the services offered. Some international government departments and organizations are now contributing their reports to NTIS. Access to NTIS reports is available through the printed index and online services noted above. Products added to NTIS within the last thirty days can be searched at no cost through *NTIS Order Now*. You can access this service and find out what new services NTIS is offering through its Web site at http://www.ntis.gov.

CONFERENCE PROCEEDINGS

Conferences are meetings where scholars or practitioners come together to share ideas and research findings. Conferences can be annual meetings of organizations, such as the annual meeting of the Academy of Criminal Justice Sciences, or they can be special meetings called by a government or organization to discuss a pressing topic, such as the National Conference on Substance Abuse and the Courts, held in 1993.

Conference papers appear at an early stage in the flow of criminal justice information. New theories and techniques are often first described at conferences, where they can be discussed and critiqued before being submitted for publication. During conferences new ideas can be shared, societal issues aired, and buzzwords born. They are often the locus for movement into the formal information network. Conference proceedings contain the printed text of the papers presented at these meetings. They may be published as a monograph (book), particularly for conferences that are called once to discuss a unique problem. They may be part of a series of proceedings of annual conferences. Occasionally, proceedings of a conference called by an organization are published as part of a journal issued by that organization. Some conference proceedings may appear on the Internet while the conference is in session and for an indefinite period afterward.

Unfortunately, most conference proceedings are not published at all, because the volume of material makes publication prohibitively expensive. Yet both published and unpublished conference papers are often cited by researchers who have attended the conference or acquired a copy of the paper from its author. How can these be located?

The simplest first step is to check your library's catalog to find out if it owns a copy of the published proceedings of the conference where the paper was presented. Rarely is there an entry in the catalog for individual conference papers. To locate the proceedings use an author keyword search of the online catalog for the name of the organization sponsoring the conference, or a title search for a unique title that might have been given to the conference. Conference proceedings are notoriously difficult to locate in a catalog, so don't hesitate to ask a librarian for help.

If you find nothing in the catalog, then use the following sources to see if the proceedings have been published and where they are available. If it appears that the papers were never published, it may be possible to get a copy of an individual paper from its author, but the older the paper, the more unlikely that becomes.

Guides to Conference Papers and Proceedings

Sociological Abstracts. San Diego, CA: Sociological Abstracts Inc., 1952– . Five issues a year. Also available on CD-ROM (*sociofile*) from EBSCO, and
 SilverPlatter, 1974– , updated three or four times a year; and online from Ovid
 Technologies, DIALOG, CompuServe (Knowledge Index), DataStar, DIMDI,
 and OCLC (EPIC and FirstSearch), 1963– , updated bimonthly.

Sociological Abstracts includes a section of conference paper abstracts in
each issue. Conferences regularly covered include the American Sociological Association (ASA), the Society for the Study of Social Problems (SSSP),
and the International Sociological Association (ISA). Regional conferences
are included with less regularity. Many of the conference papers indexed in
Sociological Abstracts can be ordered directly from Sociological Abstracts,
Inc. Topics regularly discussed include criminology, delinquency, public opinion, the sociology of law, human relations aspects of criminal justice, and
research methodology. Further information on *Sociological Abstracts* can be
found in Chapter 7.

Index to Social Sciences and Humanities Proceedings (ISSHP). Philadelphia, PA: Institute for Scientific Information, 1979– . Quarterly, with annual cumulations.
 Also available on CD-ROM, 1990– , quarterly.

ISSHP indexes proceedings published as books, reports, sets of reprints, or
in journals. It gives complete bibliographic information including name of
conference, sponsors, citation to book or journal in which proceedings appear, author and title of published papers, and ordering information where
appropriate. There are indexes of place of conference, authors, editors, and
keyword in title of paper or conference. It is difficult to use, but it is one of the
few sources providing this information.

Bibliographic Guide to Conference Publications. Boston: G. K. Hall, 1975– . Annual.

This guide lists published conference proceedings cataloged during the
year by the Research Libraries of the New York Public Library and the Library of Congress. Proceedings are listed by name of conference, editor, title,
series title, and subject. This is not an index to individual papers in a conference, but it tells you if the proceedings have been published and are available.

PapersFirst. Dublin, OH: OCLC Online Computer Library Center, Inc. Online from
 OCLC (EPIC and FirstSearch), 1993– , updated monthly.
ProceedingsFirst. Dublin, OH: OCLC Online Computer Library Center, Inc. Online
 from OCLC (EPIC and FirstSearch), 1993– , updated monthly.

These two databases are compiled from information received from the British Library Document Supply Center. *PapersFirst* contains descriptions of
papers from worldwide conferences, professional meetings, and symposia.
ProceedingsFirst has documentation on the conferences themselves.

10

Statistics

Statistics is a word that strikes terror into the heart of many students and even some researchers and practitioners. Do not panic. This chapter is not a crash course in statistical analysis, but rather a guide to the many sources of criminal justice statistics and statistics relevant to criminal justice. Whether you are looking for a simple figure to bolster an argument, or a dataset that you can use for advanced statistical analysis, the chances are you can locate what you want using these sources.

STATISTICS DEFINED

Statistics have been collected for centuries. The word statistics has its origin in the word "state," implying a government-sponsored, systematic compilation and study of demographic and political facts. Facts so collected were used for political purposes, and often for taxation. Mary and Joseph went to Bethlehem to be "counted" in a Roman census. William the Conqueror listed both inhabitants and animals for his 1068 *Doomsday Book*. London officials in 1532 noted the number of dying citizens and their diseases. Since numbers were involved in these early compilations, the word statistics evolved to mean the assembly and analysis of numbers.

Statistics achieved greater credibility when recognized as a branch of applied mathematics. In the twentieth century, statistics have played a major role in the research of the sciences, the social sciences, and even the humanities. Over the last four decades, computers, with their rapid and efficient calculations, have increased the use of statistics by making them easier to manipulate and analyze. Students and practitioners are now expected to be able to understand and use statistics in their work.

This is particularly true in criminal justice, a field that is heavily dependent on numbers. Crimes must be counted if we are to know if they are increasing or decreasing. Penologists, politicians, and the general public need to know how many people are in prison and what it costs to keep them there. When there is a call for more police on the streets, the questions are: more than what? more than when? Are people more fearful of crime then they used to be? Is anyone counting now? Did anyone count before?

Criminal justice statistics emanate from a variety of sources. The FBI, the Bureau of the Census, the Bureau of Justice Statistics, and the Administrative Office of the U.S. Courts are all among the federal agencies that collect and disseminate criminal justice statistics. States have their own statistical analysis centers to feed information to the Uniform Crime Reporting Program and to examine their own problems. Added to these sources are thousands of state and local agencies, research centers, academic units, and professional organizations that collect, analyze, disseminate, and use criminal justice data.

Statistics thus compiled are used by lawmakers, public administrators, law enforcement personnel, correctional officers, researchers, students, the media, and the public. Among the most important uses of statistics are to validate planning and budgeting decisions, to evaluate policies, and to project future trends. As laws change to throw new light on stalking, hate crimes, and crime on college campuses, statistical collecting agencies are changing their reporting requirements to count and track these new areas of interest.

Your research may require you to find and use many statistics or only a few. Regardless of the number, those you use must be credible, appropriate, applicable to your topic, and easily interpreted by your intended audience. Be wary of using statistics taken from varying sources or times. Time periods may not be consistent, terms may be defined differently by different individuals or agencies, and sources may vary in quality and comprehensiveness. Know and cite the source of every statistic you use.

With the growth of the Internet, statistics that were previously unpublished or available only in obscure sources may now be easily found on the World Wide Web, often in a form that can be downloaded and analyzed in a spreadsheet or a database. The usual caveat applies: verify and evaluate the source of the data before relying on it, and always cite your source.

GENERAL U.S. STATISTICS

Many agencies of the U.S. government collect, analyze, and publish statistics. These figures report on individual states, cities, counties, and the country in total. Statistics on business, employment, health, education, and birth and death rates can tell a great deal about communities as a whole, and help you understand how criminal justice issues relate to the larger society. The following sources make it easy to find these general statistics:

Statistical Abstract of the U.S. Washington, DC: U.S. Dept. of Commerce, Bureau of the Census; for sale by the Supt. of Docs., U.S. Govt. Print. Off., 1878– . Also available on CD-ROM.

1996 Statistical Abstract of the U.S. Washington, DC: U.S. Dept. of Commerce, Bureau of the Census. PDF file. Available [Internet] at http://www.census.gov/prod/2/gen/96statab/96statab.html

Probably the most useful general source for finding statistics on all aspects of the United States, the *Statistical Abstract* includes population and vital statistics, health, education, government finance, social welfare, income, employment, commerce, and criminal justice data. The CD-ROM version contains tables that are not offered in print and files that can be downloaded to a spreadsheet or database for statistical manipulation. Frequently requested tables are available for viewing or downloading in spreadsheet format over the Internet at the *Statistical Abstracts'* own home page, http://www.census.gov/statab/www/. In addition, the *1996 Statistical Abstract of the U.S.* is available in PDF format for viewing or printing for those with the Adobe Acrobat® Reader and the time and patience to download large files.

Historical Statistics of the United States, Colonial Times to 1970. Washington, DC: U.S. Dept. of Commerce, Bureau of the Census; for sale by the Supt. of Docs., U.S. Govt. Print. Off., 1975.

Provides historical statistics on all aspects of life in the United States, including crime. It is valuable for longitudinal studies of social indicators.

County and City Data Book. Washington, DC: U.S. Dept. of Commerce, Bureau of the Census; for sale by the Supt. of Docs., U.S. Govt. Print. Off., 1949– . Released every six years. Also available on CD-ROM.

An excellent source for official statistics for cities over 25,000 and for all counties. The sole crime figure included is the crime rate per 100,000 population, but other subjects include education, health, labor force, income and poverty, and vital statistics. Selected tables are available over the Internet for viewing or downloading in spreadsheet format from the Census Bureau at http://www.census.gov/statab/www/ccdb.html.

USA Counties. Washington, DC: U.S. Dept. of Commerce, Bureau of the Census, Data User Services Division, 1992– . CD-ROM. Also available [Internet] from the Government Information Sharing Project of Oregon State University Libraries at http://govinfo.kerr.orst.edu/usaco.stateis.html

This valuable new data source includes all the data published for counties in the last three editions of the *State and Metropolitan Area Data Book* (1991, 1986, 1982) and the last three editions of the *County and City Data Book* (1994, 1988, 1983), as well as a number of data items not previously published. The emphasis is on providing extended time series in such areas as population, housing, health care, education, earnings, ancestry, income, labor force, vital statistics, poverty level, and crime. Information from such nongovernmental sources as the American Medical Association and the Elections Research Center are also included. The crime information comes from the Uniform Crime Reports, with statistics often retrospective to 1977. A useful feature of this source is that you can download the data in various formats for your own statistical analysis.

Government Information Sharing Project. Oregon State University Information Services. Available [Internet] at http://govinfo.kerr.orst.edu/

Although not an official U.S. government Internet site, this excellent World Wide Web resource was developed by Oregon State University with the help of a grant from the Department of Education. It provides easy access to demographic, education, and economic data from the federal government.

White House Social Statistics Briefing Room. Available [Internet] at http://www.whitehouse.gov/fsbr/ssbr.html

This service of the President's office brings together highlights of the social statistics gathered by various federal agencies. The color charts are particularly striking, and there are links to the agencies that gather the data. This is a useful site for the beginning researcher, or for those who merely want to find a few good figures.

FEDERAL CRIMINAL JUSTICE STATISTICS

Outside of the Federal Bureau of Investigation, which collects the official crime statistics, the single most important source of criminal justice statistics in the United States is the Bureau of Justice Statistics. Most of the sources listed below are their publications. In addition, they put out a truly astonishing number of bulletins, press releases, and special reports. Their publications can usually be found through the library catalog either by searching on "United States. Bureau of Justice Statistics" as an author, or by doing a keyword search for "justice statistics"; ask a librarian for help if you need it. If your library is a government depository library it may be receiving all BJS publications automatically, but they may not be listed in the catalog. Again, ask the reference librarian or the government documents librarian for assistance. If you have access to the World Wide Web you can also read and download BJS documents directly.

Bureau of Justice Statistics Internet site. U.S. Dept. of Justice. Available [Internet] at http://www.ojp.usdoj.gov/bjs/

The Bureau of Justice Statistics has been publishing all of its current documents on the World Wide Web in both ASCII and Adobe Acrobat® (PDF) format. Included are statistics about crimes, victims, law enforcement, courts, sentencing, and corrections. The site is arranged by topic and includes summary findings and recent press releases as well as the more formal documents.

Sourcebook of Criminal Justice Statistics. Washington, DC: U.S. Dept. of Justice, Bureau of Justice Statistics; for sale by the Supt. of Docs., U.S. Govt. Print. Off., 1973–. Annual. Also available [Internet] at http://www.albany.edu/sourcebook/

This sourcebook is the single most important compendium of U.S. statistics on criminal justice. Note that it is a compilation, a secondary source of information that presents statistics gathered nationwide from other sources: government agencies, academic institutions, research organizations, and public opinion polling firms. The criteria for inclusion are that the data be nationwide in scope and methodologically sound. Different sections include data on characteristics of the criminal justice system, including numbers and types of agencies and employees, expenditures, and so forth; public attitudes toward crime, including public opinion polls on victimization, gun control, and the death penalty; nature and distribution of known offenses; characteristics of persons arrested; judicial processing of defendants; and persons under correctional supervision, including prison and jail population and parolees. Because this is a secondary source, and one which usually appears at least six months after the date it purports to cover, some of the information will be quite dated by the time you use it. The source of the statistics is always clearly indicated, however, and this usually provides the information you need to find more recent data. Note that the World Wide Web version of the *Sourcebook* requires the Adobe Acrobat® Reader, free software available over the Internet. Note also that the Web version of the *Sourcebook* is updated throughout the year as new tables become available.

Uniform Crime Reports (UCR): Crime in the United States. Washington, DC: U.S. Department of Justice, Federal Bureau of Investigation, 1930– . Annual.
1995 Crime in the United States. Washington, DC: U.S. Department of Justice, Federal Bureau of Investigation. PDF file. Available [Internet] at http://www.fbi.gov/ucr/crimeus/crimeus.htm

When the news media trumpet that crime is down across the United States or Sin City is the new murder capital of America, it is because a new edition of the *Uniform Crime Reports* has appeared. Sixteen thousand jurisdictions (cities, counties, states) in the United States voluntarily report information to the Federal Bureau of Investigation. The offenses covered in the crime index include murder, rape, robbery, aggravated assault, burglary, larceny, motor vehicle theft, and arson. This is a very valuable source for analyzing crime over time and across states or localities. The press releases that announce the preliminary and final annual crime statistics are available at http://www.fbi.gov/, and some of the data files on which the reports are based are available for analysis from the National Archive of Criminal Justice Data (NACJD) at http:/

/www.icpsr.umich.edu/nacjd/. The most recent volume of the *Uniform Crime Reports* is available on the WWW, complete with color charts, as a PDF file. It is a very large file and works best for those who have a very fast computer with a high-speed Internet connection.

Criminal Victimization in the United States. Washington, DC: U.S. Department of Justice, Bureau of Justice Statistics, 1973– . Also available [Internet] at http://www.ojp.usdoj.gov/bjs/cvictgen.htm

This annual series provides information from the National Crime Victimization Survey, administered for the Bureau of Justice Statistics by the U.S. Census Bureau. As the name suggests, these reports provide information not on crimes reported to police, but on crimes as perceived by the victims, thus providing a very different measure of crime in the United States than that provided by the *Uniform Crime Reports.* Some of the most interesting tables report the percentage of crimes that are actually reported to the police. The datafiles from which this series is derived are available from the National Archive of Criminal Justice Data at http://www.icpsr.umich.edu/nacjd/.

STATISTICS ON CORRECTIONS

Correctional Populations in the United States. Washington, DC: U.S. Department of Justice, Bureau of Justice Statistics, 1987– . Annual. Recent issues also available [Internet] at http://www.ojp.usdoj.gov/bjs/prisons.htm

Correctional Populations is probably the most comprehensive source on the number of persons under some form of correctional supervision: jail, probation, state or federal prison, and parole. Most figures are provided by states with many statistics reported by sex, Hispanic origin, and race. It includes figures on capital punishment. Each year there is a special section; for example, in 1994 this section was devoted to persons held in U.S. military confinement facilities. Over the Internet, recent volumes can be viewed in Adobe Acrobat® (PDF) format; some years are available as ASCII (plain text) format or are accompanied with downloadable zipped (compressed) spreadsheet files. Codebooks and datasets for these statistics and other studies of corrections are available from the National Archive of Criminal Justice Data at http://www.icpsr.umich.edu/nacjd/.

Corrections Statistics. Washington, DC: U.S. Department of Justice, Bureau of Justice Statistics. Available [Internet] at http://www.ojp.usdoj.gov/bjs/correct.htm

This useful government site provides links to official documents and datafiles related to prisons, jails, probation and parole, and capital punishment.

Capital Punishment. Washington, DC: U.S. Department of Justice, Bureau of Justice Statistics, 1971– . Annual. Recent issues also available [Internet] at http://www.ojp.usdoj.gov/bjs/cp.htm

Provides characteristics of persons under sentence of death and executed. Tables present data on offenders' sex, Hispanic origin, race, education, marital status, age at time of arrest for capital offense, legal status at time of capital offense, methods of execution, trends, and time between imposition of death sentence and execution.

Vital Statistics in Corrections. Laurel, MD: American Correctional Association, 1984– . Irregular.

Concerned with correctional personnel rather than prisoners, the most recent volume released was for 1991. Provides data on education, training, and pay of corrections officers.

American Correctional Association. *Directory, Juvenile & Adult Correctional Departments, Institutions, Agencies & Paroling Authorities.* Lanham, MD: American Correctional Association, 1979– . Biannual.

The prefatory material in this annual provides excellent summary statistics on expenditures, capital expenditures, numbers of adult and juvenile prisoners under supervision, correctional personnel, and so on. In addition, most of the entries for individual correctional institutions supply daily or annual figures for the cost of care per inmate.

Corrections Yearbook. New York, NY: Criminal Justice Institute, 1981– .

The data reported here were compiled by the Criminal Justice Institute from questionnaires sent to federal and state correctional agencies. These are not official government statistics, and the response rate of the questionnaires is unclear, but the questions asked gather data that are not easily available any other way, such as the cost of maintaining a prisoner, the types of work programs, and the number of escapes.

Cahalan, Margaret Werner. *Historical Corrections Statistics in the United States, 1850–1984.* Washington, DC: U.S. Department of Justice, Bureau of Justice Statistics, 1986.

Some of the statistics reported here date back to the nineteenth century. Among the more instructive tables are those that report on executions by race.

STATISTICS ON LAW ENFORCEMENT

Law Enforcement Statistics. U.S. Department of Justice, Bureau of Justice Statistics. Available [Internet] at http://www.ojp.usdoj.gov/bjs/lawenf.htm

Included on this official government Web site are summary statistics and links to documents on federal, state, local, and campus law enforcement. A useful feature is the inclusion of links to related government and nongovernment sites.

Law Enforcement Management and Administrative Statistics. Data for Individual State and Local Agencies with 100 or More Officers. Washington, DC: U.S. Department of Justice, Bureau of Justice Statistics, 1990– . Also available [Internet] at http://www.ojp.usdoj.gov/bjs/abstract/lemas93.htm

Provides information on police and other law enforcement personnel. The tables present data on race and sex of sworn personnel, agency functions, type of 911 system, lockup facilities, operating expenditures, starting salaries, vehicle use policies, educational and training requirements, types of sidearms and nonlethal weapons authorized, automated fingerprint identification system (AFIS) facilities, types of computers and their functions, complaint review processes, drug enforcement activities, and employee drug testing policies. The volume with 1993 data that is available over the Internet comes with supporting spreadsheets that can be downloaded and analyzed.

Campus Law Enforcement Agencies, 1995. Washington, DC: U.S. Department of Justice, Bureau of Justice Statistics, 1996. Also available [Internet] at http://www.ojp.usdoj.gov/bjs/abstract/clea95.htm

In 1995 the Bureau of Justice Statistics undertook a survey of the campus law enforcement agencies of all U.S. four-year universities or colleges with 2,500 or more students. The resulting report describes nearly 600 campus law enforcement agencies in terms of their personnel, expenditures and pay, operations, equipment, computers and information systems, policies, and special programs. The WWW version offers supporting spreadsheets that may be downloaded.

STATE AND LOCAL STATISTICS

Many states, and a few localities, publish their own statistical abstracts that may include criminal justice figures not collected by the FBI or the Bureau of Justice Statistics. To find these, try searching the library catalog under the geographic name with the subheading "Statistics," or try a keyword search on the state or locality and the word "statistics." These searches can be tricky, so ask a librarian for help if you need it. Local statistics may be found in local government publications, in a municipal reference library, in a local newspaper, or in the file drawers of a local agency. The printed works listed below are good sources for comparative statistics on states and municipalities. Many of the resources described in the sections of Chapter 9 on state documents and local documents (pp. 112–115) also provide statistical information.

A particularly valuable index for finding state and local statistics is the *Statistical Masterfile*, discussed in the next section (pp. 131–132).

Finally, many states and localities are making some local statistics available over the Internet as part of their WWW pages. Since their major function is to promote tourism and business, however, these sites tend to accentuate the positive and criminal justice statistics do not fit that image. If you want to spend the time to see what is available, the best place to start would be the Library of Congress Web page *State and Local Governments*, or *State and Local Government on the Net* from Piper Resources, both described later (p. 130) and also discussed in Chapter 9 (p. 115).

Book of the States. Lexington, KY: The Council of State Governments, 1933– . Biennial.

Statistical tables accompany narrative discussions of trends in state activities. Sources of statistics are noted. Sections on the "Judiciary" and "Criminal Justice/Corrections" yield limited statistics but prove valuable because statistics for all states are collected in a single table. Useful essays often examine criminal justice issues from the perspective of state government.

Municipal Year Book. Washington, DC: International City Management Association, 1934– . Annual.

Better known for its overview of current issues in local government and its data on cities and counties, this yearbook also offers detailed statistical tables on police. Figures for cities, arranged by population size, reveal personnel, expenditures, and salaries.

Crime in America's Top-Rated Cities: A Statistical Profile. Boca Raton, FL: Universal Reference Publications, 1995– . Biennial.

This useful work brings together criminal justice statistics by city. Included is information on major crime categories, hate crimes, illegal drugs, correctional facilities, law enforcement personnel, gun laws, and victimization.

Crime State Rankings. Lawrence, KS: Morgan Quitno Corp. 2nd ed. 1995.

A useful compilation of criminal justice statistics by state in alphabetical and ranked order, mostly taken from statistics gathered by the U.S. Department of Justice. Includes tables on arrests, corrections, drugs and alcohol, finance, law enforcement, and offenses. Some tables are calculated by the publisher from public data sources; sources of all the tables are provided.

Criminal Justice Data for New York State. New York State, Division of Criminal Justice Services. Available [Internet] at http://criminaljustice.state.ny.us/crimnet/data.htm

This easy-to-use, comprehensive site is a model for the distribution of state criminal justice statistics. The site includes current criminal justice statistics as well as ten years of statistics on crime, arrests, convictions and sentences, and felony prosecutions for counties and cities in New York State. Users can select a geographic area and two separate years to custom-design comparison tables.

Dallas Police Crime Statistics. Available [Internet] at http://www.ci.dallas.tx.us/dpd/

Providing maps and crime statistics down to the sector and beat level, this is a rare model of the information that can be made available by localities over the Internet. Select "crime stats" from the icons displayed at the URL listed above.

State and Local Governments. Library of Congress. Available [Internet] at http://lcweb. loc.gov/global/state/

Provides links to meta-indexes for state and local government information and a directory of state government information.

State and Local Government on the Net. Piper Resources. Available [Internet] at http:// www.piperinfo.com/state/states.html

An excellent, searchable or browsable directory of state and local government resources available on the Internet. Sites are reviewed before they are added, and the directory is updated frequently.

INTERNATIONAL CRIMINAL JUSTICE STATISTICS

International criminal justice statistics are very difficult to find and even more difficult to compare. Every country has its own definitions for crimes and standards for the reporting of crime. In addition to the sources listed here, many of the resources listed in Chapter 15, Resources for the Study of Criminal Justice in Other Countries, contain statistical information.

International Criminal Police Organization. *Statistiques Criminelles Internationales. (International Crime Statistics).* Paris: International Criminal Police Organization, 1950/52– .

The statistics published here by INTERPOL of affiliated countries remain the best printed compilation in the field, despite numerous drawbacks. The data are often sketchy or incomplete and crime categories are poorly defined, making comparisons difficult. In addition, much of the information is three or four years old when published.

United Nations Crime and Justice Information Network. *United Nations Surveys of Crime Trends and Operations of Criminal Justice Systems.* Available [Internet] at http://www.ifs.univie.ac.at/uncjin/mosaic/wcs.html

The United Nations has undertaken five World Crime Surveys of Crime Trends and Criminal Justice covering 1970 to 1994. The results of these surveys are not widely available in print, but the data sets can be retrieved from this site in ASCII, Lotus 1-2-3, and SPSS formats. In addition, information from the fourth survey, covering the years 1986–1990, is available here in a form that can be read and printed online. Statistics were gathered from over seventy countries for crimes, criminal justice expenditures, police, courts, prisons, and prisoners. For further discussion about the World Crime Surveys, see Chapter 15 (p. 214).

The World Factbook of Criminal Justice Systems. Washington, DC: U.S. Department of Justice, Bureau of Justice Statistics. Available [Internet] at http://www.ojp. usdoj.gov/bjs/abstract/wfcj.htm

Narrative information with some statistics is provided for over forty countries.

U.S. Census Bureau. *International Data Base.* Available [Internet] at http://www. census.gov/ipc/www/idbnew.html

The International Data Base is a computerized databank containing statistical tables of demographic and socioeconomic data for all countries of the world.

INDEXES AND FINDING GUIDES FOR STATISTICS

Statistics Sources. 20th ed., 1997. Ed. Jacqueline Wasserman O'Brien and Steven R. Wasserman. Detroit: Gale Research Co., 1996.

An alphabetically arranged guide to over 2,000 current sources of statistical information in over 20,000 subjects. Most sources are readily available; many are federal documents. A particularly useful feature is the list of federal statistical contacts, which includes the name and telephone numbers of subject specialists dealing with particular aspects of criminal justice.

American Statistics Index (ASI). Washington, DC: Congressional Information Service, 1974– . Monthly. Also available on CD-ROM, updated quarterly; online from DIALOG.
Index to International Statistics (IIS). Washington, DC: Congressional Information Service, 1983– . Monthly. Also available on CD-ROM, updated quarterly.
Statistical Reference Index (SRI). Washington, DC: Congressional Information Service, 1980– . Monthly. Also available on CD-ROM, updated quarterly.
Statistical Masterfile. Washington, DC: Congressional Information Service, 1974– . CD-ROM. Quarterly.

These indexes provide fast and easy access to statistical publications. Each index identifies publications within its parameters, classifies them by their source, and indexes and summarizes their contents. Each index is accompanied by a collection in microfiche of all or part of the documents it indexes. This is a very expensive set, so only the largest research libraries are likely to have all of these tools plus the microfiche sets, but if you are lucky enough to be able to use such a library, your search for statistical information will be immeasurably easier.

Different groups of sources are covered by each index. *ASI* extracts statistical information located in publications from more than 500 federal government agencies. *IIS* covers statistics published by approximately 100 international intergovernmental organizations including the United Nations, the Organization for Economic Cooperation and Development, the European Union, and the Organization of American States. *SRI* indexes publications from American sources outside the U.S. government, including some 1,000 associations and institutes, businesses and commercial publications, state government agencies, and independent and university research centers.

ASI, IIS, and *SRI* are each published monthly, with quarterly, annual, and multiyear cumulations. Each issue has two parts: an abstract and an index. Start with the index. Look in the subject index under "crime and criminals." In addition to entries on that topic you will find a "see also" list of related topics used in the index. Reading this list gives you a good idea of the criminal justice topics covered in each set. *ASI, IIS,* and *SRI* have specialized indexes following the general subject index. These help you refine your subject by breaking down information into geographic, economic, or demographic categories.

A number following the subject in the index volume leads to a succinct synopsis of that item in the abstract volume. The abstracts provide the actual pages of the cited document where the specific information or tables appear. The abstracts are a great time saver, since they are frequently informative enough for you to decide whether or not the item will be useful for your research. If your library purchases the microfiche collection that accompanies the index, you have access to the information immediately. If not, check the library catalog or your local government documents collection to find out if your library owns the publication you need, or request it via interlibrary loan.

The *Statistical Masterfile* brings together the indexes and abstracts of all three printed products into one simple searchable database. It is possible to search a term such as "juvenile corrections," for example, and find statistics from federal, state, and international sources. Boolean AND, OR, and NOT operators are available to enable you to further refine your search for information, and you can search either a controlled vocabulary of descriptors or free text on any word or words appearing in the index or abstract. As with the printed volumes, there are abstracts providing more detailed information on the publication.

If the statistical information you are seeking cannot be easily found in the more common sources of criminal justice statistics mentioned earlier in this chapter, you should try to use the *Statistical Masterfile* to locate the information, even if it means going to another library.

Statistics on Crime and Punishment. Detroit: Gale Research Co., 1996.

This is a good place to start for the beginning researcher. The charts, graphs, and tables in this volume are all taken from other sources which, paradoxically, is the strength of this publication. The editors explain the significance of the statistics and also describe the strengths and weaknesses of the sources, and how the statistics are collected.

PUBLIC OPINION POLLS

Public opinion on specific issues is determined by interviewing a segment of the population. Elaborate sampling procedures have been developed over the years to produce poll results that eliminate bias and accurately reflect public views. Sophisticated computer methodology has enhanced polling techniques. First developed for private business enterprises, public opinion polls have moved onto university campuses and into the offices of leading newspapers and television companies. Pollsters often turn the spotlight on crime and the justice system. The resulting reflections of public opinion can prove useful to your research. Surveys have been conducted on topics such as sentencing, the fear of crime, gun control, capital punishment, the public level of confidence in the police and the courts, law enforcement, legalization of marijuana, and victimization. Poll results are broadcast on radio and television, and printed in newspapers, periodicals, special publications, and over the Internet.

Printed results of polls frequently appear in newspapers and periodicals. Thus they are indexed along with the other articles in newspaper and periodical indexes. If you are using a printed index, look under the subject heading "Public Opinion" or "Public Opinion Polls," or look for the term "public opinion" as a subheading under the topic of the poll; for example, "Capital Punishment—public opinion." If you are using an online or CD-ROM index, try a keyword search using "public opinion" plus the subject of the search; for example, **public opinion and capital punishment**.

Several printed sources and one Internet-accessible source are devoted to public opinion polls:

American Public Opinion Index. Bethesda, MD: ORS Publishing, 1981– . Annual.
American Public Opinion Data. Bethesda, MD: ORS Publishing, 1981– . Annual.
Polling the Nation. ORS Publishing, 7200 Wisconsin Ave., Bethesda, MD 20814; 800–462–8913. CD-ROM.

The annual *American Public Opinion Index* lists questions asked on polls conducted in America. Questions are arranged by subject and are followed by a code for the polling source. Part II provides full information about the poll, including the date of the survey, sample size, method, universe, and special topic. A microfiche set, *American Public Opinion Data*, accompanies the printed index and provides the responses to the questions asked. The CD-ROM, *Polling the Nation*, contains the complete text and aggregates answers from 1986.

Public Opinion Quarterly. New York: Elsevier Science Publishing, 1937– . Quarterly.

This scholarly journal presents articles on polling methodology and on specific polls and poll results from various survey organizations. It is the most heavily indexed of the polling journals, appearing in *Criminal Justice Ab-*

stracts, Current Contents, Public Affairs Information Service Bulletin, Psychological Abstracts, and *Social Sciences Index* among others.

Gallup Poll Monthly (Formerly *The Gallup Opinion Index, The Gallup Political Index,* and *The Gallup Report*). Princeton, NJ: The Gallup Poll, 1989– . Monthly.
Gallup Poll Monthly Index, 1965–1995. Princeton, NJ: The Gallup Poll, 1996.

Since its inception, questions about crime and criminal justice related topics have been among the mainstays of the Gallup Poll. The results of recent polls are reported monthly in this fascinating periodical. Indexed in *PAIS International,* the *Gallup Poll Monthly* is the most widely available and easiest to use source of public opinion polls. If your library owns the *Gallup Poll Monthly Index, 1965–1995,* then finding past surveys on criminal justice topics is easy.

Public Opinion Index. Institute for Research in Social Science, University of North Carolina. Available [Internet] at http://www.irss.unc.edu:80/data_archive/pollsearch.html

The Institute for Research in Social Science (IRSS) at the University of North Carolina at Chapel Hill, maintains an online Public Opinion Index available at no cost over the Internet. You can search for individual questions asked by the following sources: Carolina Polls, General Social Surveys, 1972–1994; Latin American Public Opinion; Louis Harris Polls; National Network of State Polls (a consortium of organizations that perform polls on a statewide basis); Southern Polls; and USA Today Polls. Up to four words or phrases can be connected with Boolean ANDs or ORs and the results are returned as an onscreen list or a downloadable file.

Sourcebook of Criminal Justice Statistics. Washington, DC: U.S. Department of Justice, Bureau of Justice Statistics, 1973– . Annual. Also available [Internet] at http://www.albany.edu/sourcebook/

As mentioned earlier in this chapter, this important criminal justice source also reports the results of public opinion polls on criminal justice topics.

Analyzing Public Opinion Polls

For those who are comfortable with statistical analysis, it is possible to get raw survey results of public opinion polls and do your own analysis. Many universities are members of the Inter-university Consortium for Political and Social Research (ICPSR) or have agreements with ICPSR or the Roper Center for Public Opinion Research to provide their researchers with access to the data maintained by these organizations, both of which have extensive holdings of public opinion surveys. Check with your library or data center to find out if it can provide you with access to this information and review the following section on Criminal Justice Datasets.

CRIMINAL JUSTICE DATASETS

Increasingly, criminal justice students and researchers are expected to be comfortable carrying out statistical analyses. This often means conducting small surveys and analyzing the results. However, researchers often need to compare their own statistics with other figures (e.g., how the opinion of a small sample of college students about date rape compares with a national sample), or wish to analyze crime statistics in light of economic or social trends, or want to test a new hypothesis relating to an older study. It has already been noted that many of the statistical sources discussed earlier in this chapter provide data in the form of spreadsheet tables that can be downloaded or analyzed. In addition, criminal justice researchers have a definite advantage over researchers in other fields because they have free access to the National Archive of Criminal Justice Data.

National Archive of Criminal Justice Data. Available [Internet] at http://www.icpsr. umich.edu/nacjd/

The central mission of the National Archive of Criminal Justice Data is to facilitate and encourage research in the field of criminal justice through the preservation and sharing of data resources and the provision of specialized training in quantitative analysis of crime and justice data. It archives and disseminates computerized data, documentation, and software for the quantitative study of crime and the criminal justice system. NACJD was established in 1978 under the auspices of the Inter-university Consortium for Political and Social Research (ICPSR) and the Bureau of Justice Statistics (BJS), U.S. Department of Justice. NACJD currently holds over 500 data collections relating to criminal justice. Their website at http://www.icpsr.umich.edu/nacjd/ provides browsing and downloading access to most of this data and documentation. If your college or university is a member of ICPSR, it may already have the codebooks and datasets from NACJD. Find out who your data librarian is and check with him or her about availability, or browse the NACJD website yourself.

Data Resources of the National Institute of Justice/U.S. Department of Justice, Office of Justice Programs, National Institute of Justice, 1985– . Irregular.

This printed directory lists all the datasets available from the National Institute of Justice through the National Archive of Criminal Justice Data (discussed above). For each dataset information is provided on the purpose of the study, the methodology, the file structure, and reports that resulted. This is a very usable directory describing data that is available at no charge from ICPSR or the *National Archive of Criminal Justice Data.*

11

Printed Bibliographies

There is nothing wrong with taking the easy way out when doing bibliographic research. One of the most efficient ways to add to the list of titles you are collecting for your research is to locate a useful bibliography compiled by a scholar who has had the time to search the literature of the field thoroughly. In truth, finding a good bibliography is like having someone else do some of your work for you.

PRINTED BIBLIOGRAPHIES

Kinds of Bibliographies

Bibliographies are as varied as the persons who create them. They may be short, long, selective, comprehensive, simple, or complex. They may be arranged alphabetically, by author or title, or clustered under certain topics. Bibliographies may pull together items on a specific subject, by a single author, in a specified format, or in a special collection. They may vary in length from a simple list of a few items to a multivolume set of bound volumes. They may cite only current items; or older items, in which case they are called retrospective bibliographies; or a combination of both. By definition, bibliographies are lists of works, parts of works, or documents with a common factor among them. Many of the research tools we have been discussing, such as indexes and abstracts, or checklists of documents, are technically bibliographies. In this chapter we will be discussing bibliographies that have appeared as printed books.

When to Use Printed Bibliographies

Bibliographies often provide an overview of a discipline because representative works of subject authorities in the field are selected for inclusion. In a certain sense bibliographies are analogous to encyclopedias in the information flow. While encyclopedias offer synthesis and analysis of the content of a subject, some bibliographies offer synthesis and analysis of items available in the literature of a particular subject.

Other bibliographies are valuable less for their analysis than for their coverage of material from different disciplines. As we have seen, criminal justice issues are discussed in the literature of psychology, sociology, anthropology, and economics, among others. A bibliography on a subject like family violence, or drug abuse, which crosses many disciplines, can save hours of searching the indexes and abstracts of each field.

The researcher must decide the role that bibliographies should play in any particular project. If a paper is short, if the library has an abundance of material on the subject, or if indexes provide more than adequate coverage, there is really little advantage to seeking out bibliographies. When the research should be exhaustive, when very little information is readily available, when there is adequate time to use interlibrary loans, or when the topic seems to fall between disciplines or overlap disciplines, bibliographies will greatly enhance the research.

How to Find Bibliographies

Libraries with inadequate collections in a particular subject often purposely collect bibliographies in that subject area. Such bibliographies then provide users with access to titles and possibly to sources for obtaining those titles through interlibrary loan. Research libraries collect bibliographies as part of their attempt at comprehensiveness. As you work in your library and with your librarian, you will soon discover the role bibliographies can play in your research.

Locating bibliographies is not difficult. If you find a scholarly journal article, book, or report that is valuable for your research, examine the list of sources used in the research. Many of those sources can be equally valuable for your research. Doctoral dissertations have particularly good bibliographies, since part of the requirement of dissertation work is usually a review of the literature of the field.

In library catalogs, book-length bibliographies form the subdivision "Bibliography" under specific subjects. It is a subdivision that can be used with any subject. If your library's online catalog offers keyword searching (and most do) try combining your subject using the Boolean AND with the word **bibliography**. Try combinations like **ex-convicts and bibliography**, **criminal justice and bibliography**, or **police wives and bibliography**. Remember, even when doing a keyword search, you will probably find more relevant citations if you use subject heading terms as your keywords.

How to Use Bibliographies

Use printed bibliographies skillfully. Check the publication date and examine the introduction to find the dates the compiler says that it covers; then skim the entries to find the earliest and latest dates.

Bibliographies may be annotated with short summaries describing the contents and value of the works included, or they may aim for comprehensiveness with thousands of citations but no annotations. Critical annotations can help you decide which citations are most important for you to pursue. Conceivably, however, a bibliography may reflect a compiler's bias. You must always use your own judgment in evaluating a source to determine its usefulness for your work.

Occasionally, you may find enough information from an annotation to eliminate the need to view the original work. It is permissible to cite the annotation as it appears in the bibliography; never, however, cite a work that you have not actually seen.

SELECTED BIBLIOGRAPHIES

General Bibliographies

Bibliographic Index. New York: H. W. Wilson, 1938– . Quarterly.

By now it should not surprise you that there can be an index to bibliographies. Easy to use, this is an alphabetical subject and author index to bibliographies of fifty or more entries. The bibliography indexed may be published separately or as part of a book, pamphlet, or article. The index is cumulated annually. General in scope, it contains such criminal justice entries as "rape victims," "victims of crime," "crime prevention," and "rehabilitation of criminals." Check also under other standard criminal justice topics.

International Bibliography of the Social Sciences: International Bibliography of Sociology. London: Tavistock; Chicago: Aldine, 1952– . Annual.

This is a multilanguage classified listing of books, chapters in books, pamphlets, articles, and official publications, with a subject index. There are no annotations, but it affords excellent international coverage. It is scholarly and selective.

Selected Criminal Justice Bibliographies

Denno, Deborah W., and Ruth M. Schwarz. *Biological, Psychological, and Environmental Factors in Delinquency and Mental Disorder: An Interdisciplinary Bibliography.* Westport, CT: Greenwood Press, 1985.

Although this bibliography aims for comprehensiveness, with over 2,000 entries arranged alphabetically by author with a subject index, it has no annotations, limiting its usefulness.

Engeldinger, Eugene A. *Spouse Abuse: An Annotated Bibliography of Violence Between Mates*. Metuchen, NJ: Scarecrow Press, 1986.

This is a bibliography of almost 1,800 references to popular and scholarly
books, parts of books, articles, dissertations, government documents, conference papers, pamphlets, and other sources published in English through 1983.
Its arrangement is alphabetical by author, but there is a subject index. The
annotations offer substantial information.

Harding, Jim, and Beryl Forgay. *Breaking Down the Walls: A Bibliography on the
Pursuit of Aboriginal Justice*. Regina, Saskatchewan: Prairie Justice Research
Center, University of Saskatchewan, 1991.

This bibliography compiles citations, without annotations, to books, journal articles, magazine and newspaper articles relating to Canadian Native
Americans and the criminal justice system.

Hewitt, John D., Eric D. Poole, and Robert M. Regoli. *Criminal Justice in America,
1959–1984: An Annotated Bibliography*. New York: Garland, 1985.

Under each of three main types—Law Enforcement, Courts, and Corrections—
the authors have subdivided entries by history, organization, process, and issues.
Its almost 1,000 entries are indexed by personal name and subject.

Jerath, Bal K., and Rajinder Jerath. *Homicide: A Bibliography*. 2nd ed. Boca Raton,
FL: CRC Press, 1993.

The authors aim for completeness in this bibliography, which is an interesting
mix of popular news magazines, scholarly and professional journals, and international journals. There are no annotations. The entries are arranged by specific
subject in a classified arrangement and there is a subject index in addition.

Radelet, Michael L., and Margaret Vandiver. *Capital Punishment in America: An Annotated Bibliography*. New York: Garland, 1988.

Including books, articles, Congressional publications and Supreme Court
decisions, the material in this bibliography is mostly post–1972 with some
earlier citations. The arrangement is by author, with a subject index.

Suvak, Daniel. *Memoirs of American Prisons*. Metuchen, NJ: Scarecrow Press, 1979.

Annotated entries reveal experiences of civil, voluntary, and military prisoners. Indexed by name, title, and prison name, this is a good resource for a
hard-to-find genre.

Bibliographies on Terrorism

The spate of terrorist activities beginning in the 1960s has spawned a rash
of bibliographies to cover the literature of the field.

Lakos, Amos. *International Terrorism: A Bibliography.* Boulder, CO: Westview Press, 1986.
Lakos, Amos. *Terrorism, 1980–1990: A Bibliography.* Boulder, CO: Westview Press, 1991.

These two complementary bibliographies contain no annotations. They are arranged by specific topics in terrorism, such as "terrorist tactics," and by geographic area. The earlier volume covers resources through 1979. Both titles include good subject indexes.

Mickolus, Edward F. *The Literature of Terrorism: A Selectively Annotated Bibliography.* Westport, CT: Greenwood Press, 1980.
Mickolus, Edward F., and Peter A. Flemming. *Terrorism, 1980–1987: A Selectively Annotated Bibliography.* Westport, CT: Greenwood Press, 1988.
Mickolus, Edward F. *Terrorism, 1988–1991: A Chronology of Events and a Selectively Annotated Bibliography.* Westport, CT: Greenwood Press, 1993.

These three works offer comprehensive coverage of the literature of terrorism from the late 1960s to 1991. Entries are rather generally arranged by tactics, terrorist infrastructure, geographic area, and responses to terrorism. Mickolus indexes books, parts of books, articles in journals and professional newsletters, and government documents. As noted in the titles, the bibliographic entries are selectively annotated. None of the volumes contains a subject index.

SELECTED OLDER, BUT STILL USEFUL BIBLIOGRAPHIES

Beyleveld, Deryck. *The Effectiveness of General Deterrents against Crime: An Annotated Bibliography of Evaluative Research.* Cambridge: University of Cambridge, Institute of Criminology, 1978.

This is an unusually thorough bibliography on this topic. Annotations are quite detailed and a good system of cross-references make this source a very productive one.

Culver, Dorothy Campbell. *Bibliography of Crime and Criminal Justice, 1927–1931.* 1934. Montclair, NJ: Patterson Smith, 1969.
Culver, Dorothy Campbell. *Bibliography of Crime and Criminal Justice, 1932–1937.* 1939. Montclair, NJ: Patterson Smith, 1969.
Thompkins, Dorothy Campbell Culver. *Sources for the Study of the Administration of Criminal Justice, 1938–1948: A Selected Bibliography.* 1949. Montclair, NJ: Patterson Smith, 1970.
Thompkins, Dorothy Campbell Culver. *Administration of Criminal Justice, 1949–1956.* 1956. Montclair, NJ: Patterson Smith, 1970.

This series of classified bibliographies emanated from Berkeley's Bureau of Public Administration (now the Institute of Governmental Studies). Coverage is comprehensive for books and journals, including some in foreign languages. All are indexed. Follow-up bibliographies were done by the author: *The Offender* (1963), *Probation Since World War II* (1964), *White Collar Crime* (1967), *Sentencing the Offender* (1971), and *The Prison and the Prisoner* (1971).

Cuming, Sir John. *Contribution towards a Bibliography Dealing with Crime and Cognate Subjects.* 3rd ed. 1935. Montclair, NJ: Patterson Smith, 1970.

Considered to be the basic nineteenth- and early twentieth-century police bibliography, this British classified list covers fifty years and is international in scope. It includes both author and combined subject and geographical indexes.

Doleschal, Eugene, Anne Newton, and William Hickey. *A Guide to the Literature on Organized Crime: An Annotated Bibliography Covering the Years 1967–1981.* Hackensack, NJ: National Council on Crime and Delinquency, 1981.

The title says it all. This bibliography documents the major change in scholarly thought on the origins, nature, and control of organized crime, particularly after publication of the President's Commission on Law Enforcement and Administration of Justice *Task Force Report.*

Economics of Crime and Correction. Washington, DC: American Bar Association, Correctional Economics Center, 1974.

This brief bibliography pulls together material on meeting the challenge of fiscal responsibility and on planning based on sound fiscal principles—an example of a specialized bibliography dealing with a specific aspect of criminal justice.

Johnson, Emily, and Marjorie Kravitz, comps. *Basic Sources in Criminal Justice: A Selected Bibliography.* Washington, DC: U.S. National Criminal Justice Reference Service, 1978.

General in scope, this bibliography contains extensive discussions of each of its 259 items. Particularly helpful are descriptions of individual commission reports.

Klein, Fannie J. *Administration of Justice in the Courts.* 2 vols. Dobbs Ferry, NY: Oceana Publications, 1976.

These two volumes cover books and journals through early 1975, dealing with courts and criminal justice in the courts. Annotations note distinctive features of titles. Indexes include name, subject, and table of cases.

Kuhlman, Augustus F. *Guide to Material on Crime and Criminal Justice.* 1929. Montclair, NJ: Patterson Smith, 1969.

An author index was added to this comprehensive reprint list of books, pamphlets, and articles in a classified arrangement. Covers American and British materials published before 1927. The subject index is at the front of the volume.

Radzinowicz, Leon, and Roger Hood. *Criminology and the Administration of Criminal Justice: A Bibliography.* Westport, CT: Greenwood Press, 1976.

The authors carefully selected and evaluated contemporary books, articles, and reports through August 1974, then bound a lengthy supplement into the volume to update selections to February 1976. Annotations are brief. Entries are classified and arranged in each class from earliest to most recent. Focus is sociological with an emphasis on policy.

Rank, Richard. *The Criminal Justice Systems of the Latin-American Nations: A Bibliography of the Primary and Secondary Literatures.* South Hackensack, NJ: Fred B. Rothman, 1974.

More than 9,000 entries are arranged in classified order under individual areas including Central and South America, Cuba, the Dominican Republic, Haiti, and Puerto Rico.

Simpson, Antony E., and Nina Duchaine. *The Literature of Police Corruption.* 2 vols. New York: John Jay Press, 1977–1979.

Both a review of the literature and a bibliography of 600 titles comprise Volume 1. Dissertations and textbooks are included in the four hundred titles noted in Volume 2.

Triche, Charles W., III. *The Capital Punishment Dilemma, 1950–1977: A Subject Bibliography.* Troy, NY: Whitson, 1979.

This lists books and essays, and indexes periodical literature under broad subjects. Some foreign-language entries are included.

Vom Ende, Rudolf. *Criminology and Forensic Sciences: An International Bibliography, 1950–1980.* 3 vols. Munich: Saur, 1981.

This alphabetical author index to journals and monographic materials has no subject index, so you may find it useful mostly if you are checking the works of a specific writer.

Whitehouse, Jack. *Police Bibliography.* New York: AMS Press, 1980.

Contains 17,400 book and article entries that cover the wide spectrum of police activity.

Wolfgang, Marvin E., Robert M. Figlio, and Terence P. Thornberry. *Criminology Index.* 2 vols. New York: Elsevier Science Publishing, 1975.

This two-volume citation index covers periodical literature from 1945 to 1972. It is a challenge to use because of its arrangement, but it includes valuable citations.

Part III

SOME SPECIAL
PROBLEMS

12

Research in Legal Resources

The purpose of this chapter is not to teach "legal research" as the term is used by lawyers; rather it is to help criminal justice researchers exploit legal resources to buttress and enrich studies in their own field.

After mastering the material in this chapter you should be able to use legal resources to do the following:

1. Find a citation if you know only the name or popular name of a case, statute, or regulation;
2. Locate the latest additions to the law;
3. Locate all the cases or current law in force on a particular topic;
4. Determine if what you have found is still valid, or "good law";
5. Locate discussions of general legal topics;
6. Locate discussions of specific laws, cases, and regulations.

Do not think that after reading this chapter you will be able to defend yourself in a court of law. The law is extremely complex and full of unfamiliar terms and concepts. That is why law school lasts three years and why lawyers can command such high salaries. If your money or your freedom hang in the balance, consult a lawyer. If you need to study some law for a term paper, read on.

THE AMERICAN LEGAL SYSTEM AND ITS PUBLICATIONS

American law has four basic components, each of which exists on the federal and state levels:

1. The Constitution;
2. Statute Law—the statutes, or laws, passed by the legislatures;
3. Regulatory Law—rules and regulations promulgated by government agencies, which have the force of law;
4. Case Law—the interpretations of the other three made by the courts as a result of cases brought to them on appeal.

The law is a living entity, with statutes, regulations, and case law constantly being nullified, added to, and revised. Understanding the manner in which these changes and additions progress through the various types of legal publications—the information flow—enables you to plot the research strategy that will best serve your needs.

Legal resources are often a pleasant surprise for the first-time user. They follow a logical and thoroughly consistent pattern of publication. Once that pattern is understood, it is relatively simple to choose the proper source to solve your problem.

Because it is essential for lawyers, politicians, and the public to have access to the most current additions and changes, all new and revised elements of the law appear fairly quickly in published form. The first appearance is chronological, with the publication arranged simply by the date of the decision or ruling. Such chronological publications however, do not cumulate and are difficult to use to locate all the law on a particular topic. Thus, there are frequent republications of the law in subject format.

STRATEGIES FOR THE USE OF LEGAL RESOURCES

Before Starting

Your work will be easier if you decide before starting whether your research involves federal or state sources; whether it involves statute, regulatory, or case law; and the level of information needed—historical precedent, law currently in force, or only the most recent revisions or additions.

Reading Legal Citations

Although they look as if they were designed to bedevil the uninitiated, legal citations are actually simple to decipher. A legal citation is just a standardized way of referring to a specific element in the law. It has three basic parts: a volume number, an abbreviation for the title of the legal set, and a page or section number. These are sometimes followed by the date.

The following are examples of legal citations:

Supreme Court Case: 383 US 463 (1966). This means Volume 383 of the *United States Reports*, page 463, decided in 1966.

Federal Law: 42 USC §1437. This means Title 42 of the *United States Code,* section 1437.

Federal Regulation: 28 CFR §42.6. This means Title 28 of the *Code of Federal Regulations*, section 42.6

Journal: 131 U.Pa.L.Rev 353–387, Dec '82. This means Volume 131 of the *University of Pennsylvania Law Review*, pages 353 to 387, from December, 1982.

Using Indexes in Law Books

There are significant differences between the index of a law book and that of other books. Law books tend to use broad rather than narrow terms as index entries, with the narrower concepts used only as subdivisions of the more encompassing word.

It is helpful to begin your search by compiling a list of all possible synonyms, broader terms, and narrower terms which apply to your topic. Expect to check most of them before finding exactly what is needed. Although this may be surprisingly time consuming, in the end it will save you from wasting time reading irrelevant material.

Exploring Tables of Contents

Most legal publications that have a subject arrangement, such as encyclopedias, digests, and codified arrangements of statutes and regulations, have very detailed tables of contents before each section or article. In some cases there is a general table of contents followed by one or more increasingly detailed analytical tables of contents. It is not unusual for these tables to be over ten pages. Do not rush through them; they give an overview of the entire topic, and can help isolate the specific paragraph that will help to answer your question. In general, time spent reading an analytical table of contents yields a greater saving of time that might have been wasted reading material not relevant to your research.

Updating with Pocket Parts

Lawyers need to have the most up-to-date information. Chronological publications are automatically updated each time a new volume is issued. Publications that are arranged by subject are more difficult to keep up to date. Legal publishers, however, make use of a nifty device for keeping their alphabetically arranged publications current. Called a *pocket part*, it is a separate part, or pamphlet, that is inserted into a pocket in the back cover of the volume that it updates. Never consider that you have finished using a legal publication until you have consulted the pocket part to see whether or not the information you have just read is still valid. Lawyers generally look at the pocket part first. Remember, index volumes also have pocket parts.

GAINING ACCESS TO LAW BOOKS

Law Libraries

Legal resources are more widely available than many people think. Many academic and public libraries maintain small, basic law collections. If your library does not have the material you need, ask your librarian for advice on where to go, or contact the closest federal, state, or county courthouse. Often the lawyers who use court system libraries (and the librarians who run them) view the resources as their exclusive property. In many cases, however, these libraries, because they are supported by public funds, are indeed open to the public. You may find access to libraries in law schools more difficult to achieve but many of them do permit outsiders to use their resources. A letter of introduction or a telephone call from your own librarian may help.

First encounters with law libraries are frequently intimidating even to experienced library users. The books are overwhelming in number and appearance; the librarian, although knowledgeable, may not be accustomed to helping those who are learning to use legal materials; and the other patrons somehow all look as if they know exactly what they are doing.

Before going to a law library, read this chapter carefully, get as much help as you can from your own librarian, and if possible, consult one of the legal research guides listed at the end of this chapter. When you get to the law library remember: Do not be intimidated by either the people or the books.

Computerized Access to the Law

There are two major commercial systems which provide online access to all facets of U.S. law. WESTLAW, a product of the West Publishing Company, now a division of the Thomson Corporation, and LEXIS, developed by Mead Data Central and now a division of Reed Elsevier, are both complex systems, providing a variety of search options and indexes and the full-text of federal and state statutes, regulations, and case law—usually with commentary and notes. Both can be accessed only through subscriptions and both are quite expensive. However, both are now often available to students through limited-service academic subscriptions in college and university libraries.

Taking full advantage of these systems requires training and a thorough knowledge of the law. But it is possible to make more casual use of them. Both WESTLAW and LEXIS provide computer-assisted tutorials and both provide a simplified end-user system for the occasional user. WEST calls it "EZ Access"; LEXIS "Easy Search." Ask your librarian if either of these systems is available to you and how to access it. If they are not available, you can probably find what you need in other ways; in fact, many students find that without the context that a physical volume provides, legal research is often more confusing online. Students who do not understand the difference between statutes, regulations, and cases are probably better off beginning their research with printed volumes.

Law over the Internet

One of the most extraordinary results of the development of the Internet has been to bring the law closer to the American public. Until recently these laws, passed by our own representatives, have all too often been locked away in law libraries available only to lawyers. Now, the full-text of the *United States Code*, recent Supreme Court decisions, some lower court decisions, and many state statutes and cases are available to anyone with a computer and a modem, or access to a library that provides Internet connections.

While you cannot do sophisticated legal research on the Internet—that continues to require expensive commercial services like WESTLAW and LEXIS—you can find and read the law. However, it is still necessary to comprehend the American legal system and its publications to understand what you are reading. Throughout this chapter, if a resource is available over the Internet it will be noted.

The following sites have excellent collections of their own legal materials and maintain comprehensive links to some of the best legal resources available on the Internet:

FedLaw: Legal Resources on the Internet. U.S. General Services Administration. Available [Internet] at http://www.legal.gsa.gov/

FedLaw was developed by the General Services Administration as an attempt to reduce overhead in the GSA Office of General Counsel. It provides links to selected resources of use to those doing federal legal research—primarily federal laws, rules and regulations, judicial decisions, and some general research and reference materials.

Findlaw. Available [Internet] at http://www.findlaw.com/

One of the highlights of this site is its collection of searchable and browsable Supreme Court cases dating back to 1906. *Findlaw* also has one of the Net's best collections of links to federal, state, and international legal resources.

Internet Law Library. U.S. House of Representatives. Available [Internet] at http://law.house.gov/

The U.S. House of Representatives *Internet Law Library* has organized more than 8,900 Internet resources related to federal, state, and international law. It provides its own full-text searchable copies of the *United States Code* and the *Code of Federal Regulations*, and full-text of House *Hearings*; but most of the links are to resources on other servers.

Legal Information Institute. Cornell University Law School. Available [Internet] at http://www.law.cornell.edu/

Cornell Law School's Legal Information Institute is a well-known repository for recent and historic Supreme Court cases, the *United States Code* in hypertext, and other federal and New York State materials. It also has an excellent collection of links to legal resources by subject.

THE CONSTITUTION

A constitution defines a government's basic principles and organization. In the United States, laws passed by legislatures can be nullified if the judiciary finds that they violate these basic principles. The Constitution of the United States is reproduced in almost every American almanac and encyclopedia. Thorough exposition of the Constitution, and of the legal decisions that have shaped it, can be found in most constitutional law textbooks, but the following sources take a particularly encyclopedic approach.

The Constitution of the United States of America: Analysis and Interpretation: Annotations of Cases Decided by the Supreme Court of the United States to June 29, 1992. Prepared by the Congressional Research Service, Library of Congress. Washington, DC: Govt. Print. Off., 1996. Also available [Internet] at http://www.access.gpo.gov/congress/senate/constitution/

Also known as the *Annotated Constitution*, this enormous one-volume work—published regularly by order of Congress—is the official treatise on the history of the U.S. Constitution and its shaping by court decision. It provides the full-text of the Constitution and the amendments with discussion of the shaping of each idea by the original framers and subsequent reinterpretations by events and jurists. The Internet version is both searchable and browsable.

Encyclopedia of the American Constitution. 4 vols. New York: Macmillan, 1986. *Supplement I*, 1992.

As discussed earlier (page 74), this comprehensive encyclopedia was issued to commemorate the bicentennial of the Constitutional Convention. This is an excellent source to begin any detailed examination of issues of constitutional law. It highlights the important themes and cases in scholarly, well-written articles that are remarkably free of legal jargon.

STATUTE LAW

Statute law is that body of law passed by a legislative unit.

Federal Statutes

At the federal level, a bill normally becomes a law after it is passed by both houses of Congress and is signed by the President. Most American almanacs and encyclopedias describe how a bill becomes a law. A very detailed discussion titled *How Our Laws Are Made* is available over the Internet at http://thomas.loc.gov/home/lawsmade.toc.html.

Chronologically Arranged Publication

United States Public Laws (Slip Laws). Washington, DC: Government Printing Office.
United States Statutes at Large. Washington, DC: Government Printing Office, 1937– .

After passage, laws are given two-part numbers, the first part indicating the number of Congress, the second its sequential place. PL 104–210 would be the 210th law passed by the 104th Congress. Laws are printed first by the U.S. Government Printing Office as *slip laws.* Included in this publication, following the text of the law, is the legislative history, including information about House and Senate Reports, conference reports, *Congressional Record* notations (when it was discussed or debated on the floor of the House or Senate), and presidential statements that appear in the *Weekly Compilation of Presidential Documents.* All of these may be consulted to help understand the reasons for enactment, to discover background information, and to shed light on the social and political environment of the deliberations.

At the end of a Congressional session, slip laws are reprinted in numerical order in *U.S. Statutes at Large,* also published by the Government Printing Office. Each volume of *Statutes* is indexed by subject and contains a table listing how each public law in the volume affects any previous public law. Recently passed laws are also published in a timely fashion in:

U.S. Code Congressional and Administrative News Service. St. Paul, MN: West Publishing Co., 1939– .

This service also includes the full-text of some of the Congressional reports related to the laws.

Advance Sheets, United States Code Service, Lawyer's Edition. New York: Lawyer's Co-op, 1972– .

The fastest, and possibly easiest, way to find the text of current laws is through the following two World Wide Web sites:

Thomas. Library of Congress. Available [Internet] at http://thomas.loc.gov
GPO Access. Government Printing Office. Available [Internet] at http://www.access.gpo.gov/su_docs/

Thomas is a World Wide Web site developed by the Library of Congress at the behest of Congress. It provides full-text of recently-passed laws (slip laws) and of bills being considered by Congress. (For other services provided by Thomas, see "Tracking Current Legislation," p. 155.) The Government Printing Office provides a similar service through *GPO Access,* discussed in Chapter 9 (p. 111). The GPO, as the official printer of the nations' laws, provides the official online version of the law and other documents in both plain text and Adobe Acrobat® (PDF) format.

Publications Arranged by Subject

The next published format of the U.S. law is the *Code*. The codification process brings together into "titles" all the laws on a subject that are in effect as of the publication date, unites the original law with all changes, and eliminates repealed, superseded, or expired laws.

> *United States Code.* Washington, DC: U.S. Government Printing Office, 1926– . Also available in CD-ROM, and [Internet] from *GPO Access* at http://www.access. gpo.gov/su_docs/aces/aaces002.html or from the Legal Information Institute at http://www.law.cornell.edu/uscode/

The first official *U.S. Code* was not published until 1926 when all non-repealed sections of the *Revised Statutes of 1875* and all subsequent volumes of *Statutes at Large* were arranged into a single set of fifty titles. This official version of the *Code* is reissued every six years by the U.S. Government Printing Office. Bound cumulative supplements accommodate the years between each revision. Beginning in 1994, the Government Printing Office began issuing the *Code* on CD-ROM as well.

The *U.S. Code* is available on LEXIS if you have access to it, or over the Internet. Cornell University's Legal Information Institute offers excellent access to the full-text of the U.S. Code. You can browse this online *Code* by title, find exact citations by title and section, or perform keyword searches of particular titles or the entire code. The result of a keyword search is always displayed in the context of the title and chapter of the *Code* in which the section appears. The Legal Information Institute uses the latest version available from the U.S. government on CD-ROM, but the Institute has created WWW forms that allow you to search Congress' *Thomas* to find out if a particular section has been amended. The *Code* is also searchable from the *GPO Access* WWW site.

> *United States Code Annotated (USCA).* St. Paul, MN: West Publishing Co., 1927– .
> *United States Code Service, Lawyer's Edition (USCS).* Rochester, NY: Lawyers' Co-op, 1972– .

Because the meaning of a law is not always clear, its interpretation frequently is clarified by court decisions. Annotated codes, published by commercial firms, include brief summaries of such cases. These annotated codes provide more detailed indexing than the official one; are more current because they are updated by pocket parts, pamphlets, and replacement volumes; and are enriched by federal and state court decisions plus citations to the *Code of Federal Regulations*, opinions of Attorneys General, and historical notes. Easier to use, the annotated versions give the researcher access to not only the law but also supplementary information vital to its interpretation.

Locating Acts by Popular Name

Statutes often are known by popular names, usually based on the subject of the act or its authors. The name "Omnibus Crime Control and Safe Streets Act," does not reveal its year of passage, its public law number, or the title where it is encoded. Neither does an act name based on authors' names, such as the Stevenson-Wydler Technology Innovation Act. All versions of the *Code* contain indexes to acts by their popular names.

A separate publication is

Shepard's Acts and Cases by Popular Names, Federal and State. Colorado Springs, CO: Shepard's, 1979– .

Both federal and state acts are listed alphabetically by name with the citation given to locate the source.

Tracking Current Legislation

Thomas. Available [Internet] at http://thomas.loc.gov/

The easiest way to track current legislation, if you have access to the World Wide Web, is through *Thomas. Thomas* was created by the Library of Congress at the request of Congress and announced with a great deal of fanfare. The object of Congress is to provide open access for the American public to federal legislative information. The site debuted in January, 1995 with the text of current bills, followed by the full-text of the *Congressional Record. Thomas* now provides information on the current week's activities in Congress, including bills that are expected to receive floor action; discussion of major bills introduced in Congress; full-text of all bills; information about current status of all bills, including sponsors and cosponsors, legislative history, and committees and subcommittees of referral; the full, searchable text of the *Congressional Record* and the *Congressional Record Index*; information about Congressional committees and full-text of committee reports; selected historical documents; and links to other Congressional, Library of Congress, and Government Printing Office sites.

The full-text of bills (in ASCII text and the "official" PDF form) can also be found on the GPO Access site at http://www.access.gpo.gov/su_docs/aces/aaces002.html.

• • •

If you lack good Internet access or desire analysis and interpretation, the following easy-to-find and easy-to-use sources provide exhaustive coverage.

Congressional Index. Chicago: Commerce Clearing House, 1953/54– .

Updated weekly, this looseleaf publication summarizes legislation for each Congress and indexes it by subject, author, and bill number. It includes summaries, the progress and status of bills, and voting records.

Congressional Quarterly Weekly Report. Washington, DC: Congressional Quarterly,
1971– . Weekly.

This news weekly features articles about legislation, revealing its intent by
providing background material. It includes summaries of bills and voting
records on the bills and of the legislators. Weekly and cumulated indexes
make finding information easy.

State Statutes

State laws follow the same general pattern of organization and publication
as federal laws. Laws are passed by the legislature, published in chronological order, then incorporated into a code. Often the publication in chronological order carries the title "session laws." The code usually has "revised,"
"compiled," or "consolidated" in its title. Most volumes of state law include
the state's constitution, its laws arranged by subject, historical notes, annotations, and tables. Many sets of state laws are now also published in CD-ROM
format by the major legal publishers. For some states, published guides, often
written by law librarians, contain the legal history and organization of the
state government. Such resources clarify areas of confusion and lead you to
useful avenues of research. Ask your librarian if a guide is available, since it
will save you time and effort.

You may have difficulty finding state laws, particularly those of states other
than your own. Generally only law libraries will have printed or CD-ROM
versions of the laws of all fifty states. Public and academic libraries are likely
to have only the laws of their own state. If you are lucky enough to have
access to *LEXIS* or *WESTLAW*, this is the preferred method of doing comparative research in state laws.

An alternative is to try to access state codes over the Internet. Many, if not
most, states are now making the full-text of their laws available on the World
Wide Web or through gopher. The sites listed below are excellent places to begin.

United States. House of Representatives. *Internet Law Library, U.S. State and Terri-
torial Laws.* Available [Internet] at http://law.house.gov/17.htm

United States. House of Representatives. *Laws of All Jurisdictions, Arranged by Subject.* Available [Internet] at http://law.house.gov/90.htm, with a section on crime,
and so forth.

Cornell University Legal Information Institute. Available [Internet] at http://www.law.
cornell.edu/statutes.html#state

Findlaw. Available [Internet] at http://www.findlaw.com/11stategov/

Some useful printed resources are

Martindale Hubbell Law Directory. New York: Martindale Hubbell, 1931– . Annual.
Also available online through LEXIS-NEXIS.

Its "Law Digest" volumes provide digests of state laws on many subjects. Uniform subject headings are used under each state. Most of the summaries, written by lawyers, include the citations to the state statutes.

Shepard's Acts and Cases by Popular Names, Federal and State. Colorado Springs, CO: Shepard's, 1979– .

Discussed earlier, this resource is mentioned here because it indexes statutes of all states and can be used to locate similar legislation from state to state.

Municipal Statutes

Municipal or local governments operate under powers granted to them by the state. Their legislative activities center on (1) a charter, which is analogous to a state constitution; (2) ordinances, the legislative enactments of the local city council or board of supervisors; and (3) a code which arranges ordinances in force in some logical form. Few city codes are annotated. It is usually necessary to work directly with such primary sources to do legal research at the local level.

If a municipal library exists in your town, either as a section of the public library or in an office at city hall, use its resources. If not, work with the city clerk or various department heads. Always remember that the smaller the unit of government, the less likely it is that information will be arranged in an easily accessible fashion. Remember also that although the information should be publicly available, there may not be many requests from the public to use it, and the civil servants who will be helping you probably have many other duties to attend to. Be tactful but persistent.

REGULATORY LAW

Federal Administrative Agencies

Concerned with the public or private rights and obligations of private parties, administrative agencies work out the details in the laws passed by Congress. Their authority, vested and controlled by legislative action or presidential executive order, promulgates faster and more efficient enforcement of public policy. First used by states during the last half of the nineteenth century, administrative agencies centered their activities on the regulation of private economic activity. The Depression and New Deal ushered in a watershed period in the growth of federal regulatory agencies, as they focused on economic recovery. By the 1960s and 1970s, regulation of aspects of social life such as health, welfare, and education became an important concern of administrative agencies. In spite of the antiregulatory trend since the late 1970s, agencies continue to formulate and administer public policy through rules and regulations, to provide an adjudicative procedure through hearings, and to subject their regulatory functions to judicial review. Administrative agencies have various labels: boards, commissions, bureaus, offices, departments, divisions, or corporations.

Federal Administrative Rules and Regulations

Because rules and regulations passed by administrative agencies have the effect of law, have important consequences for our private lives, and are constantly changing, it is imperative to have effective access to current rules and regulations.

Chronologically Arranged Publications

Federal Register. Washington, DC: U.S. Government Printing Office, 1936– . Daily. Also available in microfiche; online through DIALOG, LEXIS-NEXIS, and WESTLAW; and through *GPO Access* [Internet] at http://www.access.gpo.gov/nara/index.html

Administrative agency issuance of rules is a fairly simple process. For any administrative rule or regulation to become effective, it must first be published in the *Federal Register.* Thus the *Federal Register* is the administrative agencies' counterpart to Congress's *Statutes at Large.* Both include new statements of law or regulation as they are promulgated, but do not compile rules or statutes by subject. The *Federal Register* differs from the *Statutes* because it also includes proposed actions.

The *Federal Register* is published daily, Monday through Friday, and indexed monthly, quarterly, and annually. The Internet version, available through the Government Printing Office's *GPO Access* system, is fully searchable. Searches can be limited by date or by section of the *Federal Register.*

Publications Arranged by Subject

Code of Federal Regulations (CFR). Office of the Federal Register. National Archives and Records Service. Washington, DC: U.S. Government Printing Office, 1936– . Annual. Also available in microfiche; online from LEXIS-NEXIS and WESTLAW; and through *GPO Access* [Internet] at http://www.access.gpo.gov/nara/index.html

In order to arrange federal regulations and amendments in force by subject, they are entered into the *Code of Federal Regulations*, published in fifty titles (subject areas), with each title updated once a year. Besides a cumulated index, each title volume has its own index, plus a detailed table of contents. What has been said about using law books is also applicable here; regulations tend to be indexed under their broader aspects. Plan to spend extra time exploring *CFR* tables of contents and indexes.

Keeping Current

The easiest way to stay current is through online access to the *Federal Register* or the *Code of Federal Regulations*, listed above. The following print sources are also available:

List of CFR Sections Affected. Office of the Federal Register. National Archives and Records Service. Washington DC: U.S. Government Printing Office, 1936– . Monthly.

The currency of each title of *CFR* depends on the date. Each year titles 1 through 16 are revised as of January 1; titles 17 through 27, April 1; titles 28 through 41, July 1; and titles 42 through 50, October 1. If regulations have been added, amended or revoked, such changes will be noted in the monthly *List of CFR Sections Affected* and in "Cumulative List of Parts Affected," which is printed in the *Federal Register*.

CIS Federal Register Index. Bethesda, MD: Congressional Information Service, 1984– .

Its weekly publication allows this index to promptly demystify the complexity of the *Federal Register*. Proposed rules, rules, and notices of agencies responsible for developing and implementing federal regulations are indexed in detail by subject and name, including issuing agencies, geographic areas, chemical substances, popular names of authorizing legislation, and names of industries, organizations, corporations, and individuals. Other indexes are by *CFR* section numbers and by federal agency docket numbers.

State and Municipal Regulations

Rules and regulations of state agencies tend to follow the same publication schedule as federal sources. Regulations first appear in a chronological format, then are compiled into a subject, or title, arrangement. The form of publication of state agency regulations varies greatly across the states. Many of the state regulations are published in CD-ROM format by the major legal publishers.

Regulations of municipal agencies often are enacted by the legislative body of the municipality and hence are incorporated into the ordinances and code. Others appear in such documents as policy manuals, either cumulated for various agencies or issued for a single agency.

Your sources for help in locating state and municipal regulations continue to be a state legal guide; a state or municipal library; the state or municipal agency; and, as always, your librarian.

CASE LAW

Case law is law evolving from judicial interpretations of the constitution, the statutes, and the regulations. These judicial interpretations are rendered only when a case is brought before a court on appeal. A case may have majority, minority, concurring, and dissenting opinions.

Case law, like statute and regulatory law, follows a logical publication pattern, although some of its forms may be less familiar to you.

Chronologically Arranged Publication: Reporters

Reporters contain the written decisions of the courts in cases brought to them on appeal. Published chronologically, they are the primary sources—the building blocks—of case law. Decisions are usually published first in slip format soon after they are rendered and then in bound volumes at the end of each court term. There are separate sets of reporters for the various levels of federal and state courts and for groups of states.

Reporters, arranged by jurisdiction and by date of decision, are thus equivalent to *Statutes at Large*. Each volume lists the cases contained, and most also contain an alphabetical case name index. These indexes, however, do not cumulate; thus, if you do not know the year in which your case was decided (as well as the court), you will have to go through hundreds of individual reporter indexes to locate the case.

Court decisions may be published directly by the governmental jurisdiction concerned, in which case they are called *official reporters*, or by a commercial publisher, in which case they are called *unofficial reporters*. In some instances, a commercially published set has been designated by the jurisdiction to be its official reporter. In general, unofficial reporters contain helpful additional information such as reference aids, additional summaries, and referrals to related material in other publications that does not appear in the official reporters. However, the actual case decisions, with any minority, majority, dissenting or concurring opinions, must obviously be identical to those appearing in the official reporters.

All U.S. federal and state court decisions are available from the two major online legal services, WESTLAW and LEXIS. Almost all federal, and most state, court decisions are now also available on CD-ROM from the major legal publishers. And many federal and state court decisions are now available over the Internet. Find out from your librarian which case law the library makes available and what form it takes.

United States Supreme Court

United States Reports. Washington, DC: U.S. Govt. Print. Off.

This is the official reporter.

United States Supreme Court Reports: Lawyers' Edition. Rochester, NY: Lawyers'
    Co-op.

Decisions to 1956.

United States Supreme Court Reports: Lawyers' Edition. 2nd series. Rochester, NY:
    Lawyers' Co-op.

Decisions since 1956.

Supreme Court Reporter. St. Paul, MN: West Publishing Co.

All Supreme Court decisions.

United States Law Week. Washington, DC: Bureau of National Affairs, 1932– .

Prints the most recent Supreme Court decisions and provides information
on cases and issues coming before the Court.

Decisions of the U.S. Supreme Court. Ithaca, NY: Cornell University Legal Informa-
    tion Institute. Available [Internet] at http://supct.law.cornell.edu/supct

Searchable, full-text decisions of the U.S. Supreme Court beginning with 1990.

Selected Historic Decisions of the U.S. Supreme Court. Ithaca, NY: Cornell Univer-
    sity Legal Information Institute. Available [Internet] at http://supct.law.cornell.
    edu/supct/cases/historic.htm

Provides online access to over 325 significant decisions of the U.S. Supreme Court dating back to *Marbury v. Madison* (1803).

FedWorld/FLITE Supreme Court Decisions Homepage. Washington, DC: Office of
    Management and Budget and National Technical Information Service. Avail-
    able [Internet] at http://www.fedworld.gov/supcourt/index.htm

More than 7,000 Supreme Court opinions dating from 1937 through 1975,
from volumes 300 through 422 of *U.S. Reports.*

Project Hermes. Available [Internet] at ftp://ftp.cwru.edu/hermes

The original ftp site for Supreme Court decisions beginning in 1990.

Findlaw. Available [Internet] at http://www.findlaw.com/casecode/supreme.html

Searchable and browsable Supreme Court decisions from 1906.

• • •

All these sources provide access to United States Supreme Court decisions. *United States Supreme Court Reports: Lawyers' Edition* and *Supreme
Court Reporter* are the unofficial reporters with headnotes and annotations
provided by legal experts. Since 1990, through *Project Hermes*, the Supreme

Court has been releasing its decisions free over the Internet at the same time it releases them to WESTLAW and LEXIS. They can be accessed through the World Wide Web from Cornell University's Legal Information Institute or via gopher and ftp from Case Western Reserve. Beginning in late 1996, the U.S. government has made available the Air Force's FLITE (Federal Legal Information Through Electronics) system through its FedWorld WWW site, providing access to cases from 1937 to 1975. The *Findlaw* site is probably the most comprehensive and easiest to use of the Web sites with Supreme Court cases dating back to 1906.

Lower Federal Courts

Among the printed reporters for the lower federal courts are

Federal Reporter. St. Paul, MN: West Publishing Co.
Federal Reporter. 2nd series. St. Paul, MN: West Publishing Co.
Federal Supplement. St. Paul, MN: West Publishing Co.

Internet sources are

Judicial Opinions. Legal Information Institute. Cornell Law School. Available [Internet] at http://fatty.law.cornell.edu/opinions.html
Fedlaw: Federal Judiciary. U.S. General Services Administration. Available [Internet] at http://www.legal.gsa.gov/intro3.htm
Guide to Law Online: United States Federal Courts. United States Library of Congress. Available [Internet] at http://lcweb2.loc.gov/glin/us-court.html

Most of the recent decisions of the lower federal courts can now be found over the Internet. Cornell University Law School maintains a WWW page with direct links to U.S. Court of Appeals decisions. The Library of Congress, as part of its *Guide to Law Online* (*GLIN*), also provides a guide to federal court decisions available over the Internet. This useful list links directly to the sites (mostly law schools) for circuit court decisions and information about the federal judiciary. In most instances the online decisions begin with 1995 or 1996.

State Courts

Every state has ensured that its appellate court decisions be published in some form. Some states publish their own; others rely on commercial publications. As a general rule, only law libraries have reporters of all states or the *National Reporter System* mentioned below, and even many law libraries are abandoning print or CD-ROM subscriptions in favor of online access via WESTLAW or LEXIS. As with state statutes, it can be difficult to gain access to state court decisions, particularly for states outside of your own. The source listed here may be of use:

National Reporter System. St. Paul, MN: West Publishing Co., 1879– .

This is a mammoth system for reporting state and federal court decisions in a series of regional and national reporters. State decisions can be found in the *Atlantic Reporter, North Western Reporter, North Eastern Reporter, Pacific Reporter, South Eastern Reporter, South Western Reporter*, and the *Southern Reporter*. In some instances, coverage provided by the *National Reporter System* duplicates that available in official reporters; in others it is the only source.

The Internet provides access to court decisions from many states. In some cases these are made available by the state government, or the state court system itself. In other cases they are provided by a law school or even a private company. Some sites provide WAIS or similar indexing of the full-text of the decisions; others simply provide a list of the decisions arranged by date, which can be viewed or downloaded. As the World Wide Web becomes increasingly the "hot" place to be for state governments, more and more of them are providing access to their court decisions. However, they are very rarely providing retrospective access to older cases, and it remains to be seen if they will maintain online everything that they are now offering, or if they will save computer storage space by removing the older cases as the years go by.

The sites listed below provide comprehensive indexing or links to state judicial opinions:

State Legal Resources. University of South Carolina Law Library. Available [Internet] at http://www.law.sc.edu/st_hp.htm
Judicial Opinions. Cornell University. Legal Information Institute. Available [Internet] at http://fatty.law.cornell.edu/opinions.html
Findlaw:State Resources. Available [Internet] at http://www.findlaw.com/11stategov/index.html

Publications Arranged by Subject: Digests

A digest is a form of publication unique to case law. Digests are subject arrangements of summaries of the points of law discussed in court decisions.

There are typically several points of law discussed in a court decision. Digests summarize each of these individual points for each case and then arrange the summaries by subject, in one encyclopedic alphabetical arrangement. In order to keep the digest current without reprinting the entire set, pocket parts are issued regularly for each volume.

Unlike codes, which are subject arrangements of laws or regulations and are designed to be used alone, digests should never be used alone in the study of case law. Digests do not contain the entire case; they are designed to be used as subject indexes to the reporters.

Most digests have two indexes:

1. A subject, or word index, that leads to the areas within the digest where points at issue from relevant cases are summarized. In practice this index works in the

same way as the index to an encyclopedia; it leads you to information about a subject.

2. A case name index that lists each of the cases summarized in that digest, gives the complete citation, and gives the subject areas within the digest where elements from that case are summarized.

It is helpful to remember the dual function of the case name index to the digest: If you know the name of the case and want to locate other cases which discuss the same topic, it leads you to the proper section of the digest; it also provides the citation if all you know is the name of the case, thus enabling you to go directly to the decision in the appropriate reporter. Note that the index volumes as well as the digest volumes have pocket parts.

Federal Digests

U.S. Supreme Court Reports Digest: Lawyers' Edition. Rochester, NY: Lawyers' Co-op.

Indexes all Supreme Court cases.

U.S. Supreme Court Digest. St. Paul, MN: West Publishing Co.

Indexes all Supreme Court cases.

West Federal Practice Digest. St. Paul, MN: West Publishing Co.

Indexes lower federal court decisions. Now in the 4th series.

State Digests

Digests for state court decisions are available from various sources. If your interest is in a single state, it is simplest to use the digest system for that particular state; most states have them. If your interest is somewhat broader or a separate digest is not available for the state with which you are concerned, the regional digests, published by West and corresponding to the regional reporter series, would be the best choice. However, if you have access to LEXIS or WESTLAW, you may want to try subject searching these enormous legal databases. Both systems allow you to limit your searches to a particular jurisdiction. Both are also very complex and allow the user to perform very sophisticated searches. A simple keyword search in these huge, full-text databases will likely yield more cases than you anticipate. To search these databases effectively for cases on a particular topic, you should invest some time in training.

American Digest System

The *American Digest System* is an overwhelmingly comprehensive digest system that attempts to cover every reported case in every jurisdiction in the country from 1658 to date. Published by West, it has hundreds of volumes in multiple series. Its bulk and comprehensiveness make it difficult to use, so that most criminal justice researchers will only turn to it after trying either an individual state or a regional digest. Perhaps its most useful and interesting series is the *Century Edition*, which purports to digest every reported American case from 1658 to 1896, in fifty volumes. Again, these cases are available in full-text from WESTLAW and LEXIS, but the sheer volume of the information makes searching difficult.

SHEPARDIZING

Shepard's is a company that publishes a series of books called *citators*, each of which is keyed to one of the basic publications of the law. *Shepardizing* is a process that enables the researcher to determine if a specific case, statute, regulation, or ordinance has been discussed, cited, overturned, repealed, or affirmed in another case. There are Shepard's citators for case, statute, and regulatory law on the municipal, state, and federal levels; all are published in confusingly identical maroon bindings and are kept up to date by supplements and advance sheets.

In appearance, legal citators are like no other form of publication in the world. Consisting of columns of numbers, abbreviations, and arcane symbols, they appear to be exceedingly difficult, if not impossible, to use.

If you need to use a citator, however, do not panic. They are not nearly as difficult as they look; most people can master them fairly quickly by reading the introduction or by getting a few minutes of instruction from the librarian. The key to understanding them is to use them.

Both WESTLAW and LEXIS provide online citation searching of cases. If you have access to one of these services, you will probably find online citation searching to be much easier than using the printed volumes.

TRIAL TRANSCRIPTS

Transcripts, or verbatim records, of individual trials are generally not published. As we said earlier, case law is the judicial interpretation of the law that occurs when a case is brought before a court on appeal; this occurs after the trial phase. If a case is appealed, transcripts will be produced for the appellate court—generally by the court reporter for a significant fee. These transcripts are not widely reproduced or made available.

There are exceptions, however. Occasionally, transcripts of particularly notorious trials are published and sold through normal commercial channels. These may be found through your library's catalog or through the union catalogs discussed in Chapter 5 (p. 62). Collections of transcripts of historical trials have also appeared in sources such as:

American State Trials; A Collection of the Important and Interesting Criminal Trials Which Have Taken Place in the United States, from the Beginning of Our Government to 1920. Reprint ed. 17 vols. Wilmington, DE: Scholarly Resources, 1972.

Full transcripts of some of the trials that made the front pages of the newspapers of their time.

• • •

In the 1990s, the transcripts of particularly well-publicized trials have made their way online. WESTLAW offers access to full transcripts of such well-known trials as the Susan Smith trial, the Menendez brothers trial, the O.J. Simpson trial, plus a number of others. Some of these transcripts can also be found on the Internet at no charge. To locate them try the following sites.

Court TV Casefiles. Available [Internet] at http://www.courttv.com/casefiles/

Provides transcripts of the most famous of the cases that have appeared, are appearing, or are reported on by "Court TV," such as the O.J. Simpson criminal and civil trials, the Oklahoma bombing trial, and the Menendez brothers trial.

Yahoo: Government: Law: Legal Research: Cases. Available [Internet] at http://www. yahoo.com/Government/Law/Legal_Research/Cases/

Yahoo is a directory of World Wide Web sites. The section on law cases points to sites dealing with notable historic and recent trials, as well as highly-publicized court decisions.

Cecil Greek's Criminal Justice Resources on the Web: Criminal Justice and the Media. Available [Internet] at http://www.fsu.edu/~crimdo/media2.html

Provides links to WWW sites with transcripts of and information about the cases that are most covered by the media.

DISCUSSIONS ABOUT THE LAW

Encyclopedias

When researching legal topics, think of using encyclopedias in the same way you would for other topics. Look to them to provide overviews, general orientations to topics with which you are not familiar, and for specific information such as dates, sponsors, and summaries or discussions of particular statutes or cases.

There are two types of encyclopedias that can be helpful to the criminal justice researcher with a need for information about the law: those written to meet the needs of nonlawyers and those, traditionally called legal encyclopedias, written specifically for the legal profession.

If your need for legal information is peripheral to your main topic, or if you are totally unacquainted with the legal issues that you are researching, it may be easier to start with one of the encyclopedias designed for the nonlawyer.

Guide to American Law and the *Encyclopedia of Crime and Justice* both provide factual information and broad overviews without the use of legal jargon. Both contain bibliographies, give citations to relevant cases and statutes, and include case name indexes that are helpful in locating summaries and discussions of specific cases. If you are interested in cases of constitutional significance, the *Encyclopedia of the American Constitution* is another excellent source. These are all discussed in greater detail in Chapter 6.

Two sources that may also be of use are

Corpus Juris Secundum. St. Paul, MN: West Publishing Co. Also available online from WESTLAW.
American Jurisprudence, 2nd. Lawyers' Co-op. Also available online from LEXIS-NEXIS.

Corpus Juris Secundum, published by West, and *American Jurisprudence, 2nd*, published by Lawyers' Co-op, are the standard encyclopedias of the legal profession. Like digests, they have a basic subject arrangement by broad subject, with a separate subject index for the set.

The most efficient approach to these encyclopedias is to use the general index to locate relevant articles and then carefully scan the analytical table of contents found at the beginning of most of the articles. These detailed lists of the contents of each article will help pinpoint precisely those pages that will be most helpful to you.

These encyclopedias do not contain case table or statute indexes and thus cannot be used easily to locate discussions and summaries of specific cases. They are designed for a subject approach.

Both of the traditional legal encyclopedias are updated by pocket parts, with individual volumes being occasionally rewritten.

Do not be intimidated by the appearance of a legal encyclopedia. A typical page has dozens of closely packed footnotes, often taking up more than half the page; these footnotes cite the cases and statutes that have been used as the basis of the discussion. If you want only an overview of the topic, ignore the footnotes.

Legal Periodicals

Legal periodicals, some of which are called law reviews, are like other scholarly or professional periodicals; they contain articles written for the specialist. As with other periodicals, the best way to locate an article on a particular topic is through the use of periodical indexes.

Index to Legal Periodicals and *Current Law Index* (*Legal Resource Index* in the online version) are the two most important indexes to legal journals. Both contain case name indexes that are extremely useful in locating discussions of specific cases. Both are also available on CD-ROM and online. These indexes are discussed more fully in Chapter 7 (pp. 88–89).

Also useful is

Criminal Law Reporter. Washington: Bureau of National Affairs. 1967– . Weekly.

Criminal Law Reporter reviews changes and potential changes in the criminal law—both statute and case law—on the federal and state level. Cumulating indexes provide access to articles by subject and case.

GUIDES TO LEGAL RESEARCH

The following books, written for nonlawyers interested in legal research, are particularly helpful to those with no experience in using legal resources.

Cohen, Morris L., and Kent C. Olsen. *Legal Research in a Nutshell.* 6th ed. St. Paul, MN: West Publishing Co., 1996.
Elias, Stephen. *Legal Research: How to Find and Understand the Law.* 4th ed. Berkeley, CA: Nolo Press, 1995.

Fuller discussions of legal research can be found in the many books written for law students. Among the most widely used is

Jacobstein, J. Myron, Roy M. Mersky, and Donald J. Dunn. *Fundamentals of Legal Research.* 6th ed. Westbury, NY: Foundation Press, 1994.

13

Research in Forensic Science

Katherine B. Killoran

In the last few years, Americans have witnessed criminal investigations and trials that have increasingly relied on sophisticated forensic techniques to identify and analyze physical evidence. These cases illustrate the need for all individuals involved with the criminal justice system to have a basic understanding of crime scene processing, evidence collection procedures, and the scientific processes germane to the analysis of evidence. As results from these complex analyses are presented in courtrooms along with often conflicting expert witness testimony, judges, attorneys, and jurors must grapple with them.

The current interest in forensic science extends to the general public as well. Recent traffic on the forensic science World Wide Web sites and the electronic discussion list, FORENS-L (forens-l@acc.fau.edu), includes queries from elementary age schoolchildren and from teachers inquiring about forensic science material suitable for high school curricula. If this current excitement leads to more widespread education about forensic science among the young and the public at large, the criminal justice system stands to benefit. Increasing public awareness of and interest in forensic science can, on the one hand, drive the increasing sophistication of the science itself and, on the other hand, make it possible for the general population, all of whom are potential jurors, to attain a competent understanding of the science as it becomes more complex.

This chapter will present an overview of the basic information sources (encyclopedias and handbooks, indexes and abstracts, periodicals, and Internet resources) in forensic science and those allied fields that are pertinent to forensic science research. Appropriate electronic resources are discussed in each section.

Before starting your research, analyze your topic, giving consideration to the aspect of forensic science you wish to concentrate on and the level of sophistication appropriate for your background.

FORENSIC SCIENCE DEFINED

The term *forensic science* can be a confusing one. Taken in general it is defined as the application of the principles and techniques of the basic sciences to the problems and processes of the law. Accordingly, any science then can be considered a forensic science if it is applied within a legal context. Forensic science can also be used to describe the collection of sciences which are traditionally used in crime laboratories.

The American Academy of Forensic Sciences (AAFS), founded in 1950, is the professional body that oversees the field. Within the organization there are nine specialties recognized with separate divisions: Criminalistics, Pathology/ Biology, Toxicology, Psychiatry, Odontology, Physical Anthropology, Questioned Documents, Engineering, and Jurisprudence. Other specialties are subsumed within the General Division. Criminalistics is the broadest division, encompassing trace and transfer evidence (including fibers, hair, blood, imprints and toolmarks, accelerant and explosives residue, glass, and soil) and forensic chemistry (including drug identification). The terms "forensic science" and "criminalistics" are often used synonymously, although "forensic science" has a much wider scope that includes the other specialties listed above.

Forensic science is an interdisciplinary field incorporating material from the sciences, criminal justice, law, and medicine. There are three fundamental principles that underlie the discipline of forensic science: identification, comparison or classification, and individualization.

Identification involves the application of analysis techniques to physical evidence to confirm that a substance is what it appears to be. For example, when a drug arrest occurs, analysis is done to confirm that the white powder in the suspect's possession is indeed an illegal substance. When arson is suspected, charred wood must be analyzed for the presence of accelerant residue. Confirming that the red spots at a crime scene are indeed human blood can be essential in determining if a crime occurred. In each case, results obtained from these tests are matched with known standard values for properties of that substance.

Comparison techniques are used to determine whether evidence collected at a crime scene is consistent with a specimen from a suspect's person or possessions. Hair found at a scene can be compared to samples from a suspect to discover if they share common characteristics. Rug fibers found on a murder victim can be identified as consistent with those found in the trunk of a suspect's car. Evidence of this type cannot be definitively tied to a specific individual but can be said to be "consistent with" the characteristics of a known sample from that individual. More often, scientists analyze evidence by comparing it against characteristics of known samples to classify it by type, brand, or group. Paint chips found at the scene of a crime can be classified as coming from a specific make and model of automobile. Cigarette butts can be classified into type—menthol or low-tar—or a specific brand.

Individualization, on the other hand, is the principle which proves, with a high degree of probability, that evidence gathered at a crime scene could have come only from one individual or an item belonging to one individual. Individualization is not always possible, but it is the goal of the forensic scientist.

Individualization can occur on several levels; traditional fingerprints and DNA fingerprints can be individualized to a specific person; striations on a bullet can identify a specific firearm owned by a suspect.

Evidence of this kind can serve to incriminate a suspect, but more often it eliminates or exonerates suspects. Today, inmates are using DNA analysis to prove that biological evidence collected from crime scenes could not have come from them and are having their convictions overturned. Attorneys Barry Scheck and Peter Neufeld have established the Innocence Project, which provides DNA testing services to prisoners who cannot afford them. The project has resulted in the release of over fifteen wrongfully convicted persons.

ENCYCLOPEDIAS AND HANDBOOKS

As discussed in Chapter 6, reference books such as encyclopedias provide overviews, analysis, and summaries of knowledge in a particular field. They are invaluable tools with which to begin a research project. The sources discussed below are divided into four categories: general, criminal investigation, legal, and medical, which are presented in order of importance.

General Sources

Saferstein, Richard, ed. *Forensic Science Handbook*. Englewood Cliffs, NJ: Prentice-
Hall, 1982– .

This ongoing handbook is the best single reference source for forensic science. Each chapter, written by noted experts, constitutes an authoritative review of a particular aspect of the discipline. Chapters discuss examination techniques for physical evidence, including blood, hair, fibers, paint, glass, soil, petroleum products, gunshot residue, explosives, alcohol and drugs, and questioned documents. Analytical methods in use in crime laboratories, such as high-performance liquid chromatography, microscopy applications, capillary gas chromatography, and infrared and mass spectrometry, are also covered. The latest volume, published in 1994, devotes three chapters to the forensic uses of DNA typing. Some chapters are quite technical, but others are appropriate for the layperson. References are included in each chapter, and some have long bibliographies.

McGraw-Hill Encyclopedia of Science and Technology. 8th ed. New York: McGraw-
     Hill, 1997. 20 vols.

This twenty-volume encyclopedia provides broad, comprehensive coverage of the sciences and technology. The generally brief articles are written by
subject specialists in a readable style. Forensic science topics include: "Death,"
"Autopsy," "Forensic Anthropology," "Hair," "Forensic Dentistry," "Natural
and Man-Made Fibers," "Forensic Medicine," "Genetic Mapping," "Chromatography," "Ballistics," and "Ink." A detailed index volume is provided.

Handbook of Forensic Science. Washington, DC: Federal Bureau of Investigation Li-
     brary, 1975– . Irregular.

This slim handbook is published periodically by the FBI to familiarize law
enforcement personnel with the techniques, capabilities, and limitations of
crime laboratories. It is arranged in outline format and covers legal and practical procedures for collecting, preserving, and handling different types of
physical evidence. Information furnished is brief. Laboratory services of the
FBI are discussed. There is no index but the table of contents is helpful. This
handbook is a basic source that is approachable by the layperson.

Evans, Colin. *The Casebook of Forensic Detection: How Science Solved 100 of the
     World's Most Baffling Crimes.* New York: John Wiley & Sons, Inc., 1996.

Students who want to do research on a specific incident where scientific
evidence was vital to solving the crime will welcome this recently published
volume. One hundred brief case studies were chosen for their forensic significance and appeal.

Criminal Investigation Sources

These sources provide a wealth of information about crime scene processing and preservation, and the handling and collection of evidence.

O'Hara, Charles E., and Gregory L. O'Hara. *Fundamentals of Criminal Investigation.*
     6th ed. Springfield, IL: Charles C. Thomas, 1994.

This one-volume treatise comprehensively introduces readers to the foundations of investigative work, and describes the application of scientific methods to this field. The authors discuss investigation techniques for specific
crimes, including arson, narcotics violations, sex offenses, burglary, forgery,
and homicide. Now in the sixth edition, this source is a classic in the field of
criminal investigation. A bibliography and subject index are provided.

Fisher, Barry A. J. *Techniques of Crime Scene Investigation.* 5th ed. New York: Elsevier,
     1993.

This latest revision of the classic text by Svensson and Wendel introduces concepts, procedures, and technical information on crime scene investigation to the nonspecialist. A good overview of crime scene processing and the techniques used to collect different types of evidence is provided. Specific crimes such as sexual assault, burglary, and homicide are discussed. The appendix lists equipment that may be needed to process a crime scene. The bibliography is particularly useful.

Ingraham, Barton L., and Thomas P. Mauriello. *Police Investigation Handbook*. New York: Matthew Bender, 1990– .

This very thorough looseleaf treatise was created to help investigators increase the courtroom effectiveness of the evidence they collect. The treatise is divided into four parts. Part I deals with general legal principles and rules of evidence. Part II concisely covers the methods and techniques used in criminal investigation, crime scene processing, and the collecting of physical evidence like fingerprints, firearms and ballistics, tool marks, questioned documents, and trace evidence. DNA fingerprinting is covered, as is police interrogation of suspects using hypnosis or the polygraph. Part III details the presentation of evidence in court and the testimony of expert witnesses. Part IV covers the collection of evidence for specific crimes such as homicide, robbery, drug investigations, and rape and other sexual offenses. The text is replete with references that include citations to statutes and cases. A table of cases and a subject index are provided.

Grau, Joseph J., ed. *Criminal and Civil Investigation Handbook*. 2nd ed. New York: McGraw-Hill, Inc., 1993.

This 1,000-page handbook provides practical advice from experienced professionals on the techniques and procedures of investigation. Unique in its scope, it briefly addresses the fundamentals of investigation, and then details different types of investigations, such as insurance, environmental, missing persons, immigration, computer crime, and stolen art, in which forensic scientists may play a role. Chapters of particular interest deal with homicide, the investigative role of the medical examiner, and forensic investigation. Subject and case citation indexes are provided.

Kirk, Paul L., and John I. Thornton. *Crime Investigation*. 2nd ed. New York: Krieger, 1974.

Another classic text on crime investigation, this volume comprehensively presents the basics of the handling of physical evidence. Kirk explains the physical properties of different types of evidence and how to investigate them. Laboratory operations and techniques are included, along with sections on casting, fingerprinting, and photography. The first edition (1953) contains certain sections that have been omitted from the second, but are still valuable. Brief references and index are included.

Legal Sources

The sources below provide a general overview of the legal principles that govern the introduction of scientific evidence in the courtroom. Their target audience is primarily attorneys, but parties interested in criminal investigation and forensic science will also find them of value.

Giannelli, Paul, and Edward J. Imwinkelried. *Scientific Evidence*. 2nd ed. 2 vols. Charlottesville, VA: Michie Co., 1993.

Although not as comprehensive as *Forensic Sciences* by Wecht (listed below), this two-volume legal text provides more depth for the topics it covers. It is written in plain language and is appropriate for the layperson but sophisticated enough to be of use to the specialist. The first ten chapters generally explain the legal issues that effect scientific evidence: admissibility, discovery, expert testimony, and chain of custody. The remaining chapters cover specific forensic topics such as fingerprints, DNA evidence, firearms, tool marks, and the like. Each chapter gives a general overview of the topic, historical or scientific background, appropriate analytical procedures or techniques, and admissibility of that type of evidence. A selected bibliography is included for each chapter. The set is indexed by subject and has a table of cases. Updated annually with pocket parts.

Wecht, Cecil H., ed. *Forensic Sciences: Law/Science, Civil/Criminal*. New York: Matthew Bender, 1981– . 4 vols.

Forensic Sciences is a four-volume looseleaf treatise that comprehensively covers the legal applications of forensic science. It provides general overviews of forensic procedures; rules, precedents, and advice for presentation of scientific evidence in court; and information on selecting and questioning expert witnesses. References to cases, statutes, legal encyclopedias, and articles abound. The fourth volume provides transcripts of actual testimony by forensic experts. There is a subject index and a list of expert witnesses by forensic discipline. The set is updated annually by the colored pages at the beginning of each volume.

Moenssens, Andre A. et al. *Scientific Evidence in Civil and Criminal Cases*. 4th ed. Westbury, NY: Foundation Press, 1995.

This book presents the expected results and capabilities of laboratory procedures that are performed on scientific evidence. It also discusses the admissibility of that evidence and the changes that may evolve in the law because of advances in scientific methods. Intended, in part, for students of criminal justice, it is not a technical treatise. Although coverage is spotty, with some topics presented in detail while others are treated only superficially, this is still a worthwhile source for researchers. The fourth edition has an expanded scope which includes civil as well as criminal cases. Lengthy bibliographies conclude each chapter although some are dated. A table of cases is provided.

Imwinkelried, Edward J., ed. *Scientific and Expert Evidence.* 2nd ed. New York: Practicing Law Institute, 1981.

The aim of this collection of articles is to explain the value and limitations of scientific evidence. Arranged differently from the other sources discussed, this volume is divided into three parts: instrumental techniques producing numerical results, instrumental techniques producing nonnumerical results, and techniques such as hypnosis that do not result in such tangible outcomes. The editor prefaces each article with a critical commentary describing the legal problems associated with each technique and outlines tactics for introducing evidence in court. This book should be used along with sources that are more current, since it was published in 1981 and includes reprints of some articles from the 1970s. Information is presented in straightforward language and is appropriate for the general user. A subject index is provided.

Medical Sources

Spitz, Werner U., ed. *Spitz and Fisher's Medicolegal Investigation of Death: Guidelines for the Application of Pathology to Crime Investigation.* 3rd ed. Springfield, IL: Charles C. Thomas, 1993.

This authoritative treatise comprehensively summarizes the theories and techniques of death investigation and forensic pathology in a practical manner. The highly respected experts who have edited this volume present their information in an easily accessible format with little specialized jargon, making this source productive for a wide audience. The text is liberally supplemented with graphic black and white photographs and drawings that illustrate modes of death. Topics of note are forensic entomology and odontology, bodily changes after death, autopsy procedures and reports, gunshot wounds, and the investigation of deaths resulting from child abuse, drugs, or alcohol. A subject index is provided.

Curran, William J., A. Louis McGarry, and Charles S. Petty. *Modern Legal Medicine, Psychiatry and Forensic Science.* Philadelphia: FA Davis Co., 1980.

Despite its date, a great deal of relevant information for students of forensic science can be found in this ambitious text. Written as a comprehensive book for nonspecialists and students as well as practitioners in law, medicine, science, and policing, the volume is very readable. Part I reviews the development and ethical issues of these fields. Parts II and III cover death investigation and special investigations, respectively. Part IV deals with forensic psychiatry. Part V covers various fields in forensic science. Chapters include discussions of crime laboratory organization, forensic toxicology and dentistry, voice identification, the polygraph, and questioned documents.

Knight, Bernard. *The Post-Mortem Technician's Handbook: A Manual of Mortuary Practice*. London: Blackwell Scientific Publishers, 1984.

Written for technicians working or training in a coroner's or medical examiner's office, this book provides detailed descriptions of autopsy procedures and methods for the collection and preservation of specimens.

INDEXES AND ABSTRACTS

Because of the multifaceted nature of forensic science, indexes and abstracts from the sciences, criminal justice, medicine, and law can yield productive results. Some of these sources have been discussed in earlier chapters, but annotations here emphasize forensic science content (see Chapter 7 for a general discussion of indexes and abstracts).

General magazine and newspaper indexes (for example: the *Readers' Guide to Periodical Literature*, the *General Science Index*, the *Social Sciences Index* and *The New York Times Index*) should not be overlooked as important resources for forensic science material, especially for undergraduate students and the layperson. Students often wish to locate information about certain crimes or events with forensic significance. Popular magazines and newspapers usually are the most timely and productive sources in which to do research of this sort. See Chapter 8 for a more thorough discussion of news sources and check with your librarian to learn what general periodical and newspaper indexes are available at your institution.

Science/Medical Indexes and Abstracts

Applied Science and Technology Index. New York: H. W. Wilson Co., 1958– . Monthly. Also available on CD-ROM; online via WILSONLINE and OCLC (FirstSearch); and on magnetic tape, 1983– .

ASTI indexes over 300 English language periodicals in all areas of the applied sciences and engineering. Forensic science researchers frequently use this source to locate references to manufactured products or chemicals (for example, deodorants or cosmetics) when attempting to classify evidence by type or brand. This index also covers the processes and techniques often used by forensic scientists to analyze evidence. Many of the journals covered in *ASTI* are highly specialized trade publications that may only be available via the interlibrary loan services at your library.

CA Selects Plus: Forensic Chemistry. Columbus, OH: Chemical Abstracts Service. 1981– . Biweekly.

This current awareness tool is created twice each month by Chemical Abstracts Service, a division of the American Chemical Society. A computer search of the *Chemical Abstracts* (see below) database is executed to gather information on selected topics—in this case, forensic chemistry. The results are collated into this pamphlet-like print index. Topics that are covered include: analytical techniques; blood chemistry; breath analysis; fiber, ink and paint identification; arson, forgery, and counterfeiting; explosives and gunshots; and drug analysis. This source is very technical and substantial knowledge of chemistry is needed. No cumulative indexing is provided.

Chemical Abstracts (CA). Columbus, OH: Chemical Abstracts Service. 1907– . Semimonthly. Also available on CD-ROM, 1987– ; and online via STN and DIALOG, 1967– .

Chemical Abstracts is the most comprehensive source for the chemical literature of the world. It is highly technical and expertise in chemistry is necessary to use it efficiently, but it is an extremely fertile service for many aspects of forensic science, especially toxicology.

Forensic Science Abstracts. Amsterdam, Netherlands: Excerpta Medica, 1975– . Six times per year. Also available as part of EMBASE (*Excerpta Medica*) on CD-ROM, 1980– ; and online via DIALOG and DIMDI, 1974– .

This abstract is subset number 49 of the vast medical database *Excerpta Medica: The International Medical Abstracting Service.* It specifically indexes scientific journals related to the fields of forensic science and medicine. This source is the major indexing tool for this field, but it is highly scientific and appropriate only for users with the necessary background. The abstract is arranged by broad subject categories with indexes by subject and author. Searching the full *Excerpta Medica* should not be overlooked, especially for topics in forensic medicine, toxicology, and biology. *Excerpta Medica* concentrates more heavily on drugs and toxicology than does *Index Medicus* (discussed below).

Forensic Science Database (FORS). Aldermaston, England: Great Britain Home Office, Forensic Science Service and Central Research Establishment and Support (CRSE), 1976– . Updated nine times per year. Available online via Data-Star.

FORS indexes conference proceedings, books, technical reports, government publications, and over 300 journals. Coverage is international and includes forensic toxicology, chemistry, biology, pathology, questioned documents, and firearms examination; relevant case law and material related to forensic laboratories; safety, analytical methods, and management. It is a good source for unpublished documents, especially British.

Index Medicus. Bethesda, MD: U.S. National Library of Medicine, 1960– . Monthly. Available online (MEDLINE) from DIALOG, STN, Data-Star, LEXIS-NEXIS, OCLC (FirstSearch), and the National Library of Medicine; also available [Internet] at telnet://medlars.nlm.nih.gov:23 and http://www.nlm.nih.gov/databases/freemedl.html, 1966– .

This comprehensive database of the world's biomedical literature can be a very rich resource for many fields of forensic science including forensic biology, serology, toxicology and pathology, DNA fingerprinting, and medical jurisprudence.

Criminal Justice Indexes and Abstracts

Criminal Justice Periodical Index (CJPI). Ann Arbor, MI: University Microfilms International. 1975– . Three times per year. Available online through DIALOG.

The practical nature of *CJPI* makes this index especially suitable for undergraduates and nonspecialists. The *Journal of Forensic Sciences* and the *Journal of Forensic Identification* are indexed here, along with articles on forensic science from criminal justice and law magazines and newsletters.

Criminology, Penology and Police Science Abstracts. New York: Kugler Publications. 1961– . Bimonthly.

This international indexing and abstracting tool provides more scholarly coverage than *CJPI,* from a broader range of periodicals including most of the major forensic science journals.

NCJRS Database. Rockville, MD: National Criminal Justice Reference Service, U.S. National Institute of Justice. 1972– . Monthly. Also available on CD-ROM; and online through DIALOG.

The National Criminal Justice Reference Service (NCJRS) collection includes much information dealing with forensic science topics, although the database emphasizes materials that address the investigative aspect of the field. A limited amount of legal and scientific material is included. This database is especially suited to the nonspecialist. Each record provides a lengthy abstract as well as bibliographic information.

Violence & Abuse Abstracts: Current Literature in Interpersonal Violence. Thousand Oaks, CA: Sage Publications, 1995– . Quarterly.

This indexing source cumulates journal articles, books, reports and conference papers on child, women, and elder abuse, domestic violence, hate crimes, interethnic/interracial conflict, gang warfare, and sexual assault and harassment. The "Forensic Issues" section primarily deals with physical evidence associated with child sexual abuse.

Legal Indexes and Abstracts

Current Law Index (CLI). Foster City, CA: Information Access Corp., 1980– . Monthly. Also available on CD-ROM (LegalTRAC); and online (Legal Resource Index) from WESTLAW, DIALOG, and Data-Star.

A substantial amount of the scholarly literature concerned with the legal aspects of forensic science is indexed here. Since law review articles contain citations to relevant cases and statutes, they are a good way for researchers unaccustomed to legal research to locate important cases on a subject. The table of cases can be helpful for locating articles on a specific legal case.

LEXIS-NEXIS Database. New York: Reed Elsevier. Daily.
WESTLAW Database. St. Paul, MN: West Publishing Co. Daily.

The *WESTLAW* and *LEXIS-NEXIS* electronic legal databases include the text of legal cases, statutes, and law review articles as well as legislation, briefs, regulations, and the like. Law review articles and the text of law cases can be of great use to individuals interested in the legal aspects of forensic science. Both databases have natural language search capabilities and user-friendly search engines that can be employed by beginning searchers. Both *WESTLAW* and *LEXIS-NEXIS* offer access to the *Forensic Services Directory* (see print version listed under directories below).

FORENSIC SCIENCE PERIODICALS

Like most of the sciences, forensic science relies predominantly on journal literature to communicate research in the field. There is a strong core of forensic science journals that adequately provide platforms for the dissemination of research results and issues. It should be noted that forensic scientists also publish their findings in the science journals within their specialization or in the prestigious general science journals such as *Nature*, *Science*, and *Scientific American*.

Forensic science newsletters are a rich source from which to garner information on new developments and changes in the field, including the impact of specific cases and legislation. Since newsletters are often not included in major indexes, they are listed below.

Crime Laboratory Digest. U.S. Department of Justice, Federal Bureau of Investigation Laboratory, FSRTC, FBI Academy, Quantico, VA 22135. 1984– . Quarterly.

Published by the FBI in cooperation with the American Society of Crime Laboratory Directors, this quarterly covers laboratory techniques and services and is intended to aid communication between crime laboratories. Each issue is under twenty-five pages and contains one or two feature articles, but most items published are brief.

Forensic Drug Abuse Advisor. Forensic Drug Abuse Advisory Service, Box 5139, Berkeley, CA 94705. 1989– . Updated ten times per year.

This newsletter contains brief articles on the medical, legal, and legislative aspects of drug abuse. Subjects covered include physiological effects, toxicity, testing, and toxicological analysis. Content emphasizes the forensic significance of these subjects and how they are applied in the U.S. legal system.

INTERfaces. The Forensic Science Society, 18-A Mount Parade, North Yorkshire, Harrogate, ENG HG1 1BX. Quarterly.

INTERfaces presents a lighthearted look at the news and views of the members of the Forensic Science Society. Recent issues (in PDF format) can be accessed via their Web site at http://www.demon.co.uk/forensic/intertop.html.

Scientific Sleuthing Review; Forensic Science in Criminal Law. Scientific Sleuthing, Inc., c/o J. E. Starrs, George Washington University, National Law Center, Washington, DC 20052. 1976– . Quarterly.

Scientific Sleuthing Review is published by a nonprofit corporation devoted to the study of forensic science in law enforcement. Each issue contains one long article and many short ones that discuss recent developments in the various branches of this field. Many of these short articles summarize recently published research and point to the original source. Recent court decisions relevant to forensic science are also discussed. This publication affords an accessible, fun, and interesting way to stay abreast of developments.

Academy News/American Academy of Forensic Science. The Academy, Box 669, Colorado Springs, CO 80901. 1982– . Bimonthly.

Academy News communicates news and events, upcoming conferences, and employment opportunities. Activities of the Forensic Sciences Foundation, which is the educational branch of the AAFS, are also included.

DIRECTORIES

Forensic Services Directory. Princeton, NJ: National Forensic Center, 1981– . Annual. Also available on CD-ROM; and online from *WESTLAW* and LEXIS-NEXIS, updated daily.

This national register of experts lists persons and organizations in the United States with expertise in a broad range of specialties that go far beyond the fields traditionally associated with forensic science. The directory is arranged by subject, with indexes by name and geographical location. Part II is a list of organizations that can provide access to specialized information.

World List of Forensic Science Laboratories and Practices. 8th ed. Harrogate, ENG: Forensic Science Society, 1997. Published irregularly.

Lists addresses and phone numbers for forensic laboratories by country and city.

American Academy of Forensic Sciences. *Membership Directory.* Colorado Springs, CO: The Academy, 1979– . Annual.

Members of the academy are listed alphabetically within specialties and geographically by state. Officers, meetings, and bylaws of the academy are included. Some of this information can also be found on the AAFS Web site at http://www.aafs.org.

LIBRARY CATALOGS

A useful research strategy in a highly specialized field such as forensic science is to search the catalogs of libraries that are known for the strength of their forensic science collection. Listed below are several college and university libraries in the United States that have particularly rich holdings of material relating to forensic science. Each can be accessed via the Internet. Once you have located relevant material, consult the interlibrary loan department at your library. (For a general discussion of the library catalog, see Chapter 5.)

The most useful subject headings for general information are "Forensic Sciences" or "Criminal Investigation." Appendix A includes many Library of Congress subject headings that are useful for forensic science research. A significant portion of the materials on these subjects are classified in the Library of Congress call numbers, HV 8073 and RA 1001, so that browsing the shelves in an appropriate library or performing a call number search in the OPAC can be a fruitful technique.

The Lloyd Sealy Library of John Jay College of Criminal Justice (part of the City University of New York) has a strong collection of general forensic science materials, with emphasis on criminalistics, toxicology, forensic biology, and criminal investigation. Access CUNY+, the catalog of the City University of New York:

tn3270 to cunyvm.cuny.edu
At VM/ESA screen, tab twice to command line, type **dial vtam** <ENTER>
Select "CUNYPLUS" from menu <ENTER>
Clear screen and type **lnav**
[Please note: your computer must have TN3270 emulation software to access CUNY+].

George Washington University, a member of the Washington Research Library Consortium OPAC, offers graduate programs in forensic science. Access the WRLC ALADIN catalog:

telnet to xlibris.wrlc.org or telnet to aladin.wrlc.org or tn3270 to aladin.wrlc.org
Type **cats**
To exit, type **stop**

Michigan State University. Access the MAGIC catalog:

tn3270 to magic.lib.msu.edu
Tab twice to command line, type **dial magic**
Choose option **1**, MSU Libraries LCAT
To exit, type **stop**
[Also accessible via the Web at http://web.msu.edu/library/]

The University of California, Berkeley. Access the GLADIS catalog:

telnet to gopac.berkeley.edu
Type **gladis**
To exit, type **logoff**
[GLADIS is also accessible via the Web at http://infolib.berkeley.edu/ or http://www.lib.berkeley.edu/Catalogs/RemoteAccess.html]

All libraries of the University of California may be searched via the MELVYL catalog:

telnet to melvyl.ucop.edu
At terminal type prompt, type **vt100**
Type **cat** for the full MELVYL catalog—Type **e guide** for instructions on using MELVYL
To exit, type **end**
[MELVYL also accessible via the Web at http://www.dla.ucop.edu/]

California State University at Los Angeles, John F. Kennedy Memorial Library. Access the CSLA OPAC:

telnet to 130.182.123.5
At terminal screen, type **v** then **y** to confirm
To exit, return to the main menu and type **d**
[Also available via the Web at http://web.calstatela.edu/library/opacte.htm]

California State University at Sacramento. Access the EUREKA catalog:

telnet eureka.lib.csus.edu
At the login prompt, type **library**
At terminal id screen, type **v**
Clear screen
Type **e** to access EUREKA
To exit, type **q**

INTERNET RESOURCES IN FORENSIC SCIENCE

Forensic scientists, like other academics and researchers, are becoming increasingly interested in the powerful communication capabilities of the Internet. In fact, recent meetings of the American Academy of Forensic Sciences have featured Internet workshops (see Chapter 4 for a general introduction to the Internet). A fair number of forensic science organizations now have Web pages, and two police department crime laboratories [the Metro-Dade (Miami) Police Department (http://www.mdpd.metro-dade.com/crimelab.html) and the Sacramento County Police Laboratory (http://users.aol.com/LCTOX/lfshome.htm)] are using their Web sites to describe their laboratory services.

Listed below are some worthwhile Web sites and electronic discussion groups. A useful strategy for locating forensic sites and keeping abreast of new sites is to periodically access the Yahoo subject directory (http://www.yahoo.com), which has a subdirectory */Science/Forensics/* for forensic science, and one for expert witnesses */Business_and_Economy/Companies/Law/Consultants/Forensics/*.

Zeno's Forensic Page (http://zeno.simplenet.com/forensic.html) has an extensive array of links and some unique sources arranged by subspecialties such as DNA, hair and fiber, forensic chemistry, firearms, shoeprints and toolmarks, handwriting, forensic medicine, forensic entomology, and forensic anthropology. A directory of e-mail addresses of forensic experts has recently been added.

Forensic Web (http://www.eskimo.com/~spban/forensic.html) assembles forensic resources not just on the Web but on the entire Internet, drawing together links to electronic mailing lists, ftp sites, gopher sites, and other Web sites. It also provides an unofficial copy of the *World Directory of Criminological Institutes* and some valuable text files that cover forensic organizations and forensic education.

Carpenter's Forensic Science Links (http://www.public.usit.net/rscarp/forensic.htm) provides a short set of links to general forensic science sites and an extensive bibliography of the forensic science literature and many of the subdisciplines.

Michigan State University Forensic Science Homepage (http://www.ssc.msu.edu/~forensic/) is a well-constructed site that not only provides detailed information about the MSU program, but offers a directory of forensic science programs worldwide, as well. A lengthy list of links to a wide variety of sites broadly associated with forensic science is provided.

Forensic Science Reference Page (http://ash.lab.r1.fws.gov). The U.S. Fish and Wildlife Service (USFWS) forensic laboratory in Portland, Oregon serves federal, state, and international wildlife law enforcement agencies. This site provides links to other forensic Web resources and includes pages that describe USFWS laboratory services and research interests. (http://ash.lab.r1.fws.gov/labweb/for-lab.htm).

Crime Scene Investigation Page (http://police2.ucr.edu/csi.htm) includes full-text documents written by a forensic scientist from the Louisiana State Police Crime Laboratory covering crime scene photography, organization, and the collection of evidence. The page is hosted by the Police Department of the University of California at Riverside.

Forensic Entomology Page (http://www.uio.no/~mostarke/forens_ent/forensic_entomology.html). Full-text documents introduce the field of forensic entomology, including common insects associated with forensic evidence, case histories, and a short bibliography. A similar page can be found at the Web site of the Council of American Forensic Entomologists (http://www.missouri.edu/cafnr/entomology/index.html).

Questioned Document Examination Page of Emily Will (http://www.webmasters.net/qde/default.htm) is a fascinating site detailing the basic theory, applications, and famous cases in questioned document examination.

TC Forensic Arson Investigation Page (http://www.ozemail.com.au/~tcforen/) is a commercial site from Australia that presents an overview of the basics of fire investigation through full-text reprints of articles and conference papers. A lengthy list of other fire investigation sites is provided.

Experts Page (http://expertpages.com) is a commercial Web site that lists expert witnesses arranged geographically and by area of expertise. Each specialty has a varying number of experts listed.

Organizations

Each site listed below presents information describing the organization, membership requirements, officers, and activities:

American Academy of Forensic Sciences (http://www.aafs.org)

American Society of Crime Laboratory Directors (http://www.shadow.net/~datachem/ascld.html) offers guidelines for forensic laboratory management practices, a code of ethics, and information on their voluntary accreditation program for crime laboratories. An employment directory searchable by state and recent issues of *ASCLD NEWS*, the society's newsletter, are also available.

California Association of Criminalists (http://www.criminalistics.com/CAC/) provides the table of contents of the most recent issue of the *CAC Newsletter*, and links to other forensic science sites.

Canadian Society of Forensic Science (http://home.istar.ca/~csfs/)

Forensic Science Society Home Page (http://www.demon.co.uk/forensic/index.html) includes information about the society's journal *Science and Justice* (subscriptions, rates, and the table of contents and selected articles of recent volumes), full-text version of their newsletter, *INTERFaces* (in PDF format), and a long list of links to other sites.

For a more extensive listing of forensic associations, consult

Zeno's Forensic Page (http://zeno.simplenet.com/forensic.html)

Electronic Discussion Group

FORENS-L (forens-l@acc.fau.edu) is the main discussion list for forensic science. Subscribers include academics, practitioners, attorneys, expert witnesses, and students. Discussion can involve some highly technical exchange, but general discussion has also taken place on ethics within the profession, DNA evidence and statistics, presentation of scientific evidence in court, and certification. Unfortunately, this list is not archived.

To subscribe to FORENS-L send an e-mail message to

postmaster@acc.fau.edu. Leave the subject line blank. The text of the message should read: **subscribe forens-l** your name

14

Historical Research with Primary Sources: Nineteenth-Century America

What and how much did our ancestors think about criminal behavior? How did they define it? How did they dispense justice, punish the offender, or reform the delinquent? Was criminal behavior viewed by the public as common or uncommon? Did they believe it could be eradicated, or that it would always be with them? Were some people destined to be criminal? Some of the answers to these questions may be found in these titles: "On the Effects of Secluded and Gloomy Imprisonment on Individuals of the African Variety . . . ," *Journal of Prison Discipline and Philanthropy* (1847); "Crime and Pauperism," *DeBows Review* (1854); "Jury Trial," *North American Review* (1860); "Whippers and Anti-Whippers," *Journal of Prison Discipline and Philanthropy* (1850); "Increase of Crime in the U.S.," *Evangelical Review* (1860); "Juvenile Depravity," *Christian Examiner* (1825, 1830, 1849); "Gasocution," *Scientific American* (1893); "Care of Truants and Incorrigibles," *National Education Association Proceedings* (1894); "Report on the Ohio Penitentiary," *Moral Advocate* (1821).

PRIMARY SOURCES AND SECONDARY SOURCES

You can learn about criminal justice history by selecting from the many fine, recent books and articles that have been published on the subject. Perhaps more interesting is reading some of the primary sources upon which that secondary literature is based. This is not to say that every researcher should undertake large-scale historical research. But using historical sources—looking at a century-old annual report, reading the proceedings of the first conference of the American Correctional Society, browsing the magazines and newspapers in which our great, great grandparents expressed their opinions on the social problems of the day—can be surprisingly satisfying to both beginning and experienced researchers.

The primary-source versus secondary-source issue is much clearer when considering historical studies than it is when dealing with present-day research. If the item was written during the period of history you are investigating, you should have more confidence that it is a primary source; if it was written later, it is almost always a secondary source. As with research on today's problems, the closer the source is to the event the greater its authority.

The purpose of this chapter is to introduce some of these primary sources. For reasons of space, general interest, and availability of materials, this discussion will be limited to selected sources for the study of criminal justice in the United States during the nineteenth and early twentieth centuries, a time, as Professor Sagarin noted in his Foreword, of difficult social conditions and of the genesis of the disciplines of criminology and criminal justice.

For centuries the use of primary sources for historical research was limited to individuals who had the time and finances for long trips away from home, and the credentials that would allow them access to rare and often fragile documents. Today, because of the wonders of micropublication and the efforts of reprint publishers, many primary sources (including all those discussed in this chapter) are widely available, and can be used as easily by beginning undergraduates as by experienced researchers. If the particular item you want to consult is not in your own library or another library in your region, it will be available through interlibrary loan.

STRATEGIES FOR THE USE OF PRIMARY SOURCES

The basic strategy for using primary sources, either contemporary or historical, is the old adage "read between the lines."

- For whom was the document written? By whom was it written?
- All the information included in the document, whether true, partially true, or untrue, is obviously of some significance; the information not included may be of equal significance.
- The document should be examined for implicit assumptions; did the original readers know or assume things that are not immediately obvious to you? For example, decisions about how to organize police forces in mid-nineteenth century American cities were often very political ones. The researcher needs to be aware of the political undertones of such decisions.
- The document can be analyzed on two levels—for the meaning it had to its contemporaries and for the hindsight researchers can bring to it today.

In attempting to uncover the real content of a primary source, comparisons can frequently yield great insights. Wherever possible, consider comparing

- a series of documents; for example, annual reports of a particular state prison system, across a number of years;
- annual reports of similar systems in different parts of the country for the same years;
- newspaper or periodical reports about a particular institution with the official reports of that institution;
- newspaper or periodical articles on a topic (e.g., youth gangs, capital punishment, prison labor, lynching) for different time periods, or for the same period in different parts of the country;
- what was said about these topics in professional conferences compared to what was said in the popular press.

The basic publication formats of the nineteenth century were similar to those with which we are familiar. However, there were fewer publications, and most were written by and for people with less rigidly defined specializations and interests than is true today. The following types of sources will be discussed: periodical articles, newspapers, reports and documents, conference proceedings, trial transcripts, books, archives, and Internet resources.

PERIODICAL ARTICLES

Periodical articles are probably the most widely available group of sources and in many ways may be the most satisfying to use.

Nineteenth-Century Criminal Justice Periodicals

Journal of Prison Discipline and Philanthropy. 1845–1920. Wilmington, DE: Scholarly Resources. Microfilm.

Printed in Pennsylvania, this is a substantial and long-lived publication, with close ties to organizations devoted to prison reform. Although a nineteenth-century tone of moral uplift is clearly evident, especially in the early period, the general orientation of this periodical reflects an increasingly professional outlook. It contains complete reprints of many official documents and summaries of others; original articles; and reprints of articles, sermons and speeches; as well as news reports of interest to its readers. Items are from all over the Old World, as well as the New.

Moral Advocate; a Monthly Publication on War, Duelling, Capital Punishment, and Prison Discipline. Vols.1–3, March 1821–1824. Ann Arbor, MI: University Microfilms International. Microfilm.

A short-lived publication whose basic tone is reflected in its title, this is largely the work of one man and was published in Mt. Pleasant, Ohio. Issues contained original articles; reprints from other magazines, both American and foreign; news reports of relevant activities; extracts of sermons and speeches;

and summaries of reports from prisons and agencies in many states, as well as extensive reports on Ohio prisons.

National Police Gazette. 1845–1906. Ann Arbor, MI: University Microfilms International. Microfilm.

Originally, a gazette was a government journal reporting official news. The concept of a gazette as a way of officially reporting crimes goes back at least to eighteenth-century England; in the nineteenth century the term *gazette* was adopted by commercial publishers. For some years the *National Police Gazette* did contain official lists of army deserters, but it was part of the sensationalist crime press and never a government document.

The value of this periodical for the researcher is as a picture of popular attitudes toward crime and sensationalism. In the first few years emphasis was placed on violent crime and criminal biographies, but there was a gradual movement toward prostitution and other salacious topics. Occasional appearances of a police blotter and some statistics may be useful in getting a picture of types and numbers of reported crimes.

These sample headlines give the flavor of the *Gazette*: "A Brutal Assault; A Gang of Grain Laborers Attack One of Their Number; He is Beaten Unmercifully, and His Ear Bit Off; The Perpetrators of the Outrage Still At Large" (December 8, 1866, page 3); "A New York Pugilist Set Upon by Rowdies; He is Beaten and Almost Cut to Pieces in a Brothel; Not Expected to Survive" (September 21, 1867, page 3); "Audacity's Acme; A Wealthy Lady Assaulted, Garroted and Robbed of Her Diamond Earing [sic] on Fifth Avenue; in Broad Daylight; Amid a Throng of People, Who, with Her Companion are Paralyzed by the Bold Attack of the Thief" (March 1, 1879, page 11).

The journal is illustrated with woodcuts, some of which are exceedingly fine.

Indexes to Nineteenth-Century
General Interest Popular Periodicals

Many of the hundreds of popular general-interest periodicals published in the nineteenth century were concerned with issues of crime, justice, and law and order. The keys to locating such articles in these periodicals, including most of those listed at the beginning of this chapter, are these two indexes:

Poole's Index to Periodical Literature, 1802–1906. 6 vols. Rev. ed., reprinted, Gloucester, MA: Peter Smith, 1958.

Mr. Poole began compiling his index in 1848. The third edition of the basic volume, covering 1802 to 1881, was published in 1882, and is the basis for the reprint edition. Although not difficult to use, the indexing does not have the consistency or uniformity which we have come to expect in periodical indexes; use with care and imagination.

19th Century Readers' Guide to Periodical Literature. 2 vols. New York: H. W.Wilson, 1944.

Covering only the period from 1880 to 1900, this index was actually compiled in 1944, and is identical in format and indexing policies to the current *Readers' Guide* with which you may be familiar.

Indexes to Nineteenth-Century Scholarly Periodicals

The development of scholarly disciplines in the nineteenth century, and the related development of publications written exclusively by and for academics, have been briefly described in the introductory chapters of this book. Many of these early academic periodical articles can be located through use of the sets described below. Articles written during the time period you are researching can be considered primary sources if they document contemporary events; secondary sources if they describe those of earlier periods.

CRIS: Combined Retrospective Index to Journals in History, 1838–1974. 11 vols. Washington, DC: Carrollton Press, 1977.
CRIS: Combined Retrospective Index to Journals in Political Science, 1886–1974. 8 vols. Washington, DC: Carrollton Press, 1977.

See especially Volume 3, *Public Administration*, and the section on crime and law in that volume.

CRIS: Combined Retrospective Index to Journals in Sociology, 1895–1974. 6 vols. Washington, DC: Carrollton Press, 1978.

See especially Volume 5, *Social Disorganization*, and Volume 2, Part 2, *Institutions, Law, and Legal Systems.*

• • •

Nontraditional in form and appearance, these are computer-generated indexes that combine some of the advantages of computer searching with those of traditional printed indexes.

NEWSPAPERS

The only American newspaper covering the period we are discussing for which both the newspaper and its index are widely available is *The New York Times.*

The *Times*, considerably more sensational in tone in its early days than it is now, has always shown an interest in crime and criminals, justice and punishment, and has always made attempts at national coverage.

There are some frustrations involved in using the indexes for the early years because of inconsistent indexing policies and a constantly shifting arrangement of material into four, six, and sometimes as many as sixteen different alphabets for a single year. However, persistence and imagination in the use of the index will pay off.

As a daily newspaper in the nineteenth century, the *Times* was primarily a recorder of events and seems to have carried few articles dealing with problems of crime in general, but the numerous entries under specific topics such as "Murders," "Blackmails," "Poisonings," and "Assaults and Affrays"—with a cross reference: "For those terminating fatally, see Murders"—are thought provoking and sobering. In addition, there is generally a considerable list of articles grouped conveniently around the word "prison," with the entries covering news from all over the country. Information about police is most often under the name of the city rather than the general heading of police.

REPORTS AND DOCUMENTS

Annual reports may contain statistical information, narrative descriptions of conditions and events, case histories, organizational charts, illustrations, or financial statements. They may present the barest, briefest possible picture, or go on and on for many pages. As sources of official information they are frequently as interesting for what is omitted as for what is included. Information presented, and not presented, needs to be carefully assessed. As we have said, comparing an annual report for a specific institution with newspaper and periodical articles dealing with that institution for the same period can be instructive, as can comparisons of reports for similar institutions in another state, or the same institution during another time period.

The most accessible group of relevant reports is

State Reports on Correction and Punishment, Poverty and Public Welfare, prior to 1930. Milwood, NY: Kraus Microfilm, 1973. Microfiche.

Among the reports included in this series are: California State Board of Prison Directors, 1879–1930 (includes San Quentin and Folsom prisons); Colorado State Board of Pardons, 1893–1922; Georgia Board of Public Welfare, 1920–1921, and Prison Commission, 1897–1930; Ohio Board of Commissioners for Reform Schools, 1856–1913, and the State Board of Pardons, 1893–1922; and, from Massachusetts, the reports of the Agents for Aiding Discharged Prisoners, 1846–1929, the General Superintendent of Prisons Report Concerning Prison Labor, 1887–1900, and the Commission on Probation, 1909–1927.

• • •

Other annual reports, either complete or summarized, can be located through newspaper and periodical indexes. They may be listed either under the name of the institution or body, under the location, or under the more general subject. The *Journal of Prison Discipline and Philanthropy* and the *Moral Advocate*, mentioned above, regularly published excerpts and summaries from official annual reports.

There is as yet no historical series of police department annual reports available in microform. However, such reports in their original format are frequently available in public libraries and in the libraries of local historical societies. If you are interested in using them, talk to your reference librarian, who will probably be able to give you some leads.

CONFERENCE PROCEEDINGS

Conference reports have always served the same purpose: they reflect the current concerns of those people most active in the field. Criminal justice researchers are fortunate to have two sets of conference proceedings that began publication in the late nineteenth century.

American Correctional Association. Annual Congress on Corrections. *Proceedings, 1870–1946.* Milwood, NY: Kraus Reprint, 1975. Microfilm with printed index.

Particularly for the years prior to formation of the International Association of Chiefs of Police, these congresses were the forum for discussions of policing and law enforcement as well as corrections.

The index to this set is particularly thorough. The indexing level is that of a book rather than periodical articles; discussions as well as formal presentations are included.

Among the topics covered are: sterilization of criminals, political influence in prison administration, insanity plea, physical characteristics of criminal and degenerate, contract system of prison labor, recidivists, prisoners' aid associations, probation, and parole.

National Conference on Social Welfare. *Proceedings.* 1874– .

This organization, founded in 1874, has undergone numerous name changes. Known originally as the Conference on Boards of Public Charities, it has also been called Conference of Charities, Conference of Charities and Correction, and National Conference of Charities and Corrections. In 1917 the name was changed to National Conference of Social Work, and in 1956 the current name, National Conference on Social Welfare, was adopted.

The proceedings of the annual conference were published and distributed widely. In addition to the original bound versions of these proceedings, there are now several microform editions available, published with slight title variations. (New York: Datamics; Ann Arbor: University Microfilms; Westport, CT: Greenwood Press; Princeton: Princeton Microform.)

This organization had much broader interests than the American Correctional Association. Along with problems of criminality and prisons, members were concerned with paupers, public health, orphans, child welfare, delinquents, and what they called "defectives"—a term that members understood to refer to the insane, crippled, blind, deaf, retarded, and epileptic.

Each volume of the proceedings until 1913 contains a section labelled "Report from the States." This was information reported to the association by state officials. Arranged by state, the amount (and probably the reliability) of information varies considerably from state to state and from year to year. There are a considerable number of statistics, along with narrative descriptions for all the categories of concern.

Among the items which may be of interest are: from 1889, an entire section on "The Ideal Prison System for a State," which included a report from the standing committee, formal papers, plus a discussion on prison regulation and on personnel; from 1899, a section on "Politics in Charitable and Correctional Institutions"; and from 1912, a paper by Professor Roscoe Pound on "Social Problems and the Courts" and one by the Honorable William McAdoo, former New York City Police Commissioner, on "Women Offenders in New York."

TRIAL TRANSCRIPTS

High-profile crimes fascinated the American public long before the 1990s. In the eighteenth and nineteenth centuries, newspapers reprinted in their entirety the closing arguments (or pleas to the jury) of the most famous lawyers, and pamphlet reports of cases were sold to an eager public.

Transcripts of criminal court trials held in the nineteenth century provide fascinating glimpses into the court system, crime, and everyday life of the period. They are also interesting for reviewing criminal procedure, and the roles of police, prosecutors, defense attorneys, coroners, and judges at the time. While most such transcripts were never published, and have probably been lost forever due to the disintegration of the paper on which they were written, a number of the most notorious cases were collected and printed in the following:

American State Trials; A Collection of the Important and Interesting Criminal Trials Which Have Taken Place in the United States, from the Beginning of Our Government to 1920. Ed. John D. Lawson. Reprint ed. 17 vols. Wilmington, DE: Scholarly Resources, 1972.

Lawson points out in his introduction that these trials present "a record of the lives, the customs and manners of the American people." He includes cases of piracy and insubordination on the high seas, murder and prosecutions based on religious bigotry, tragedies caused by poor housing, and arson (with no personal injury) resulting in hanging. *American State Trials* includes newspaper reports and reprints of pamphlet reports of cases, as well as the actual records of the trial with verbatim transcripts.

BOOKS

Many of the most influential books published during the nineteenth and early twentieth century have been reprinted; others are still available in their original format in larger public libraries, older university libraries, historical societies, and through interlibrary loan.

If you are interested in looking at primary sources in book form, the easiest way to locate them is through lists of the reprint series. The major ones are *Foundations of Criminal Justice* (AMS Press), which includes a reprint of the 1867 *Report on the Prison and the Reformatories of the United States & Canada . . .*, by E. C. Wines and T. W. Dwight; *The Patterson Smith Reprint Series* (Patterson Smith), which includes a reprint of the 1869 *Half Century with Juvenile Delinquents, or the New York House of Refuge & Its Times* by B. K. Peirce; and the *Police in America* series (Arno Press), which includes a reprint of William McAdoo's 1906 *Guarding a Great City*. Complete lists of these series can be found in *Books in Series* (R. R. Bowker, 1980–).

ARCHIVES

Archives are the one form of material which are used only for historical research. Archives are the noncurrent working files and records of an organization, government, individual, or committee. They can contain correspondence, reports, budget information, memos, speeches, photographs; that is, anything that was either generated or received. The main principle of organization for an archive is that the material retain the same organization and arrangement that it had when it was in use.

A number of archives containing information of interest to the criminal justice researcher have been filmed commercially and are available through purchase or interlibrary loan.

Rockefeller University. Archives. *Bureau of Social Hygiene Project and Research Files, 1913–40.* Wilmington, DE: Scholarly Resources, 1979. Microfilm with printed guide.

The Bureau of Social Hygiene, founded and funded by John D. Rockefeller, sponsored research in the broad field of social hygiene, including health care, prostitution, alcoholism, crime, police, and penology. The various folders of correspondence and reports from 1913 to the mid-1930s, when the Bureau's activity basically stopped, seem to contain every famous name in the field of criminal justice: Sheldon Glueck, Roscoe Pound, Bruce Smith, Edwin Sutherland, Raymond Fosdick, J. Edgar Hoover, Thorsten Sellin, and George W. Wickersham.

Perhaps typical of the range of material to be found in this archive is folder 288, titled *Criminology, 1914–28*. It includes reports on the then current status of crime statistics gathering, summaries of criminological research, proposals for the development of major programs for research into criminal justice administration, questions and reports about the drop in British prison inmates in the preceding fifteen years, and correspondence and reports dealing with prison industries, police schools, and women police.

University Settlement Society of New York City Papers. Sanford, NC: Microfilming Corporation of America, 1972. Microfilm, with printed guide.

The Bureau of Social Hygiene was involved in large-scale national and international projects; the province of the activities of the University Settlement Society was a neighborhood of perhaps several dozen square blocks. Yet they were concerned with many of the same issues.

The University Settlement was founded in 1891. Its goal was to alleviate the evils resulting from the concentration of large masses of poor, uneducated, unskilled immigrants within the densely populated, noisy, dirty, urban environment that was New York's Lower East Side. Those concerned with juvenile delinquency, the relation of crime to poverty, and community crime prevention programs will find this archive of the correspondence, reports, and records of one of America's largest and oldest social settlements unparalleled in its richness.

SOME HELPFUL REFERENCE BOOKS

The following books may be helpful in providing a quick orientation and some background information about the period being researched.

Bliss, William D. T., ed. *The Encyclopedia of Social Reform, including Political Economy, Political Science, Sociology, and Statistics, covering Anarchism, Charities, Civil Service, Currency, Land and Legislation Reform, Penology, Socialism, Social Purity, Trades Unions, Woman Suffrage, etc.* Reprint of 1897 edition. Westport, CT: Greenwood Press, 1970.

This is probably the first English-language social science encyclopedia. The articles were written by many of the leading scholars and reformers of the period, and are useful in giving an overview of the ideas and opinions of the late nineteenth century. Many of the longer articles include bibliographies.

Farmer, J. S., and W. E. Henley. *Slang and its Analogues.* New York: Arno Press, 1970. Reprint of the 7 volume set issued 1890–1904.

Goldin, Hyman E., Frank O'Leary, and Morris Lipsius. *Dictionary of American Underworld Lingo.* Boston: Twayne, 1950.

Partridge, Eric. *The Macmillan Dictionary of Historical Slang.* New York: Macmillan, 1974.

Schlesinger, Arthur M., Jr., ed. *The Almanac of American History.* New York: G. P. Putnam's Sons, 1983.

Gives the highlights of American history in short, year-by-year sequences. Very useful for a fast orientation to the key issues in the news.

The World Almanac, 1868–1893. Cleveland, OH: Bell & Howell Microphoto Division, 1973. Microfiche.

Almanacs, because they are not written from an historical perspective, are useful for pinpointing what was considered newsworthy in the year in which they were published. Almanacs of the nineteenth century, like those of today, also contain statistics, including many relating to crime and social problems, and biographies.

Wright, A. J. *Criminal Activity in the Deep South, 1700–1930.* New York: Greenwood Press, 1989.

This annotated bibliography of printed sources—including monographs, theses, journal articles, and newspaper articles—covers crime in eight Southern states before the advent of the FBI's *Uniform Crime Reports.* It contains interesting chapters on fiction, film and drama, and provides author, personal name, and subject indexes.

PRIMARY RESOURCES ON THE INTERNET

Libraries and archives are beginning to make some of their historical collections available for viewing via the World Wide Web. These resources are difficult to find, but the Internet directories and search engines discussed in Chapter 4 can be used. Perhaps most helpful in finding sources such as those listed below is the Argus *Clearinghouse* (formerly the University of Michigan *Clearinghouse of Internet Resources)* section on "Social Sciences and Social Issues" (available [Internet] from http://www.clearinghouse.net/). Some particularly interesting sites are

Making of America. University of Michigan and Cornell University. Available [Internet] at http://www.umdl.umich.edu/moa/

The *Making of America* is an ambitious joint project of the University of Michigan and Cornell University with support from the Andrew W. Mellon Foundation. Its aim is to digitize, and make available over the Internet, original documents relating to the social history of the United States from 1850 to 1877. When complete, more than 5,000 volumes will have been scanned; as of June 1997, more than 1,000 volumes—over 250,000 pages—have been made available. Documents are scanned as images and also converted into searchable files via an optical character recognition process. Thus, for some documents, the entire text of the document can be searched for individual words or phrases. A result of the emphasis on American social history is that a considerable amount of material relating to crime, prisons, poverty, and related subjects is accessible.

American Memory: Historical Collections for the National Digital Library. Library of Congress. Available [Internet] at http://lcweb2.loc.gov/ammem/ammemhome. html

The Library of Congress's Web site provides access to the American Memory project. Found here are text and reproductions of documents, pictures, sound files, and moving images from the collections of the Library of Congress that are intended to be the beginning of a National Digital Library. Of particular note for nineteenth-century history is the Murray African-American Pamphlet Collection, 351 pamphlets published between 1818 and 1907 that relate to the life of African-Americans, including their role as victims or perpetrators of crimes.

The American Memory Collection can be searched by keywords, and a wide variety of materials can be found by searching terms such as "crime," "criminal," "prison," and so on. The collection is expanding rapidly, and should be checked periodically to see what criminal justice-related material may have been added.

"She Is More to be Pitied than Censured": Women, Sexuality and Murder in 19th Century America. John Hay Library, Brown University. Available [Internet] at http://www.brown.edu/Facilities/University_Library/publications/RLCexhibit/ shes/she_is_morems.html

These Web pages reproduce some of the illustrations on display at an exhibition from the collections of the John Hay Library of Brown University, April 1–May 15, 1996. The exhibition focused on sexual scandals and murders in nineteenth-century America that involved women in a significant way: as victims, as perpetrators, or as involved bystanders. There is little primary text here, but the illustrations are from magazines and other publications of the period, and the stories are fascinating.

On the Lower East Side: Observations of Life in Lower Manhattan at the Turn of the Century. William Crozier et al., compilers. Available [Internet] at http://tenant. net:80/Community/LES/contents.html

This Web site consists of a collection of articles, documentary sources, and study guides that was compiled to accompany a course, An Urban Experience: New York City's Lower East Side, 1880–1920. Documents include personal narratives, government reports, and contemporary magazine articles depicting the crowded, difficult, and often crime-ridden immigrant life of the time.

New Perspectives on The West. Public Broadcasting Corporation. Available [Internet] at http://www3.pbs.org/weta/thewest/

From the standpoint of the criminal justice historian, the most interesting part of this Web site is "Archives of the West," a collection of diaries, letters, memoirs, and other documents that were used in the production of the well-known PBS television series, *The West.* The archive is searchable and terms such as "crime," "outlaw," and "murder" yield contemporary accounts and memoirs of the criminal acts of that time and place.

15

Resources for the Study of Criminal Justice in Other Countries

Studies of criminal justice systems in other countries are enlightening both for the information they give about those countries and for the perspective they can give about our own country. Attitudes toward crime, as well as crime rates, vary greatly in different societies. Even within fairly similar industrialized Western nations, there are great differences. Cross-national comparisons of crime and violence are one way of testing theories about crime causation and social control.

Although in recent years interest in such studies has been growing, comparative criminal justice research is still not easy because of the paucity of material, particularly in English. What is available is often widely scattered and ineffectively indexed or cataloged. Further complications arise because methods of gathering statistics are inconsistent and because the data may be unreliable.

This chapter will discuss materials designed specifically to aid research in comparative criminal justice and will also highlight those previously discussed resources most likely to be useful in research projects of this type. Strategies for the most efficient use of these sources in comparative studies will be explored.

OVERVIEWS

Library of Congress. Federal Research Division. *Country Study Series* (formerly Area Handbook Series). Washington, DC: Superintendent of Documents. Irregular. Also available [Internet] at http://lcweb2.loc.gov/frd/cs/cshome.html

The *Country Study* series, prepared by the Library of Congress, consists of authoritative one-volume studies of most of the countries of the world. Almost all volumes have a section on the criminal justice system of the country. To find them in your library catalog, do a title search under the name of the country, followed by "A Country Study" or do a keyword search on the name of the country and the phrase "country study." The Library of Congress's Web site contains the most recent study of each country in a format that can be browsed or searched.

The World Factbook of Criminal Justice Systems. Washington, DC: U.S. Department of Justice, Bureau of Justice Statistics. Available [Internet] at http://www.ojp. usdoj.gov/bjs/abstract/wfcj.htm

This factbook, developed under a Bureau of Justice Statistics grant by the State University of New York at Albany, provides narrative descriptions of the criminal justice systems of forty-two countries around the world. These descriptions are written to a common template so that comparisons of similar functions in different countries can be easily made. The descriptions were completed in mid-1993, although the most recent data available for inclusion date from a year or two earlier. Information provided about each country generally includes a description of the political system, the legal system, history of the criminal justice system, classification of crimes, crime statistics, victims, police, the judicial system, and the penal system. Additional information on these countries has been provided by links to country profiles in the United Nations Criminal Justice Information Network (UNCJIN) (see next entry).

There is a very interesting, long introduction by the editors of the *Factbook* discussing what is meant by a "criminal justice system."

UNCJIN—Countries of the World. Available [Internet] at http://www.ifs.univie.ac.at/ uncjin/mosaic/country.html

The resources listed here were compiled by the United Nations Criminal Justice Information Network. The section arranged by country contains pointers to Internet resources such as the *CIA World Factbook*, State Department human rights reports, and the Yahoo and EINet Galaxy Indexes. For many countries there is also a "UN Country Profile," a summary of the criminal justice system of the country that was prepared in the late 1980s under a Bureau of Justice Statistics grant.

Cole, George F., Stanislaw J. Frankowski, and Marc G. Gertz. *Major Criminal Justice Systems: A Comparative Survey.* 2nd ed. Newbury Park, CA: Sage Publications, 1987.

Divided into countries by their legal systems—common law, civil law, and socialist law—this resource provides fairly extensive overviews of the criminal justice systems in the United States, England, Nigeria, the Federal Republic of Germany, Sweden, Japan, the Soviet Union, and Poland. Probably less useful now for countries like Germany and Russia, which have undergone major upheavals. There is an extensive bibliography at the end.

Fairchild, Erika S. *Comparative Criminal Justice Systems*. Belmont, CA: Wadsworth Publishing, 1993.

This textbook covers all aspects of the criminal justice system—police, courts, prisons—from an international, comparative perspective. Abortion law, terrorism, and organized crime and drugs are covered in depth as "modern dilemmas."

Encyclopedia of Crime and Justice. 4 vols. New York: The Free Press, 1983.

See Chapter 6 (pp. 68–69) for a full discussion. Many articles in this set include a comparative approach to their topics. However, geographic entries in the index are given only as subdivisions of subjects. There are no entries directly under the name of a country.

United Nations Surveys

Since 1978, the United Nations, working with its regional criminal justice institutes, has conducted regular surveys of the criminal justice systems of UN member countries. The surveys, officially called United Nations Survey of Crime Trends and the Operation of Criminal Justice Systems, collect both narrative and statistical information. The Fourth Survey (1986–1990) and the Fifth Survey (1990–1994) collected data from more than seventy countries and are the most extensive so far, including information on crime reporting, arrest, pre-trial detention and diversion, juvenile justice, prison population, and women in the criminal justice system.

The statistical data for all five UN Crime Surveys can be found on the World Wide Web Site, *United Nations Surveys of Crime Trends and Operations of Criminal Justice Systems* at http://www.ifs.univie.ac.at/uncjin/mosaic/wcs.html (described in more detail on page 214). Data sets for the Fifth Survey are being modified as member states validate the information.

Publication of the narrative descriptions and analysis of the surveys have been left to the regional institutes. Some of the reports that have been published are:

Profiles of Criminal Justice Systems in Europe and North America. Helsinki: European Institute for Crime Prevention and Control, affiliated with the United Nations (HEUNI), 1995.

Most of the information in this valuable compendium comes from the national responses to the Fourth United Nations Survey of Crime Trends and the Operation of Criminal Justice Systems, covering the years 1986–1990. The quantity and quality of information provided for each country varies greatly, but generally includes the background of the criminal justice system, selected statistics, and sanctions. HEUNI has also published individual criminal justice profiles of selected European countries.

Crime and Criminal Justice in Europe and North America 1986–1990. Helsinki: European Institute for Crime Prevention and Control, affiliated with the United Nations (HEUNI), 1995.

This companion volume to *Profiles of Criminal Justice Systems in Europe and North America* contains an analysis of the Fourth United Nations Survey of Crime Trends and the Operation of Criminal Justice Systems by an international expert working group. The analysis includes interesting cross-cultural comparisons.

Criminal Justice Profiles of Asia: Investigation, Prosecution and Trial. Fuchu, Tokyo, Japan: UNAFEI, 1995.

Discusses systems of prosecution in eleven Asian countries: Australia, China, India, Indonesia, Japan, Malaysia, Pakistan, Philippines, Republic of Korea, Singapore, and Sri Lanka. From the United Nations Asia and Far East Institute for the Prevention of Crime and Treatment of Offenders.

Comparative Policing Systems

Andrade, John. *World Police and Paramilitary Forces*. New York: Stockton Press, 1985.

Arranged alphabetically by country. Provides information on police organization and operations, as well as addresses for police organizations and security companies. Information ranges from one paragraph to several pages. Use with caution, since it is more than twelve years out of date.

Becker, Harold K., and Donna Lee Becker. *Handbook of the World's Police*. Metuchen, NJ: Scarecrow, 1986.

For practically every country in the world, includes brief information on its demography, history, government, and police systems. The information on the police systems is often quite detailed, although somewhat dated now.

Comparative Corrections

Kurian, George Thomas. *World Encyclopedia of Police Forces and Penal Systems*. New York: Facts on File, 1989.

Describes the national law enforcement and corrections systems of 183 countries. For each country, information is provided on the history and background of the police forces; their structure and organization; recruitment, education, and training of police; and the penal systems. The amount of information provided varies greatly from country to country, but in some cases there is an impressive amount of detail, particularly on organization. Crime statistics from 1984 are listed for most countries.

Prisons Around the World: Studies in International Penology. Ed. Michael K. Carlie and Kevin I. Minor. Dubuque, IA: William C. Brown Publishers, 1992.

A compendium of twenty-four articles, primarily from leading journals, that deal with prisons, prison administration, prison management, and prisoners around the world. Most of the articles are from the early to mid-1980s.

FINDING BOOKS

As we saw in Chapter 5, the library catalog is a very sophisticated tool for finding information. The online library catalog is one of the best resources available for finding both comparative criminal justice studies and books about criminal justice in other countries. The advantage of the keyword searching ability of online public access catalogs can uncover books that were effectively hidden in the old card catalogs.

As we have discussed earlier, OPACs vary in their keyword searching capabilities. The most flexible will search all fields of a book's record for the specified word, including subject headings and subheadings, titles, and contents notes. If you think carefully about your topic, and both the subject headings and the terms that might be used by authors to describe it, you can construct an effective keyword search that will find not just books about your subject but often chapters or essays in books as well.

Comparative Studies

The Library of Congress uses the subject subdivision "cross-cultural studies" to describe a book that compares two or more countries, yet book titles more frequently contain the words "comparative" or "international." If you are looking for comparative analyses of a particular aspect of criminal justice, and your OPAC allows the use of the Boolean operator OR, use all three terms:

cross-cultural OR comparative OR international

Ask your librarian how hyphenated words are treated in your particular OPAC.
Combine this with the criminal justice topic you are looking for, for example:

violence and (cross-cultural or comparative or international)

(police or policing) and (cross-cultural or comparative or international)

Truncate words if you can, when it is appropriate:

(prison? or corrections) and (cross-cultural or comparative or international)

Find out what the truncation symbol is in your own OPAC.

If your library's catalog does not allow keyword or Boolean searching, then look up the subject heading for the particular aspect of criminal justice you are studying and check under the subdivision "cross-cultural studies." Use the list of criminal justice subject headings in Appendix A for guidance.

Studies of Other Countries

Books dealing with specific criminal justice topics in other countries do not appear in library catalogs listed directly under the name of the country. Instead they are listed under the topic, with a geographic subdivision for the country; for example, "Correctional institutions—Sweden" and "Law Enforcement—Japan." To make things a bit more difficult, if the book deals with the topic in a specific city, it may be under the name of the city, under the topic with a subdivision for the city, or under the topic with a subdivision for the country, followed by the city.

If a book deals with the topic in two countries, it is given two subject headings reflecting both places. For example, a book about police in France and England has two headings: "Police—France" and "Police—England." If the book deals with more than two countries, it is given the next most general heading; for example, a book comparing the police in France, Germany, and Italy: "Police—Europe"; but a book comparing police in France, Japan, and the United States: "Police."

All this makes it difficult to find those books dealing with the particular country you are interested in, unless you do a keyword search. Hopefully, a keyword search finds the name of the country as part of a title, subtitle, or chapter heading, even if it has not been used as a subject subdivision. Of course, you cannot just search under the word "France" to find books about criminal justice in France; you will retrieve all of the thousands of books about the history of France, the art of France, the customs of France, and so forth. You must also include in your search what it is about the criminal justice system in France you are researching.

For example, if you are trying to find everything you can about the police in France, your keyword search may look like this:

police and France

or, to be more thorough:

(police or policing or law enforcement) and (France or Paris)

If you are looking for information on a country for which there is very little information available, and you are trying to find *anything* you can on criminal justice in that country, then you may need to do a series of searches, like the following:

(crime? or criminal? or delinquen? or law or police or policing) and Kenya

(prison? or imprisonment or corrections or parole or probation) and Kenya

Use the subject heading lists in Appendix A to provide guidance in your use of terms.

Searching the Catalogs of Foreign Libraries

As we saw in Chapter 5 (pp. 59–62), it is both possible and useful to search the online catalogs of thousands of libraries over the Internet. Searching the catalogs of libraries outside the United States can be an excellent way to find books and documents about criminal justice in other countries. Slow Internet connections, time zone changes, differences in cataloging rules, and language barriers can all make searching foreign catalogs a difficult and time-consuming experience; but with patience, perseverance, and even a rudimentary knowledge of the language of the country to which you are connecting, your search can be richly rewarded.

Some catalogs which you may try to connect to are

University of Toronto
  telnet to library.utoronto.ca
  at Username:, type **utlink**
  when asked for library barcode number, press <ENTER>

University of Toronto Criminology Library Crimdoc Database
  Note: This database is the catalog for the government documents, reports, working
    papers, and so on in the Criminology Library.
  http://www.library.utoronto.ca/htbin/crimdoc

Cambridge University Radzinowicz Library
  telnet to ul.cam.ac.uk
  at first menu, select **3** for Union Catalogue of Departmental Libraries
  at Union Catalogue menu, type **6** to select a preferred library
  at list of preferred libraries, type **33** for Criminology (Radzinowicz) Library
  at Union Catalogue menu again, try **5** for Keyword search first unless you are search-
    ing for a known title

University of Tubingen, Germany
  telnet to opac.ub.uni-tuebingen.de
  at login prompt: type **opac**
  at Password: type **opac**

Griffiths University, Australia
  telnet to library.itc.gu.edu.au
  at login prompt: type **library**

To locate other libraries, use the following:

East, John. *National Library Catalogues Worldwide*. Available [Internet] at http://
  www.uq.edu.au/~mljeast/

Provides telnet links and instructions for accessing national library catalogs around the world.

Nelson, Bonnie R. *OPAC Directory 1997*. Medford, NJ: Information Today, 1997.

This directory of online library catalogs available over the Internet, with logon instructions and descriptions of the libraries, contains useful geographic, subject, and other indexes, and a glossary of library terms in foreign languages.

HYTELNET. Available [Internet] at http://library.usask.ca/hytelnet/

This World Wide Web site lists and links to OPACs available over the Internet. It includes logon instructions.

FOREIGN LEGAL SYSTEMS

LEXIS

LEXIS, discussed earlier in Chapter 12, contains very extensive legal material for the British Commonwealth and Ireland, and more selective texts for France, the European Community, Russia, and China.

American Series of Foreign Penal Codes. South Hackensack, NJ: Fred B. Rothman, 1960– .

Although this series is ongoing, many of the penal codes date from the 1970s. Each volume contains a substantial introduction discussing the historical evolution of the penal code, its general characteristics, structure, and highlights.

Redden, Kenneth Robert, ed. *Modern Legal Systems Cyclopedia*. Buffalo, NY: William S. Hein, 1984– . 10 vols.

This ongoing work covers the legal system of almost every country in the world, including many of the smaller ones for which information is difficult to locate. Information is given about the historical development of the government system, current national and local government structure, political parties, and systems for reporting legal decisions. It is arranged in ten logical volumes covering ten regions of the world, but by 1996 there were actually twenty-one physical volumes, kept up to date by revised pages and sections.

Global Legal Information Network (GLIN). Washington, DC: Law Library of Congress. Available [Internet] at http://lcweb2.loc.gov/glin/glinhome.html

The Law Library of Congress is attempting to maintain a site for "official" foreign law documents through the Global Legal Information Network, a database of national laws from contributing countries around the world. The database consists of searchable legal abstracts in English, and some full-texts of laws in the language of the contributing country. It provides information on national legislation from more than thirty-five countries, with other countries being added on a continuing basis.

Guide to Law Online. Washington, DC: Law Library of Congress. Available [Internet]
    at http://lcweb2.loc.gov/glin/worldlaw.html

This is an annotated, hypertext guide to worldwide sources of information
on government and law. Although these are not officially certified as legal
texts (unlike the database of the *Global Information Network*), they are recognized by the Library of Congress as the most useful and reliable online
sources for legal information about each country.

BIBLIOGRAPHIES

Beirne, Piers, and Joan Hill. *Comparative Criminology: An Annotated Bibliography.*
    New York: Greenwood Press, 1991.

This resource contains 500 entries from the fields of criminology, criminal
justice, the anthropology of law, the sociology of law, and the sociology of
social control; with author and subject indexes.

Friedman, Robert R. *Criminal Justice in Israel: An Annotated Bibliography of En-
    glish Language Publications, 1948–1993.* Westport, CT: Greenwood Press,
    1995.

This bibliography includes more than 820 citations to journal articles, books,
book chapters, and other published sources about criminal justice in Israel or
about criminal justice by Israeli social scientists. Arranged into twenty-one
subjects with an author, journal, and subject index, this is a very useful work
for anyone interested in criminal justice in Israel; the sources, for the most
part, are readily available in any research library.

Library of Congress. Hispanic Division. *Handbook of Latin American Studies (HLAS).*
    Austin, TX: University of Texas Press, 1935– . Annual. Also available on CD-
    ROM; online from RLIN (CitaDel), 1990– ; and [Internet] at http://lcweb2.loc.
    gov/hlas/ or telnet://locis.loc.gov (updated monthly).

HLAS is a bibliography of books, book chapters, journal articles, and conference papers in the social sciences and humanities. The entries are selected
and annotated by scholars of Latin American studies. The CD-ROM and online
versions include all volumes retroactive to 1935. The full-text of the subject
headings, titles, and annotations is searchable. There is a considerable amount
of criminal justice material included.

Zvekic, Ugljesa, and Anna Alvazzi del Frate. *Alternatives to Imprisonment in Com-
    parative Perspective Bibliography.* Chicago: Nelson-Hall Publishers, 1994.

There are nearly 3,600 entries in this bibliography of books, articles, and
reports published on alternatives to imprisonment from 1980–1989. Unfortu-

nately, the arrangement is strictly alphabetical and there are no annotations. There is, however, an index by rather broad subject headings.

INDEXES AND ABSTRACTS

See Chapter 7 for full discussions of these sources.

Criminology, Penology, and Police Science Abstracts. Amsterdam: Kugler Publications, 1992– .

This simple-to-use printed abstracting service has excellent international coverage. Simply check in the index at the back of the volume or issue under the name of the country in which you are interested. Be alert to languages, however; all the abstracts are in English, even in cases where the article itself is not.

Criminal Justice Periodical Index. Ann Arbor, MI: University Microfilms International, 1975– . Three issues per year. Also available online from DIALOG, updated monthly.

Although only English-language journals are indexed, there is still much information about other countries. However, citations are found listed not directly under the name of the country but under a geographic subheading under the specific subject; for instance, "Murder—Great Britain." Although this index is not yet available on CD-ROM, it can be searched online through DIALOG, where a keyword search by the name of a country would be easy and efficient.

Criminal Justice Abstracts. (Formerly *Abstracts on Crime and Delinquency* and *Crime and Delinquency Literature*.) Monsey, NY: Willow Tree Press, 1968– . Quarterly. Also available on CD-ROM from SilverPlatter, updated annually or quarterly; and online from WESTLAW, updated quarterly.

This is another service that includes information about foreign countries from English-language journals only. Coverage is selective with fairly long and informative abstracts. Some report literature is included, along with periodical articles. The printed index gives direct access by country name and, of course, the CD-ROM index can be searched by country name as a keyword.

National Criminal Justice Reference Service (NCJRS) Document Data Base. Rockville, MD: NCJRS, 1972– . Annual. CD-ROM. Also available online from DIALOG, updated quarterly.

This CD-ROM index can be easily searched by country name. Contrary to the impression given by its name, *NCJRS* is an excellent source of information about criminal justice in other countries.

International Bibliography of the Social Sciences: International Bibliography of Sociology. London: Tavistock; Chicago: Aldine, 1952– . Annual.

This multilanguage classified listing includes scholarly books, chapters in books, pamphlets, articles, and official publications, with a subject index. There are no annotations. Although this index is difficult to use, its coverage of international resources is excellent. Unfortunately, there is no indexing by country, rendering this most useful as a source for obtaining "balance" or for finding sources to help avoid a total U.S. bias in your research on a particular criminal justice topic.

PAIS International in Print (formed from merger of *PAIS Bulletin*, 1915–1990 and *PAIS Foreign Language Index*, 1972–1990). New York: Public Affairs Information Service, 1991– . Monthly. Also available on CD-ROM (*PAIS*) from PAIS, EBSCO, SilverPlatter, 1972– , updated quarterly; and online (*PAIS International*) from DataStar, DIALOG, OCLC (FirstSearch and EPIC), RLIN (CitaDel), 1972– , updated monthly.

Both the print and computer versions of this index include substantial numbers of foreign periodicals.

Sociological Abstracts. San Diego, CA: Sociological Abstracts, 1952– . 5 issues per year. Also available on CD-ROM (*sociofile*) from EBSCO and SilverPlatter, 1974– , updated three or four times a year; and online from Ovid Technologies, DIALOG, CompuServe (Knowledge Index), DataStar, DIMDI, and OCLC (FirstSearch and EPIC), 1963– , updated bimonthly.

There is excellent cross-cultural coverage here, as the indexing covers more than 2,000 journals in thirty languages from fifty-five countries. Avoid using the print version of this index; the online and CD-ROM editions are much easier.

Hispanic American Periodicals Index (*HAPI*). Los Angeles: University of California, Latin American Center, 1970– . Annual. Also available online from RLIN (CitaDel).

Contains citations to articles in more than 400 scholarly journals published in Latin America or treating Latin American topics. Coverage includes materials in English, French, German, Italian, Portuguese, and Spanish. Much of the material is in Spanish and there are no abstracts.

PERIODICALS

There are several periodicals that specialize in comparative coverage. Although their contents are accessible through indexes, it is frequently worthwhile to browse through recent issues to see the direction of current research or to get ideas for your own research. Most likely to be useful are

CJ Europe. Chicago: University of Illinois at Chicago, Office of International Criminal Justice, 1991–1996. Bimonthly.
CJ International. Chicago: University of Illinois at Chicago, Office of International Criminal Justice, 1985–1996. Bimonthly.

CJ The Americas. Chicago: University of Illinois at Chicago, Office of International
    Criminal Justice, 1988–1996. Bimonthly.
Crime & Justice International. Chicago: University of Illinois at Chicago, Office of
    International Criminal Justice, 1997– . Monthly.
OICJ Online. Chicago: University of Illinois at Chicago. Available [Internet] at http://
    /www.acsp.uic.edu/index.htm

In 1997, the Office of International Criminal Justice at the University of
Illinois at Chicago merged four newsletters into the monthly *Crime & Justice
International* to cover criminal justice news around the world. Articles are
generally short, although most issues have one longer, more in-depth contribution. Also included are book reviews and announcements of and reports on
conferences. *OICJ Online* provides the complete text of the most recent issues plus several years of archival volumes of the earlier newsletters. The
Search form provides for full-text searching of all the publications (including
back issues) on the site.

International Criminal Justice Review. Atlanta, GA: Georgia State University, Col-
    lege of Public and Urban Affairs, 1991– . Annual.

This scholarly annual journal publishes articles about systemwide trends
and problems in crime and justice issues throughout the world. Topics may
be contemporary or historical. Articles are selectively indexed in *Criminal
Justice Periodical Index; Criminology, Penology, and Police Science Abstracts;*
and *Criminal Justice Abstracts.*

International Criminal Police Review. Lyons, France: International Criminal Police
    Organization, 1946– . Bimonthly.

This professional journal is the official publication of the International
Criminal Police Organization (INTERPOL) with editions published in English, Spanish, French, and Arabic. It contains short articles and news notes
about law enforcement and criminal investigation in many different countries and
across borders. Easiest access is through *Criminology, Penology, and Police Science Abstracts.*

International Journal of Comparative and Applied Criminal Justice. Wichita, KS:
    Wichita State University. 1977– . Annual.

All aspects of criminal justice are covered for countries throughout the
world in this scholarly journal. Articles are selectively indexed in *Criminology, Penology, and Police Science Abstracts.*

NEWS SOURCES AND PUBLIC OPINION POLLS

The Times, 1788– .
Times Newspapers Ltd. Jan. 1, 1996– . Available [Internet] at http://www.the-times.
    co.uk

The Times Index, Reading, Eng., Newspaper Archive Developments Ltd., Jan./Mar. 1973– .

The Times of London has always shown considerably more interest in affairs of foreign countries than is characteristic of most American newspapers. The researcher will find fairly frequent use of subheadings such as riots and disturbances, crime, police, and prisons under the names of other countries in the London *Times* index. The Internet edition of *The Times* contains interesting "World Supplements" for selected countries, and provides full-text searching of *The Times* back to January 1, 1996.

Editor and Publisher Online Newspapers. Available [Internet] at http://www.mediainfo. com/ephome/npaper/nphtm/online.htm

This truly wonderful site listed 1,786 online newspapers (including 1,708 on the World Wide Web) as of July 1997. Coverage is international and newspapers can be located by region of the world and country, or through a name search. Each directory entry provides a description of the contents of the online paper and a direct link to the site. The great majority of the newspapers are available without charge, although some require (free) subscription.

Index to International Public Opinion. Survey Research Consultants International. Westport, CT: Greenwood, 1978/79– . Annual.

Publishes the results of important surveys conducted by leading opinion research organizations throughout the world. Surveys are grouped into single nation or multination and, within each group, arranged under broad subject areas, such as crime and justice. Indexes are by topic and by country or region. The 1993/94 volume includes surveys conducted in 64 countries by 166 survey research firms.

TRANSLATIONS OF FOREIGN-LANGUAGE INFORMATION SOURCES

United States. Foreign Broadcast Information Service. *FBIS Daily Report*. (Preceded by *JPRS Translations*, 1962–1992.) Washington, DC: National Technical Information Service, 1992– . Also available from Newsbank, New Canaan, CT: Microfiche.
FBIS CD-ROM Index. New Canaan, CT: Newsbank, 1975– .
World News Connection (WNC). Washington, DC: NTIS and FBIS. Available [Internet] at http://wnc.fedworld.gov by subscription.

In order to provide ready access to foreign-language material reflecting current concerns and activities in countries all over the world, the U.S. government publishes documents selected and translated by the Foreign Broadcast Information Service. The material covers television and radio broadcasts, news agency transmissions, newspapers, speeches, periodicals, books, and government statements. It is wide-reaching, with an emphasis on political, socioeconomic, scientific, technical, and environmental information. Eight geographic areas are covered: Central Eurasia, China, East Asia, East Europe, West Europe, Latin America, the Near East and South Asia, and Sub-Saharan Africa.

The translations are available in microfiche from the federal government for depository libraries; some large research libraries elect to purchase microfiche from Newsbank, in New Canaan, CT. Newsbank has also produced a CD-ROM index to the contents of the collection retroactive to 1975.

The World News Collection, a recent joint service of FBIS and NTIS, offers the last two years of translations over the Internet. Subscribers can search the database using full-text, Boolean, or regional or topic searches. Find out if your library has a subscription to *WNC*, or subscribe yourself for a short period of time with a credit card.

DOCUMENTS

United States Government Documents

United States government documents dealing with crime and justice in foreign countries can be located through the NCJRS database, discussed above and in Chapter 9; and through *CIS/Annual* and the *Monthly Catalog*, also discussed in Chapter 9.

Foreign Government Documents

Documents issued by foreign governments, particularly those available in English, are not easy to locate. The best sources are *PAIS International, NCJRS*, the *FBIS Daily Report*, and the Internet sources listed below:

University of Michigan. Documents Center. *Foreign Government Resources on the Web*. Available [Internet] at http://www.lib.umich.edu/libhome/Documents. center/foreign.html

The University of Michigan's Documents Center provides comprehensive links to the official World Wide Web sites of foreign governments, foreign and international laws and treaties, and background information on foreign countries. This well-organized and maintained site is a fine place to start research on foreign governments.

World-Wide Government Information Sources. Available [Internet] at http://www.eff. org:80/govt.html

The Electronic Freedom Foundation maintains a hierarchical list of government information sources available over the Internet.

Latin American Government Documents Project. Available [Internet] at http://lib1.library.cornell.edu/colldev/ladocshome.html

This Web page from Cornell University lists, describes, and points to the many government documents available on the Internet from governments in Latin America. Included are judicial and statistical sources. Most of the documents are in Spanish.

Documents of International Organizations

The United Nations and its affiliated criminal justice research institutes publish numerous enlightening but difficult to locate documents in international criminal justice. Besides the Criminal Justice Surveys discussed at the beginning of this chapter, the United Nations has also held nine international criminal justice conferences so far. The most recent was the Ninth United Nations Congress on the Prevention of Crime and the Treatment of Offenders, held in Cairo, Egypt, April 29–May 8, 1995. Some of the working papers, reports, and proceedings of that conference and earlier ones have been published individually. To find out if your library has collected any of these, try a keyword search in the online catalog using the words **united nations**, **congress**, **prevention**, **treatment**, and **offenders**. For a more thorough search for these and other UN criminal justice documents, use:

UNBIS Plus on CD-ROM. Alexandria, VA: Chadwyck-Healey, 1979– . Quarterly. CD-ROM.

An index to documents and publications of the United Nations and to non-United Nations publications acquired by the UN's Dag Hammarskjöld Library.

• • •

The United Nations Crime Prevention and Criminal Justice Programme Institutes, in affiliation with the U.S. National Institute of Justice, has developed UNOJUST, the United Nations Online Crime and Justice Clearinghouse. UNOJUST provides technical assistance to the UN-affiliated criminal justice institutes, and attempts to assist in global electronic information exchange in the criminal justice field. To that end, it has developed the UNOJUST WWW site with links to Web sites of some of the other affiliated institutes. The UNOJUST main site and some of the affiliated institute sites are listed below. You should use caution, as some of these sites exist in draft form; URLs and contents will undoubtedly change rapidly.

UNOJUST Central. [Internet] at http://www.unojust.org/

The central Web site for UNOJUST, it provides descriptions of the program, history, and "what's new." Go to "Members" for links to the individual United Nations Crime Prevention and Criminal Justice Programme Institutes Web sites.

AIC. Australian Institute of Criminology. Canberra, Australia. Available [Internet] at
http://www.aic.gov.au/
Includes an online publications catalog.

HEUNI. European Institute for Crime Prevention and Control, Affiliated with the United
Nations. Helsinki, Finland. Available [Internet] at
http://heuni.unojust.org/
Lists publications of the institute; in the future it will have a databank of ongoing
research projects.

ICCLRCJP. International Centre for Criminal Law Reform and Criminal Justice Policy.
Vancouver, British Columbia. Available [Internet] at
http://www.law.ubc.ca/centres/icclr/index.html
Includes some full-text documents of the Centre and links to international criminal
justice Web sites.

ICPC. International Centre for the Prevention of Crime. Montreal, Canada. Available
[Internet] at
http://www.crime-prevention.org/icpc/

ILANUD. Instituto Latinoamericano de Naciones Unidas para la Prevención del Delito
y el Tratamiento del Delincuente. San Jose, Costa Rica. Available [Internet] at
http://www.ilanud.or..cr/

ISPAC. International Scientific and Professional Advisory Council of the United Nations Crime Prevention and Criminal Justice Programme. Milan, Italy. Available
[Internet] at
http://www.ispac-italy.org/

UNAFRI. United Nations African Institute for the Prevention of Crime and the Treatment of Offenders. Kampala, Uganda. Available [Internet] at
http://www.unafri.or.ug/

UNICRI—United Nations Interregional Crime and Justice Research Institute. Rome,
Italy. Available [Internet] at
http://www.unicri.it/
Provides online search access to their documentation centre.

The following two sites provide comprehensive links to the World Wide
Web sites of other international organizations.

International Agencies and Information on the Web. University of Michigan, Documents Center. Available [Internet] at
http://www.lib.umich.edu/libhome/Documents.center/intl.html

International Organizations: A Library of Congress Internet Resource Page. United
States Library of Congress. Available [Internet] at
http://lcweb.loc.gov/global/ncp/io.html

STATISTICAL SOURCES

The reliability of criminal justice statistics, especially figures such as crime
rates, varies considerably from country to country. There are scholars who

contend that crime statistics reported by some foreign governments are totally suspect. Even assuming honesty and accuracy in governmental agencies, it is still exceedingly difficult to compare nations since definitions and methods of counting vary widely.

Archer, Dane, and Rosemary Gartner. *Violence and Crime in Cross-National Perspective*. New Haven, CT: Yale University Press, 1984.

About half of this book contains what the authors call a Comparative Crime Data File. In over 250 pages of small print we are given statistics for murder, manslaughter, homicide, rape, assault, robbery, and theft from 110 countries and 44 cities, from 1900 to 1974. Availability of statistics naturally varies; in some cases (for example, Bolivia), we are given only one year; in other cases there are very complete runs available, with Chile, Scotland, and Sri Lanka having the longest continuous series. Each table gives the absolute figure, rate per 100,000, and the population of the country for the year.

Current National Statistical Compendiums. Washington, DC: Congressional Information Service, 1970– .

This is a collection on microfiche of statistical yearbooks from over one hundred countries. Many of them include data on crime and corrections. The publisher regularly adds new editions of the yearbooks as they become available. Many of the yearbooks include English translations, although the alphabetical arrangement is according to the original language. Where there is no translation, a foreign-language dictionary can generally give sufficient help to enable comprehension of the statistical tables.

Index to International Statistics. Washington, DC: Congressional Information Service, 1983– . Monthly. Also available on CD-ROM as part of *Statistical Masterfile*.

An index to statistics issued by international organizations, including the United Nations. See pages 131–132 for a complete discussion of *Statistical Masterfile*.

International Crime Statistics. Paris: International Criminal Police Organization (INTERPOL), 1950/52– . Irregular.

The latest volumes contain statistics on crimes reported to the police in 115 member countries of INTERPOL. The introduction carefully cautions the user, "Our statistics cannot take account of the differences that exist between the legal definitions of punishable offences in various countries [or] the different methods of calculation," and emphasizes that the information is not intended as a basis of comparison between countries. These statistics appear irregularly and are always several years out of date.

United Nations. *Statistical Yearbook*. New York: United Nations, 1948– .

While providing basic social and economic statistics by country, this UN publication does not list criminal justice figures. Beginning with the 1993 edition, this work is also available on CD-ROM.

Statistics on the Internet

The largest and most useful collection of international criminal justice statistics on the Internet can be found at the following site:

✗ *UNCJIN—World Crime Survey Data.* Available [Internet] at http://www.ifs.univie.ac.at/
    uncjin/mosaic/wcs.html

The United Nations has undertaken five World Crime Surveys of Crime Trends and Criminal Justice. The First Survey covered the years 1970–1975; the Second, 1975–1980; and the Third, 1980–1985. The results of these surveys are not widely available in print (some reports from the Fourth Survey are noted at the beginning of this chapter), but the statistical data sets can be downloaded from this site in ASCII, Lotus 1-2-3, and SPSS formats. In addition, information from the Fourth Survey, covering the years 1986–1990, can be read here and printed. Data and code books for the Fifth Survey are also available but the data are in SPSS format only and are still being revised. For the last two surveys, statistics were gathered from more than seventy countries for crimes, criminal justice expenditures, police, courts, prisons, and prisoners.

•   •   •

Many international organizations and governments around the world are making statistical information available over the Internet, primarily through the World Wide Web. Be careful though, as currency, format, and level of detail vary greatly. In addition, Internet connections to foreign countries can be slow and unreliable; this is definitely *not* the way to collect large quantities of statistics for major cross-cultural statistical analysis. However, many of these sites provide recent statistics on population, income, and health that can add to your understanding of a country.

International Justice Statistics. U.S. Bureau of Justice Statistics. Available [Internet]
    at http://www.ojp.usdoj.gov/bjs/ijs.htm

The Bureau of Justice Statistics maintains a comprehensive WWW page with information about, and links to, analyzable datasets of international criminal justice statistics.

International Data Base (IDB). U.S. Census Bureau. Available [Internet] at http://
    www.census.gov/ftp/pub/ipc/www/idbnew.html

This Web site offers a computerized data bank containing statistical tables of demographic and socioeconomic data for all countries of the world. There are no criminal justice statistics included, but for the variables that are offered countries can be compared in user-specified online tables or downloadable spreadsheet files. Some of the statistics come from Census Bureau projections.

InfoNation. United Nations. Available [Internet] at http://www.un.org/Pubs/ CyberSchoolBus/infonation/

At this site, up to seven countries of the world can be compared with up to four variables in tables users can create themselves. Homicide is the only criminal justice statistic available, but there are many other social indicator statistics, such as life expectancy, infant mortality, spending on education, and illiteracy. All the figures are official UN statistics and the currency of the information varies greatly by country.

• • •

In addition, *The World Factbook of Criminal Justice Systems* (http:// www.ojp.usdoj.gov/bjs/abstract/wfcj.htm), discussed above, provides crime statistics for the countries profiled.

APPENDIXES, GLOSSARY, AND INDEXES

A

Selected Library of Congress Subject Headings in Criminal Justice

There are several ways that subject headings can be alphabetized. Arrangement in the catalog you are using may vary from that shown here.

The use of a dash (—) after a subject indicates that a topical subdivision follows. Remember, many of these subjects may have geographic subdivisions intervening between the subject and the topical subdivision. If your online catalog allows, it may be most efficient to use a Boolean AND search to find books with topical subdivisions; for example,

capital punishment AND religious aspects

CORRECTIONS

Afro-American prisoners
Aged offenders
Aged prisoners
Alternatives to imprisonment
Amnesty
Arrest
Arts in prisons
Bail
Bail bondsmen
Capital punishment
Capital punishment—Religious aspects
Chaplains, Prison
Children of prisoners
Children of women prisoners
Clemency
Collective bargaining—Correctional institutions
Community-based corrections
Community-based corrections—Evaluation
Community-based corrections—Law and legislation
Community service punishment
Conjugal visits
Convict labor
Convict ships
Correctional institutions
Correctional institutions—Design and construction

Correctional institutions—Fires and fire
  prevention
Correctional institutions—Health
  aspects
Correctional institutions—Law and
  legislation
Correctional institutions—Planning
Correctional issues
Correctional law
Correctional personnel
Correctional personnel—Assaults against
Correctional personnel—Attitudes
Correctional personnel—Job stress
Correctional personnel—Legal status,
  laws, etc.
Correctional personnel—Malpractice
Correctional personnel—Training of
Correctional psychology
Corrections
Corrections—Administration
Corrections—Contracting out
Corrections—Data processing
Corrections—Evaluation
Corrections—Government policy
Corrections—History
Corrections—Philosophy
Corrections—Research
Criminal anthropology
Criminals—Rehabilitation
Death row
Deinstitutionalization
Delinquent girls
Detention of persons
Discrimination in capital punishment
Early release programs
Electrocution
Electronic monitoring of parolees and
  probationers
Escapes
Ex-convicts
Ex-convicts—Economic conditions
Ex-convicts—Employment
Ex-convicts—Legal status, laws, etc.
Ex-convicts—Psychology
Ex-convicts—Rehabilitation
Ex-convicts—Services for
Ex-convicts—Suffrage
Executions and executioners

Exile punishment
False arrest
False imprisonment
Female offenders
Female offenders—Attitudes
Female offenders—Biography
Female offenders—Drug use
Female offenders—Rehabilitation
Fines (Penalties)
Forgiveness
Fugitives from justice
Galleys
Gas chambers
Grievance procedures for prisoners
Halfway houses
Hanging
Hispanic American prisoners
Home detention
Imprisonment
Imprisonment—Cross-cultural studies
Imprisonment—Government studies
Imprisonment—Moral and ethical
  aspects
Imprisonment—Philosophy
Imprisonment—Psychological aspects
Imprisonment—Religious aspects
Imprisonment—Social aspects
Imprisonment in literature
Indeterminate sentences
Information storage and retrieval
  systems—Corrections
Inmate guards
Inmates of institutions
Insane—Commitment and detention
Intensive probation
Intermittent sentences
Interviewing in corrections
Jails
Jails—Design and construction
Jails—Law and legislation
Jails—Overcrowding
Jails—Social aspects
Jails—Standards
Journalism, Prison
Juvenile corrections
Juvenile delinquents—Counseling of
Juvenile delinquents—Deinstitutional-
  ization

Juvenile delinquents—Drug use
Juvenile delinquents—Education
Juvenile delinquents—Family relationships
Juvenile delinquents—Government policy
Juvenile delinquents—Legal status, laws, etc.
Juvenile delinquents—Mental health
Juvenile delinquents—Psychology
Juvenile delinquents—Rehabilitation
Juvenile detention
Juvenile detention homes
Juvenile parole
Juvenile probation
Juvenile recidivists
Last meal before execution
Legal assistance to prisoners
Life imprisonment
Mandatory sentences
Mexican American prisoners
Military prisons
Music in prisons
Open prisons
Pardon
Parole
Parole officers
Penal colonies
Police supervision
Political prisoners
Pre-release programs for prisoners
Pre-sentence investigation reports
Pre-trial intervention
Pre-trial release
Pre-trial service agencies
Preventive detention
Prison administration
Prison contraband
Prison discipline
Prison films
Prison furloughs
Prison furloughs—Law and legislation
Prison gangs
Prison homicide
Prison hospitals
Prison hulks
Prison industries
Prison libraries

Prison periodicals
Prison psychology
Prison reformers
Prison release gratuities
Prison riots
Prison sentences
Prison theater
Prison violence
Prison visits
Prison wardens
Prisoners
Prisoners—Alcohol use
Prisoners—Attitudes
Prisoners—Biography
Prisoners—Civil rights
Prisoners—Classification
Prisoners—Correspondence
Prisoners—Counseling of
Prisoners—Death
Prisoners—Deinstitutionalization
Prisoners—Diseases
Prisoners—Drug use
Prisoners—Education
Prisoners—Family relationships
Prisoners—Health risk assessment
Prisoners—Law and legislation
Prisoners—Legal status, laws, etc.
Prisoners—Medical care
Prisoners—Mental health
Prisoners—Mortality
Prisoners—Personal narratives
Prisoners—Recreation
Prisoners—Religious life
Prisoners—Services for
Prisoners—Sexual behavior
Prisoners—Songs and music
Prisoners—Statistics
Prisoners—Substance use
Prisoners—Suicidal behavior
Prisoners—Vocational education
Prisoners, Foreign
Prisoners, Transportation of
Prisoners as artists
Prisoners as authors
Prisoners' families
Prisoners in literature
Prisoners in popular culture
Prisoners' songs

Prisoners' spouses
Prisoners' writings
Prisons
Prisons—Accounting
Prisons—Case studies
Prisons—Comparative studies
Prisons—Costs
Prisons—Cross-cultural studies
Prisons—Design and construction
Prisons—Drama
Prisons—Finance
Prisons—Food service
Prisons—Government policy
Prisons—History
Prisons—Law and legislation
Prisons—Missions and charities
Prisons—Officials and employees
Prisons—Overcrowding
Prisons—Periodicals
Prisons—Poetry
Prisons—Sanitation
Prisons—Security measures
Prisons—Standards
Prisons—Statistics
Prisons, Coeducational
Prisons and race relations
Probation
Probation officers
Punishment
Punishment in crime deterrence
Recidivism
Recidivists
Reformatories
Reformatories for women
Religious work with prisoners
Reparation
Restraint of prisoners
Sentences (Criminal procedure)
Shock incarceration
Social work with criminals
Social work with juvenile delinquents
Solitary confinement
Speedy trial
Stoning
Surety of the peace
Volunteer workers in corrections
Women correctional personnel
Women ex-convicts

Women political prisoners
Women prisoners
Women prisoners—Sexual behavior
Work release of prisoners
Work release of prisoners—Law and
   legislation
Workhouses

CRIME AND CRIMINALS

Abduction
Abused aged
Abused children
Abused gay men
Abused husbands
Abused lesbians
Abused men
Abused parents
Abused wives
Acquaintance rape
Admissions (Law)
Adult child abuse victims
Adult child sexual abuse victims
Aerosol sniffing
Afro-American criminals
Afro-American outlaws
Afro-Americans—Crimes against
Aged—Abuse of
Aged—Crimes against
Aged offenders
Alcoholism and crime
Alien criminals
Arson
Art—Forgeries
Art thefts
Asian American criminals
Assassination
Assault and battery
Assault rifles
Assault weapons
Athletes—Drug use
Automobile theft
Bank robberies
Bombings
Bribery
Brigands and robbers
Burglary
Burglary protection

Campus violence
Cargo theft
Carjacking
Casinos
Catholic criminals
Child abuse
Child prostitution
Child sexual abuse
Children and violence
Children of abused wives
Children of prostitutes
Chinese American criminals
Church work with criminals
Citizen crime reporting
Cocaine industry
Commercial crimes
Competency to stand trial
Computer crimes
Computer hackers
Confession (Law)
Conjugal violence
Corporations—Corrupt practices
Credit card fraud
Crime
Crime—Classification
Crime—Cross-cultural studies
Crime—Economic aspects
Crime—Fiction
Crime—History
Crime—Political aspects
Crime—Regional disparities
Crime—Religious aspects
Crime—Research
Crime—Seasonal variations
Crime—Sex differences
Crime—Sociological aspects
Crime analysis
Crime and age
Crime and superstition
Crime and the press
Crime and weather
Crime concern
Crime forecasting
Crime in America
Crime in literature
Crime in mass media
Crime in public housing
Crime in television

Crime in the bible
Crime laboratories
Crime prevention
Crime prevention—Citizen participation
Crime prevention—Government policy
Crime prevention—Optical equipment
Crime prevention—Youth participation
Crime prevention and architectural
    design
Crime stoppers programs
Crime writing
Crimes aboard aircraft
Crimes aboard buses
Crimes of passion
Crimes without victims
Criminal act
Criminal anthropology
Criminal behavior
Criminal behavior—Genetic aspects
Criminal behavior, Prediction of
Criminal courts
Criminal intent
Criminal justice, Administration of
Criminal justice, Administration of—
    Planning
Criminal law
Criminal methods
Criminal psychology
Criminal registers
Criminal statistics
Criminal syndicalism
Criminals
Criminals—Alcohol use
Criminals—Biography
Criminals—Drug use
Criminals—Identification
Criminals—Rehabilitation
Criminals in literature
Criminology
Dating violence
Decriminalization
Delinquent girls
Detective and mystery stories
Doping in horse racing
Doping in sports
Drinking and traffic accidents
Drug abuse
Drug abuse and crime

Drug legalization
Drug paraphernalia
Drug traffic
Drunk driving
Education and crime
Electronics in crime prevention
Embezzlement
Employee crimes
Employee theft
Escapes
Euthanasia
Exhibitionism
Extortion
False imprisonment
Family violence
Family violence in literature
Fear of crime
Female offenders
Firearms—Use in crime prevention
Forensic sciences
Forgers
Forgery
Fraud
Free press and fair trial
Fugitives from justice
Gambling
Gang members
Gang rape
Gangs
Gangster films
Gangsters
Graffiti
Handicapped—Abuse of
Hate crimes
Heroin industry
Hispanic American criminals
Homicide
Homicide—Psychological aspects
Homicide investigation
Hoodlums
Hostage negotiations
Hostages
Husband abuse
Hypnotism and crime
Illegitimacy and crime
Impostors and imposture
Incest
Incest victims

Indecent assault
Indecent exposure
Indians of North America—Crime
Infanticide
Information storage and retrieval
    systems—Crime and criminals
Informers
Insane, Criminal and dangerous
International offenses
Intravenous drug abuse
Irish American criminals
Italian American criminals
Jewel thieves
Jewish criminals
Judicial corruption
Justifiable homicide
Juvenile delinquency
Juvenile delinquency—Government
    policy
Juvenile delinquency—Prevention
Juvenile delinquency—Research
Juvenile delinquency—Sex differences
Juvenile delinquents
Juvenile delinquents—Attitudes
Juvenile delinquents—Deinstitutional-
    ization
Juvenile delinquents—Drug use
Juvenile delinquents—Education
Juvenile delinquents—Family relation-
    ships
Juvenile delinquents—Legal status,
    laws, etc.
Juvenile delinquents—Psychology
Juvenile delinquents—Rehabilitation
Juvenile delinquents—Services for
Juvenile homicide
Juvenile justice, Administration of
Larceny
Local transit crime
Lynching
Mafia
Mail bombings
Male prostitutes
Male rape
Male rape victims
Mass murder
Medellin cartel
Mentally handicapped—Abuse of

Mentally handicapped and crime
Mentally handicapped offenders
Mentally ill—Abuse of
Mexican American criminals
Military offenses
Money laundering investigation
Mugging
Murder
Murder victims
Murderers
Narcotics—Physiological effect
Narcotics, Control of
Narcotics and crime
Narcotics and youth
Narcotics dealers
Nursing home patients—Abuse of
Occasional criminals
Occult crime
Occultism and criminal investigation
Offenses against property
Offenses against the environment
Offenses against the person
Organized crime
Organized crime—Prevention
Outlaws
Parapsychology and crime
Parents of sexually abused children
Parricide
Physically handicapped and crime
Pickpockets
Pimps
Poisoning
Political corruption
Political crimes and offenses
Political violence
Prostitutes
Prostitution
Psychological abuse
Psychologically abused children
Psychologically abused women
Punishment in crime deterrence
Racketeering
Rape
Rape—Prevention
Rape—Psychological aspects
Rape—Public opinion
Rape in marriage
Rape in mass media

Rape in motion pictures
Rape victims
Rape victims—Mental health
Rape victims—Services for
Rapists
Reading disability and crime
Receiving stolen goods
Recidivism
Recidivists
Ritual abuse
Ritual abuse victims
Rogues and vagabonds
Rural crimes
School vandalism
School violence
Securities fraud
Securities theft
Self-incrimination
Serial murderers
Serial murders
Sex crimes
Sex crimes in the press
Sex offenders
Sexual abuse victims
Sexual harassment
Sexually abused children
Shoplifting
Sibling abuse
Smugglers
Social work with criminals
Sodomy
Stalking
Status offenders
Statutory rape
Sterilization, Eugenic
Stowaways
Students—Crimes against
Substance abuse
Suburban crimes
Subversive activities
Suicide
Suicide victims
Swindlers and swindling
Teenage prostitution
Terrorism
Terrorism and mass media
Terrorists
Theft from motor vehicles

Thieves
Tongs (Secret societies)
Train robberies
Transnational crime
Trials
Undercover operations
Underwater crime investigation
Unemployment and crime
Uxoricide
Vandalism
Vice
Vice control
Victims
Victims of crimes
Victims of family violence
Victims of terrorism
Vietnamese American criminals
Vigilance committees
Vigilantes
Violence
Violence—Forecasting
Violence in children
Violence in mass media
Violence in television
Violent crimes
Violent deaths
War and crime
War crimes
War criminals
White collar crime investigation
White collar crimes
Wife abuse
Women—Crimes against
Women outlaws
Women serial murderers
Yakuza
Youth—Crimes against

FORENSIC SCIENCE

Anthropometry
Arsenic—Toxicology
Arson investigation
Art—Forgeries
Automobiles—Identification
Autopsy
Blood—Analysis
Blood—Identification

Blood alcohol
Bloodstains
Bloodstains—Analysis
Body fluids—Analysis
Body fluids—Examination
Bullets
Bullets—Identification
Chemistry, Forensic
Coroners
Crime—Identification
Crime laboratories
Crime scene searches
Criminal anthropology
Criminal investigation
Criminals—Identification
Death—Causes
Death—Proof and certification
Dental jurisprudence
Dermatoglyphics
Dermatoglyphics—Data processing
Dermatoglyphics—Genetic aspects
DNA—Analysis
DNA fingerprints
Drugs
Drugs—Analysis
Drugs—Physiological effects
Drugs—Toxicology
Evidence
Evidence, Criminal
Evidence, Demonstrative
Evidence, Documentary
Evidence, Expert
Explosives—Identification
Fingerprints
Firearms—Identification
Footprints—Identification
Forensic anthropology
Forensic ballistics
Forensic genetics
Forensic hematology
Forensic hypnotism
Forensic obstetrics
Forensic osteology
Forensic pathologists
Forensic pathology
Forensic psychiatry
Forensic radiography
Forensic sciences

Forensic scientists
Forensic serology
Forensic statistics
Forensic toxicology
Forgery
Graphology
Gunshot wounds
Gunshot wounds—Pathophysiology
Hair—Analysis
Homicide investigation
Hypnotism and crime
Identification
Ink
Lead—Physiological effects
Lead—Toxicology
Legal documents
Legal documents—Identification
Lie detectors and detection
Medical examiners (Law)
Medical jurisprudence
Metals—Physiological effects
Paint—Analysis
Palmprints
Paper—Identification
Paternity testing
Pathologists
Pathology
Photography, Legal
Physiology, Pathological
Pigments—Analysis
Poisoning
Poisons
Poisons—Analysis
Poisons—Handbooks, manuals, etc.
Poisons—Metabolism
Poisons—Physiological effects
Psychology, Forensic
Serology
Serology—Handbooks, manuals, etc.
Serology—Methods
Serum—Analysis
Soils—Analysis
Soils—Bacteriology
Teeth—Identification
Textile fibers
Textile fibers—Microscopy
Textile fibers—Testing
Textile fibers, Synthetic

Textile fibers, Synthetic—Analysis
Textile fibers, Synthetic—Identification
Toxicity testing
Toxicology
Typewriting—Identification
Voiceprints
Writing—Identification

POLICE AND LAW ENFORCEMENT

Aeronautics in police work
Afro-American detectives
Afro-American police
Aged—Abuse of—Investigation
Agents provocateurs
Airport police
Animals in police work
Arrest
Arrest (Police methods)
Arson investigation
Automobile theft investigation
Auxiliary police
Bail
Bodyguards
Bombing investigation
Border patrols
Burglary investigation
Campus police
Chaplains, Police
Child abuse—Investigation
Child sexual abuse—Investigation
Citizen crime reporting
Collective bargaining—Police
Collective labor agreements—Police
Communication in police administration
Community policing
Computer crimes—Investigation
Confession (Law)
Constables
Corruption investigation
Crime analysis
Crime laboratories
Crime prevention
Crime prevention—Citizen participation
Crime prevention—Economic aspects
Crime prevention—Government policy
Crime prevention—Optical equipment

Police—Response time
Police—Salaries, etc.
Police—Selection and appointment
Police—Special weapons and tactics units
Police—Standards
Police—Study and teaching
Police—Study and teaching, Higher
Police—Supervision of
Police—United States
Police—Vocational guidance
Police, Private
Police, Rural
Police administration
Police and mass media
Police and the press
Police brutality
Police charges
Police chiefs
Police communication systems
Police corruption
Police discretion
Police divers
Police dogs
Police ethics
Police films
Police-fire integration
Police horses
Police legal advisors
Police magistrates
Police misconduct
Police murders
Police patrol
Police patrol—Mathematical models
Police patrol—Surveillance operation
Police power
Police professionalization
Police psychiatrists
Police psychologists
Police psychology
Police pursuit driving
Police questioning
Police regulations
Police reports
Police services for juveniles
Police services for the aged
Police services for the homeless

Police services for the mentally ill
Police shooting ranges
Police shootings
Police social work
Police spouses
Police stations
Police supervision
Police training
Police vehicles
Police vehicles—Automatic location systems
Policewomen
Political crimes and offenses—Investigation
Private investigators
Private security services
Public relations—Police
Radar in speed limit enforcement
Railroad police
Rape—Investigation
Riot helmets
Robbery investigation
Searches and seizures
Secret service
Self incrimination
Sex crimes—Investigation
Sex discrimination in criminal justice administration
Sheriffs
Strikes and lockouts—Police
Team policing
Tear gas
Television in police work
Tort liability of police
Trade unions—Police
Traffic police
Truncheons
Undercover operations
Vice control
Vigilance committees
Voiceprints
Volunteer workers in law enforcement
Watchmen
White collar crime investigation
Wife abuse—Investigation
Women detectives
Writing—Identification

B

Useful Directories

A directory is a list of organized data such as names, addresses, or telephone numbers. Criminal justice researchers or practitioners frequently use such resources to contact others with similar interests or in similar positions. Directories prove especially useful for conducting surveys. Most are issued annually. This list of selected directories covers diverse aspects of criminal justice activities.

GENERAL CRIMINAL JUSTICE AGENCIES AND ASSOCIATIONS

Encyclopedia of Associations. Detroit: Gale Research Co., 1961– . Annual. Also available on CD-ROM; and online through DIALOG. [General guide to national and international nonprofit organizations in all fields.]

Research Centers Directory. Detroit: Gale Research Co., 1960– . Annual. Also available online from DIALOG. [A guide to university-related and other nonprofit research organizations. The index lists many criminal-justice-related research centers.]

World Directory of Criminological Institutes. 6th ed. Rome, Italy: UNICRI (United Nations Interregional Crime and Justice Research Institute), 1995. [Provides names, addresses, contact information, and descriptions for more than 470 institutions in seventy countries. "Criminological institute" is loosely defined, and entries include academic institutions, government departments, and independent research institutes.]

LAW ENFORCEMENT

IACP Membership Directory. International Association of Chiefs of Police, 515 N. Washington St., Alexandria, VA 22314–2357. 1994. [This international directory, which lists the names, titles, addresses, and telephone numbers of members of the International Association of Chiefs of Police, is a virtual *Who's Who* of law enforcement. Issued irregularly, it is kept up to date by monthly listings in *Police Chief.*]

National Directory of Law Enforcement Administrators, Correctional Institutions and Related Agencies. National Public Safety Information Bureau, P.O. Box 365, 1308 Main St., Stevens Point, WI 54481. 1964– . Annual. [Provides state-by-state listings for law enforcement agencies such as police and sheriffs' departments, coroners, prosecuting attorneys, airport and harbor police, campus law enforcement, and others. Information in most cases is limited to names, addresses, telephone, and fax numbers.]

The Municipal Year Book. Washington, DC: International City/County Management Association, 1934– . Annual. [This general municipal information source includes names and telephone numbers of police chiefs, as well as department statistics, including salaries.]

The Jeffers Directory of Law Enforcement Officials. New York, NY: Pace Publications, 1994. [Covers municipal police, sheriffs and county police, special police, state police, and federal law enforcement agencies. Provides the names, titles, and phone numbers for key personnel in each agency. Unfortunately, it is no longer being published.]

Scroggins National Law Enforcement Directory. Scroggins National Law Enforcement Directory, P.O. Box 945, Montrose, CA 91020, 1984– . Irregular. [Contains over 36,000 listings of law enforcement agencies in the United States and Canada. For municipal police departments, listings consist of addresses and telephone numbers and, in most cases, name of the chief. Also includes state police and correctional agencies, as well as federal agencies. Last edition published so far was 1991–1992.]

COURTS

There are many different directories to American courts. Among them are

United States Court Directory. Administrative Office of the United States Courts. Washington, DC: U.S. Government Printing Office. Annual. [Judges, clerks, and circuit executives of 130 federal courts.]

Want's Federal–State Court Directory. Washington, DC: Want Publishing Co., 1984– . Annual. [Provides complete addresses and telephone numbers for federal court judges and clerks, U.S. Attorneys, Federal Administrative Law Judges, and other federal court officials. Particularly useful for the organization charts of state court systems.]

The American Bench: Judges of the Nation. Sacramento, CA: Forster-Long, Inc., 1977– . Biennial. [Arranged by state with a plethora of information about the court systems of each state as well as biographical information about the judges. The U.S. section has information for federal courts.]

CORRECTIONS

Directory: Juvenile & Adult Correctional Departments, Institutions, Agencies & Paroling Authorities. American Correctional Association, 8025 Laurel Lakes Court, Laurel, MD 20707. 1939– . Annual. [State-by-state listings of correctional institutions with officials and brief information on capacity, population, and type of supervision. Also included, for most institutions, is the cost of care per inmate at that institution. Statistical summaries precede the listings.]

National Jail and Adult Detention Directory. American Correctional Association, 8025 Laurel Lakes Court, Laurel, MD 20707. 1979– . Triennial. [State-by-state listings of jails with information on personnel, population, and operating expenses. Preceded by statistical tables.]

PROBATION AND PAROLE

Probation and Parole Directory. Laurel, MD: American Correctional Association, 1981– . Triennial. [Organizational, personnel, and statistical information on more than 760 departments, boards, and courts.]

Directory of United States Probation and Pretrial Services Officers. Washington, DC: Probation and Pretrial Services Division, Administrative Office of the United States Courts, 1989– . Irregular. [Lists personnel, with addresses and phone numbers, by region, for the vast federal probation and pretrial services division.]

LAW

Martindale-Hubbell Law Directory. New York: Martindale-Hubbell Law Directory, Inc., 1931– . Annual. Also available on CD-ROM; online from LEXIS-NEXIS; and [Internet] at http://www.martindale.com/locator/home.html [Comprehensive listings of 900,000 lawyers in the United States, its possessions, and Canada, as well as numerous lawyers and law firms abroad.]

Law and Legal Information Directory. Detroit, MI: Gale Research, 1980– . Biennial. [A comprehensive directory of organizations, courts, regulatory agencies, law schools, legal information, scholarships, grants, awards, and information sources.]

West's Legal Directory. St. Paul, MN: West Publishing Co. Online from WESTLAW. Also available [Internet] at http://www.wld.com/ [Provides information about law firms, government offices, corporate law offices, and lawyers in the United States and Canada, with searching capability by name and type of law practiced.]

INFORMATION SOURCES AND EDUCATION

Directory of Criminal Justice Information Sources. 9th ed. Washington, DC: U.S. Dept. of Justice, Office of Justice Programs, National Institute of Justice, 1994. [Directory of libraries and information services of criminal-justice-related academic, research, and social service agencies.]

World Criminal Justice Library Network Directory. Comp. John Myrtle. Available [Internet] at http://info.rutgers.edu/newark/WCJLEN/intlib2.txt [Worldwide listing of libraries with criminal justice specializations.]

Anderson's Directory of Criminal Justice Education. 2nd ed. Cincinnati, OH: Anderson Publishing Co., 1991. [Lists criminal justice programs in higher education. Arranged by state, provides information on type of programs, numbers of students and degrees awarded, personnel, course offerings, and so forth. Ceased publication with the second edition, but is still useful.]

C

Selected Major Criminal Justice Commission Reports

Criminal justice commission reports offer insights into the social, political, and economic tenor of the times. They present an overview of a major criminal justice problem and make specific recommendations. Thus, commission reports provide important information and marvelous background reading for the criminal justice researcher.

Important as these reports are, their publication patterns tend to be confusing when they include interim reports, subreports, field studies, summary reports, and final reports. Access is often equally convoluted, since listings in bibliographies and catalogs are not always consistent. Therefore, the following list includes both the SuDocs call numbers (for national commission reports) and the popular names of the commissions with the hope that this information will simplify the finding process. Popular names are usually derived from the name of the person chairing the group.

You will find this title helpful in identifying national commission reports:

Bernier, Bernard A., and Karen A. Wood. *Popular Names of U.S. Government Reports*. Washington, DC: Library of Congress, 1984.

1931 Wickersham Commission

U.S. National Commission on Law Observance and Enforcement. *Reports*. 14 vols. Washington, DC: U.S. Government Printing Office, 1931. Reprint. Montclair, NJ: Patterson Smith, 1968. (Y3:N21/7:5/#)

Valuable primary and secondary material on the social history of the United States is contained in fourteen reports on prohibition; enforcement of prohibition laws; criminal statistics; prosecution; deportation laws; child offenders; federal courts; criminal procedure; penal institutions, probation, and parole; crime and the foreign born; lawlessness in law enforcement; cost of crime; causes of crime; and police. The final volume is *The Mooney Billings Report* (on unfairness in prosecution), which was submitted to the commission but was not released by it. Commission chaired by George Woodward Wickersham.

1967 Katzenbach Report

U.S. President's Commission on Law Enforcement and Administration of Justice. *Challenge of Crime in a Free Society.* Washington, DC: U.S. Government Printing Office, 1967. (PR 36.8:L41/#)

This indexed report surveys crime and its causes and prevention in the United States, and includes statistics. Chapter headings are: "Crime in America," "Juvenile Delinquency and Youth Crime," "Police Courts," "Corrections," "Organized Crime," "Narcotics and Drug Abuse," "Drunkenness Offenses," "Control of Firearms," "Science and Technology," "Research-Instrument for Reform," and "National Strategy."

The commission, chaired by Nicholas DeBelleville Katzenbach, also published Task Force Reports, which include statistics and references: *The Police, The Courts, Corrections, Juvenile Delinquency and Youth Crime, Organized Crime, Science and Technology, Assessment of Crime, Narcotics and Drugs,* and *Drunkenness.*

Field surveys supporting the commission's findings are: *Report on a Pilot Study in the District of Columbia on Victimization and Attitudes Toward Law Enforcement, Criminal Victimization in the U.S., Studies in Crime and Law Enforcement in the Major Metropolitan Areas, Police in the Community,* and *National Survey of Police and Community Relations.*

1968 Kerner Commission

U.S. National Advisory Commission on Civil Disorders. *Report.* Washington, DC: U.S. Government Printing Office, 1968. (PR 36.8:C49/#)

This report covers causes, events, and aftermaths of the civil disorders of 1963 to 1967. It includes recommendations for improving social conditions that foment riots; city-by-city discussion of disorders; and considerations of the administration of justice under emergency conditions. It is fully indexed and has useful statistics. Commission chaired by Otto Kerner.

1969 Eisenhower Reports

U.S. National Commission on the Causes and Prevention of Violence. *To Establish Justice, to Insure Domestic Tranquility.* Washington, DC: U.S. Government Printing Office, 1969. (PR 36.8:V81/#)

This commission emphasized the historical and sociological aspects in carrying out its mission to determine the causes of violence in the United States and to find methods of prevention. Commission chaired by Milton Stover Eisenhower.

Its thirteen-volume *NCCPV Staff Study Series* includes *Task Force Reports* and *Special Investigative Reports*:

vols. 1, 2	*Violence in America: Historical and Comparative Perspectives* (Graham Report)
vol. 3	*Politics of Protest* (Skolnick Report)
vol. 4	*Rights in Concord*
vol. 5	*Shoot-out in Cleveland: Black Militants and the Police*
vol. 6	*Shut It Down: College in Crisis, San Francisco State*
vol. 7	*Firearms and Violence in American Life*
vol. 8	*Assassination and Political Violence*
vol. 9	*Mass Media and Violence*
vol. 9a	*Hearings*
vol. 10	*Law and Order Reconsidered*
vols. 11, 12, 13	*Crimes of Violence*

Volumes 4, 5, and 6 above and the following two titles comprise the *Special Investigative Reports*: (1) *Rights in Conflict: The Violent Confrontation of Demonstrators and Police in the Parks and Streets of Chicago During the Week of the Democratic National Convention of 1968* (Walker Report); and (2) *Miami Report: Civil Disturbances in Miami, Fla. During the Week of August 5, 1968.*

1970 Lockhart Reports

U.S. Commission on Obscenity and Pornography. *Report.* Washington, DC: U.S. Government Printing Office, 1970–1971. (Y3.0b7:#)

Established in 1967, the commission studied the constitutional and definitional problems relating to obscenity controls, traffic in the distribution of obscene and pornographic materials, the effects of such material (particularly on youth), and their relationship to crime and antisocial behavior. Some findings proved highly controversial. Commission chaired by William B. Lockhart.

Technical reports include: *Preliminary Studies; Legal Analysis; Marketplace, Industry; Marketplace, Empirical Studies; Societal Control Mechanisms; National Survey; Erotica and Antisocial Behavior; Erotica and Social Behavior;* and *Consumer and the Community.*

1970 Scranton Report

U.S. President's Commission on Campus Unrest. *Report.* Washington, DC: U.S. Government Printing Office, 1970. (PR37.8:C15/R29)

Special coverage of Kent State and Jackson State Universities is included in this overview of campus unrest during the 1960s. It contains an extensive bibliography. Commission chaired by William W. Scranton.

1972 Knapp Commission

New York (NY). Knapp Commission. *Commission Report:* (*with Summary and Principal Recommendations,* issued August 3, 1972). New York: The Commission, 1972. Reprint. New York: G. Braziller, 1973.

The official name of this New York City commission was the "Commission to Investigate Allegations of Police Corruption and the City's Anti-Corruption Procedures." Some of the events that led to the formation of this commission became the basis of the book and the movie *Serpico.* Commission chaired by Whitman Knapp.

1973 Shafer Report

U.S. National Commission on Marihuana and Drug Abuse. *Drug Use in America: Problem in Perspective.* Washington, DC: U.S. Government Printing Office, 1973. (Y3:M33/2:#)

Its first report entitled *Marihuana: A Signal of Misunderstanding*, includes a separate appendix volume.

The second and final report examines the roots of the drug problem and suggests ways of reducing its impact. Four volumes note the *Patterns and Consequences of Drug Use, Social Responses to Drug Use, The Legal System and Drug Control,* and *Treatment and Rehabilitation.* Commission chaired by Raymond Philip Shafer.

1973 Peterson Report

U.S. National Advisory Commission on Criminal Justice Standards and Goals. *Reports.* Washington, DC: U.S. Government Printing Office, 1973. (Y3 C86:2C#)

Regarded as the successor of the 1967 President's Commission on Law Enforcement and Administration of Justice, this commission prepared recommendations for crime reduction and prevention on the state and local level. Commission chaired by Russell W. Peterson.

An overview of commission work is given in *A National Strategy to Reduce Crime.* Standards and goals were recommended for these areas: *Community Crime Prevention, Corrections, Courts, Criminal Justice System, Police* and *Juvenile Justice.*

Other reports from this commission include

Executive Summary: Reports of the National Advisory Commission on Criminal Justice Standards and Goals, 1974.
Proceedings of the National Conference on Criminal Justice, Washington, DC, 1973, 1976.
A Call for Citizen Action: Crime Prevention and the Citizen, 1974.

1975

U.S. National Advisory Committee on Criminal Justice Standards and Goals. *Reports*. Washington, DC: U.S. Government Printing Office, 1976. (Y3.C86:2#)

Continuing the commission's work, the committee, chaired by Brendan T. Byrne, published Task Force Reports intended for the policy maker. Reports deal with: *Criminal Justice Research and Development, Disorders and Terrorism, Juvenile Justice and Delinquency Prevention, Organized Crime, Police Chief Executive*, and *Private Security*.

1976

U.S. Commission on the Review of the National Policy Toward Gambling. *Gambling in America*. Washington, DC: U.S. Government Printing Office, 1976. (Y3.G14:1/976–2)

The first national commission to deal with the complex legal, economic, political, and sociological aspects of gambling issued two interim reports previous to this final report. The Commission's charge was to examine the laws and customs that govern gambling and to draft uniform guidelines for all levels of government in developing statutory and administrative policies. The report is accompanied by three appendixes: (1) Staff and Consultant Papers, Model Statistics, Bibliography, Correspondence; (2) Survey of American Gambling Attitudes and Behavior; and (3) Summary of Commission Hearings. Commission chaired by Charles H. Morin.

1984

United States Attorney General's Task Force on Family Violence. *Final Report*. Washington, DC: U.S. Government Printing Office, 1984. (J1.2:F21/2)

The Task Force identifies various social complexities of family violence, and then discusses recommendations for ameliorative action. Commission chaired by Chief William L. Hart.

1986 Meese Commission

United States. Attorney General's Commission on Pornography. *Final Report*. Washington, DC: U.S. Government Printing Office, 1986. (J1.2:P82/v.1–2).

This year-long commission examined pornography from many different aspects: the history of pornography, first amendment constraints, the pornography industry, the question of the harm that may be caused by pornography, the difficulty of enforcement, and child pornography. The chair was Henry E. Hudson, but the commission became known as the Meese Commission after the Attorney General to whom it reported, Edwin Meese III.

1991 Christopher Commission

Independent Commission on the Los Angeles Police Department. *Report*. Los Angeles: The Commission, 1991.

This independent commission was formed in the wake of the videotaped beating of Rodney King by uniformed Los Angeles Police Department officers. Its specific mission was to evaluate and reform police procedures involving the use of force. The complete report includes a supplement, "Selected messages from the LAPD digital terminal system, November 1, 1989–March 4, 1991," and has been reproduced as part of the *Current Urban Documents* microfiche collection (fiche no. LSCA 0476). The chairman was Warren Christopher.

1993 Mollen Commission

New York (NY). Commission to Investigate Allegations of Police Corruption and the Anti-Corruption Procedures of the New York City Police Department. *Interim Report and Principal Recommendations*. New York: The Commission, 1993. *Commission Report*. New York: The Commission, 1994.

Twenty years after the Knapp Commission, police corruption was again news in New York City. This commission, chaired by Milton Mollen, was formed to investigate and make recommendations.

Glossary

Adobe Acrobat   software developed by the Adobe company that enables the computer screen to display an exact replica of a printed page.

ASCII   (American Standard Code for Information Interchange) a computer standard that limits the characters in a computer file to those that appear on a computer keyboard. This standardization, although it eliminates colors, italics, boldface, or other markings, permits a file "in ASCII" to appear legibly on any computer screen, regardless of what software the computer is running, or even if the screen is part of a "dumb" **terminal** that cannot run any software.

bookmark   a method, using the Netscape WWW browser, of storing a **URL** so that a user can return to a **World Wide Web** page later without retyping the address.

Boolean   originally Boolean algebra, took its name from the mathematician George Boole. It is one of the cornerstones of logic. Boolean logic evaluates the truth of an expression to decide whether an element (a number, letter, bibliographic citation) belongs in a set; *see* **Boolean operators** and Chapter 3.

Boolean operators   the words AND, OR, XOR, and NOT in Boolean searching. AND means that both words in a field or record must be present; OR means that either word can be present; XOR means that one word or the other, but not both, must be present; NOT means that the first word but not the second must be present.

browsable   a characteristic of a document, **database**, or other information source where the contents can be viewed sequentially, usually in alphabetical order; for example, a library catalog in which all the works of an author can be viewed alphabetically by scrolling through display screens or flipping through catalog cards.

browser   a program, such as Netscape Navigator or Microsoft Internet Explorer, that enables a user to read **hypertext** on the **World Wide Web**.

CARL   originally the Colorado Alliance of Research Libraries; now a company, owned by Knight-Ridder, that specializes in online library catalogs, **document delivery**, and online search services through the Internet.

CitaDel a service of **RLIN** that provides online searching of bibliographic **databases**, primarily indexes and abstracts, over the Internet.

client–server a form of distributed computer system in which software is split between **server** tasks and client tasks; a client sends requests to a **server**, according to some protocol, asking for information or action, and the server responds; used by **gopher**, **telnet**, and the **World Wide Web**.

database a structured set of computerized data (e.g., an online catalog or a large collection of bibliographic citations from an index); information is frequently arranged into **fields** and **records**.

DataStar a company, owned by Knight-Ridder, that provides **online** bibliographic **databases** for remote searching by dial-up telephone lines or over the Internet; popular in Europe.

descriptor a term that describes the subject content of a bibliographic work (i.e., a book or journal article); sometimes called a subject heading.

DIALOG a company, owned by Knight-Ridder, that provides **online** bibliographic **databases** for remote searching by dial-up telephone lines or over the Internet.

DIMDI a company that provides **online** bibliographic **databases** for remote searching, primarily in Europe.

discussion list an extension of electronic mail whereby a message sent to the discussion list is automatically distributed to all members who have signed up, or subscribed, to the list; *see also* **LISTSERV**.

document delivery a service, usually provided by private companies, that sends documents, primarily articles, to researchers for a fee. Delivery may be by fax, overnight mail, or electronic mail file, and is usually faster and less difficult (though more expensive) for researchers than standard interlibrary loan services.

domain name an official Internet name for an organization (e.g., loc.gov, the domain name of the Library of Congress).

domain name server a computer that matches Internet domain names with the **IP addresses** assigned to particular computers.

dumb terminal *see* **terminal**.

EBSCO a library company that distributes bibliographic **databases** on CD-ROM and over the Internet; also provides **full-text** or **full-image** information.

e-mail electronic mail; a noninteractive method of exchanging messages over a computer network, often the Internet.

emulation having a computer pretend to be another machine; for example, **terminal emulation** software enables a PC to act like a dumb **terminal** when interacting with another, often larger computer.

end-user searching the searching of bibliographic **databases** by untrained users, with software designed for the purpose.

EPIC a collection of online bibliographic **databases** from **OCLC** designed to be searched by trained (usually librarian) searchers.

field in a computer **database**, part of a **record** designed to hold a particular type of information; for example, a bibliographic database typically contains author fields, title fields, and so forth.

FirstSearch a collection of **online** bibliographic **databases** from **OCLC** available for **end-user searching**.

ftp (file transfer protocol) a computer protocol that enables a computer file to be transferred intact from one computer to another, usually over the Internet.

full-image an exact replica of a printed page displayed on a computer screen; the text on the page is usually not searchable.

full-text the entire text of an article, book, encyclopedia, or similar work available in computerized form for reading or keyword searching.

gopher document retrieval system for the Internet that began as a campus-wide information system at the University of Minnesota; enables documents to be organized into a series of menus; documents may be stored on the same **server** computer as the menu or on another.

hit a record (e.g., citation, article, WWW site) retrieved by a computer search.

HTML (HyperText Markup Language) used on the **World Wide Web** for formatting documents into attractive displays and for embedding graphics and **links** to other documents or files; *see* **hypertext**.

http (hypertext transfer protocol) the client–server protocol used on the **World Wide Web** for the exchange of **HTML** documents.

hypertext a method of linking computer files nonlinearly, at relevant points in the documents or files.

IAC (Information Access Corporation) a company that provides bibliographic **databases** to libraries on CD-ROM, and over the Internet; now also provides **links** to **full-text** files.

Internet *see* Chapter 4.

Internet Service Provider a company that provides a connection to the Internet, either for individuals dialing in from home, or for local area networks.

IP address a number that uniquely identifies a computer on the Internet.

keyword searching the ability to search for individual words in a text file or in a **database**.

Knowledge Index a set of bibliographic **databases** available for **end-user searching** through CompuServe.

LEXIS-NEXIS a collection of **full-text** legal and news files, searchable by both trained users and end-users; developed by Mead Data Central; now a division of Reed Elsevier Inc.

links words or icons (symbols) in a document that provide **hypertext** connections to other documents.

LISTSERV software that manages **discussion lists**; sometimes used as a synonym for discussion list.

mediated search a computer search performed for a library patron by someone trained in the techniques of the particular search service.

natural language searching a method of finding information in a **database** that does not require the user to have knowledge of jargon or methods of expression unique to the **search engine**. Its commands can be expressed in the language of common speech, like English.

Netscape Navigator one of the most popular WWW browsers; developed by Netscape Communications Corporation.

OCLC a company, based in Ohio, that provides shared cataloging services to libraries; also provides online bibliographic **databases** for searching by end-users (FirstSearch) or trained intermediaries (EPIC).

online generally an interactive (as opposed to "batch") connection to a computer; specifically, in this book, when a **database** is available online it resides on a large computer that can be searched remotely and without delay via telephone lines or the Internet.

Ovid Technologies a company that provides bibliographic **databases** on CD-ROM, **online**, or on magnetic tape; originally specialized in very large bibliographic files with sophisticated search capabilities.

PDF (Portable Document Format) a standard for computerized document files, defined by Adobe, that enables the text and graphics of the document to be displayed on the computer exactly as they appear on the printed page.

phrase searching searching two or more words together as a connected phrase.

positional operators *see* **proximity operators**.

protocol a set of formal rules describing how to transmit data, especially across a network.

proximity operators words that describe the physical relationship between two words in a computer search; for example, ADJ usually means that the two words must be directly adjacent and in the order specified; NEAR usually means the words must be adjacent but can be in any order (e.g., **online search** or **search online**); other possible operators are WITH and SAME.

record typically an organized group of **fields** to define a single entity; in a bibliographic **database** a record contains all the elements (or **fields**) that define a book or article—author, title, date, and so on.

relational operators *see* **proximity operators**.

relevance feedback a system for searching **databases** (primarily text) whereby the successful results of one search become the query for the next; used by **WAIS**.

RLIN   (Research Libraries Information Network) a computer service originally developed by the Research Libraries Group (RLG) for shared cataloging; also provides access to **CitaDel** bibliographic **databases** (primarily indexes and abstracts).

search engine computer software, or combination of software and hardware, for **keyword searching**; also a remotely accessible program that lets you do keyword searches for information on the Internet.

search software software for keyword searching; *see* Chapter 3.

searchable a characteristic of a document, **database**, or computer system that makes it possible to retrieve individual words (or data) and to display them in their context.

server a computer that stores information and makes it available on a network; also a computer program that exchanges information with a compatible client program running on another computer.

SilverPlatter a company formed to provide bibliographic **databases** on CD-ROM to libraries; now also provides online services over the Internet.

telnet Internet standard protocol allowing users of one computer to log into another computer; usually assumes **emulation** of a Digital Equipment Corporation model vt100 terminal.

terminal sometimes "dumb terminal"; computer equipment that allows users to obtain access to a computer and to give it commands but, unlike a personal computer, usually is not capable of running any programs or storing any information by itself.

terminal emulation computer software that allows a personal computer to act like a particular brand of **terminal** in connecting to a remote host computer.

tn3270 software, similar to **telnet**, for remote login to IBM mainframe computers; emulates an IBM TN3270 **terminal**.

truncation ending a word short of completion; many search systems allow the use of a truncation symbol (e.g., ? or *) to substitute for multiple possible endings; for example, **prison?** for **prison, prisons, prisoner**, and so forth.

UMI   (formerly University Microfilms International) a company that provides journals, magazines, dissertations, and other information sources to libraries on microform and CD-ROM, as well as online; also provides computerized indexes and abstracts on CD-ROM, online, and over the Internet.

UnCover   a bibliographic **database**, developed by **CARL**, that consists of scanned tables of contents from thousands of journals; also allows for **document delivery** (for a fee) of many of the articles listed.

URL   (Uniform Resource Locator) a standard for specifying an object (document, graphic file, computer), or the location of an object, on the Internet; *see* Chapter 4.

user interface   computer software that determines how information is presented to a user, and what choices the user can make in using a computer system.

WAIS   (Wide Area Information Server) client–server software that uses **natural language searching** to retrieve text, based on the frequency of occurrence and the relationships of the words; developed by Thinking Machines Corporation in 1990.

WESTLAW   a **full-text** legal information system developed by West Publishing; now owned by the Thomson Corporation.

World Wide Web   software that delivers **HTML**-encoded (**hypertext**) documents over the Internet via the hypertext transfer protocol (**http**).

Author and Title Index

Internet Resources Index

Subject Index

ABOUT THE AUTHOR AND CONTRIBUTOR

BONNIE R. NELSON is the Associate Librarian for Information Systems at the Lloyd Sealy Library of John Jay College of Criminal Justice. She has been helping users find information resources in criminal justice, both in print and online, for over seventeen years. Professor Nelson's earlier works include *A Guide to Published Library Catalogs*, and articles in the *Journal of Criminal Justice Education, Reference Services Review*, and *RQ*. She is also the author of the *OPAC Directory 1997*.

KATHERINE B. KILLORAN is an assistant professor and Reference Librarian at the Lloyd Sealy Library of John Jay College of Criminal Justice. She holds a B.S. in Forest Biology from the State University of New York, College of Environmental Science and Forestry; an M.L.S. in Library and Information Studies from Queens College of the City University of New York; and an M.P.S. from Adelphi University. She has published a library guide to forensic science in the journal *Reference Services Review*. Her current research interests center on the pedagogy of forensic science, and the integration of the Internet and other electronic resources into the college curriculum.